AFRICA'S EMERGING
SECURITIES MARKETS

AFRICA'S EMERGING SECURITIES MARKETS

Developments in Financial Infrastructure

Robert A. Clark

QUORUM BOOKS
Westport, Connecticut • London

Library of Congress Cataloging-in-Publication Data

Clark, Robert A., 1954–
    Africa's emerging securities markets : developments in financial
infrastructure / Robert A. Clark
        p.   cm.
    Includes bibliographical references and index.
    ISBN 1–56720–149–0 (alk. paper)
    1. Securities industry—Africa.   I. Title.
HG5828.C57   1998
332.63'2'096—dc21   98–9945

British Library Cataloguing in Publication Data is available.

Library of Congress Catalog Card Number: 98–9945

ISBN: 1–56720–149–0

First published in 1998

Quorum Books, 88 Post Road West, Westport, CT 06881
An imprint of Greenwood Publishing Group, Inc.

Printed in the United States of America

The paper used in this book complies with the
Permanent Paper Standard issued by the National
Information Standards Organization (Z39.48–1984).

10 9 8 7 6 5 4 3 2 1

Dedicated to Tricia, Sarah, and Elizabeth
The joys of my life

CONTENTS

TABLES

ACKNOWLEDGMENTS

I have always been interested in the role that financial markets play in the global marketplace. The increasing integration of the world's economies provides an interesting opportunity to examine our role in financial market development. In pursuing this research I would like to extend my appreciation to those who have had the patience to challenge me to explore the world's emerging securities markets. I would like to thank my colleagues both at the University of Vermont, where I began this undertaking, and at the University of Tampa, where I completed this phase of my inquiry. In particular I am indebted to K. Ramagopal for his discussions of the material. In addition, I would like to thank Judith Aidoo, President of the Aidoo Group, who has shared her tremendous insights into the markets of Africa with me and for the past three years has joined me in teaching a course on Contemporary African Business. Her enthusiasm is contagious and the students in those classes have deepened my appreciation for the learning and understanding of the markets.

The accuracy of my work would not be possible without the assistance of exchange representatives who have added to my market knowledge. These include, but are not limited to, Mbendi, Investments Inc.; Andrew Ashton, Vice Chairman, Botswana Stock Exchange; Russell M. Loubser, Executive President of the Johannesburg Stock Exchange; Darrell Till, Head, Research and Development, Johannesburg Stock Exchange; Tracy Botha, Johannesburg Stock Exchange; Darmanand Virahsawmy, Senior Manager, the Stock Exchange of Mauritius; Yeboa Amoa, Managing Director, Ghana Stock Exchange; Diana Okine, Assistant Marketing Officer, Ghana Stock Exchange; Charles Asembri, Ghana Stock Exchange; Geoffrey M. Bakwen, the Botswana Stock Exchange; A. F. Barfoot, Chief Executive Officer, the

Zimbabwe Stock Exchange; Peter Bennett, Bennett Capital Management; Eric Hanson, Hanson Management; Kevin McKenna, University of Vermont; Peter Yuyi, Securities Brokerage Manager, Lusaka Stock Exchange; Eric Postel, Lusaka Stock Exchange; Databank; Equity Research Group, Ghana; Botswana Stockbrokers; J. K. Kihumba, Secretary/Chief Executive of the Nairobi Stock Exchange; Rauof Boudabous, Bourse Des Valeurs Mobilieres de Tunis; R. Oladejo, General Manager & Head of Research and Info Services, the Nigerian Stock Exchange; L. Hanekom, Namibian Stock Exchange; Raoudha Salhl, Tunisia Stock Exchange; Driss Bencheikh, Secretary General, Bourse de Casablanca; Dr. Michael Matsebula, Chairman, Swaziland Stockbrokers Ltd.; Priya Deelchand, Research Officer, Stock Exchange of Mauritius; and the Casablanca Stock Exchange for providing me with information for this work.

I would also like to acknowledge the tremendous explosion of materials available to financial researchers through the internet. This tool has extended our abilities to explore topics from afar. This research has benefited from presentations at the Financial Management Associations's Annual Meetings and workshops at The University of Tampa, the Norwegian School of Management, Babson College, and the Academy of International Business.

CHAPTER ONE

INTRODUCTION

The increasing globalization of financial markets has resulted in a substantial increase in net private capital flows to developing economies. Current flows have been directed primarily at the emerging economies of Asia, Eastern Europe, and Latin America. Meanwhile, until recently investors have ignored most countries in Africa. However, African markets caught investors' attention in 1994 with Kenya's 179-percent U.S.-dollar returns leading world equity markets. This image was reinforced in 1995 when Côte d'Ivoire's 140.8-percent U.S.-dollar returns led the world. Due to the low (and even negative) levels of correlation of African markets with developed exchanges, Africa's markets present ideal opportunities to diversify one's portfolio. Rates of return for African investments are among the highest returns in the world, yet African nations have not attracted the foreign direct investment that is required to transition their economies. This work examines the continual evolution of Africa's emerging securities markets and their role in regional economic development.

The following chapters provide an overview of Africa's securities market's institutional designs and structures. The continent's trading systems represent many different trading arrangements and the rules and procedures are not standardized. Without understanding the market's microstructure and custodial arrangements, international investors will not provide African projects with the equity capital required for further development.

Chapter 2 examines the region's economic development and transitions. Chapter 3 presents an overview of each country's developing financial infrastructure and stock exchange. The securities market profiles include the recent developments, designs, regulations, and structural details pertaining to each of Africa's fourteen organized exchanges. In addition, short overviews of three emerging exchanges are provided. Chapter 4 summarizes market issues and presents policy recommendations for further financial market development. To assist the reader in gaining further insight into African market evolution, appropriate web site information is incorporated to ensure that the framework provided by the book is dynamic in this rapidly changing environment.

AFRICAN ECONOMIC DEVELOPMENT

In 1996, Africa was the second fastest growing developing region in the world after Asia. Africa's top thirteen economies averaged 6 percent growth in 1996. The indications are that Africa is adjusting to a global market economy. With the end of the Cold War, Africa emerges from the rivalry ready to concentrate on the future. Signs of democratization, good governance, and regional economic cooperation have encouraged the international investment community. Still, considerable challenges remain. African markets are small, and the continent has poor infrastructure, unskilled labor, a negative stereotype, and high levels of external debt. "Very few African countries have active equity markets, either in the form of stock exchanges or merchant banks which can provide a full range of securities related services: underwriting, brokerage dealership, corporate financial advisory services, investment management, etc. The financial policies of many countries have inadvertently had an anti-equity bias."[1]

Governments are demonstrating a commitment to creating an enabling environment for both private-sector and capital market development. Economic liberalization includes lifting of currency controls, regionalization of trade and lowering of trade barriers, privatization of state-owned enterprises, and establishment of financial institutions like stock exchanges. Securities markets emerge and become an important source of capital for many firms to develop.

"The importance of achieving macroeconomic stability prior to reform is well know, yet structural reform and institutional development in the financial sector, especially prudential financial supervision, are equally essential as liberalization proceeds."[2] In examining global economic development, Asia's successful transition to market-based economies is often cited as the model. However, as Pill and Pradhan note, Asia implemented liberalization reforms earlier and in more favorable macroeconomic environments than African countries.[3] Thus, Africa's development has been difficult in a constrained macroeconomic environment.

Africa's development of the underlying capitalistic institutions is important to international investors. Stock exchanges have been established in a number of countries as vehicles for allocating both long- and medium-term capital to productive use in the economy. Compared with traditional banking sources of debt financing, equity capital can be developed at reduced costs. Exchanges facilitate the mobilization of capital.

The evolution of securities markets is critical to government efforts to tap capital markets as a source of investment capital. Many nations have adopted the stock exchange as a privatization forum that encourages public participation in privatization programs. Africa's moves toward privatization, good local settlement, and liberalization towards foreign investment have attracted foreign investors. Foreign direct investment (FDI) is critical to future economic growth.

As the continent transitions from its Marxist orientation in the postcolonial period, which restricted foreign ownership and participation in the economy, the resultant open economic systems will increase growth rates. This development results in a shift in investor attitudes toward Africa. This shift in perceptions is critical to the ability of African economies to deliver on their promises of better living conditions. After decades of decline, only long-term efforts will foster a successful redefinition of Africa's stereotype.

The transitions have resulted in some early successes. Investment by U.S. firms in general manufacturing in sub-Saharan Africa (excluding South Africa and Nigeria) grew from $18 million in 1990 to $235 million in 1996. Sub-Saharan economies grew at an average of 4.9 percent in 1996, while Southeast Asia's economies began to slow.[4] With an increasing number of African nations opening their economies, development will accelerate and improve the lives of millions of people.

The dominance of the state-owned enterprises (SOE) in African economies is reflected by the percent of the economies' activity that is accounted for by the state-owned enterprises (see Table 1.1). The average amount of economic activity accounted for by SOEs is 15.3 percent, and if calculated based on economic weightings it would be higher, as the larger economies are more dominated by the state. The economies in Egypt, Tunisia, and Zambia are particularly dominated by state enterprises.

Privatization is critical to the economic transition of the continent. Egypt, Ghana, Nigeria, South Africa, and Zimbabwe have all moved forward with large-scale privatization efforts. Morocco's privatization program moved forward in 1996. The 1989 to 1995 proceeds total $4.8 billion (in 1995 dollars). The proceeds have been important to the development of the region's securities markets and their liquidity. Governments use proceeds for debt reduction and infrastructure investments. Despite the efforts at privatization, the SOEs continue to represent a significant percentage of Gross Domestic Product (GDP) over the period, and substantial assets in telecommunications, mining, agriculture, and manufacturing remain in government hands.

Despite its rich historical foundations, recent African history has presented the world with conflicting images as nations confront the challenges of poverty,

Table 1.1
State-Owned Enterprises

Country	Economic Activity % GDP 1980-91	Privatization Proceeds 1989-95 in 1995 $ millions
Botswana	5.9	---
Côte d'Ivoire	---	168.0
Egypt	30.0	735.0
Ghana	8.4	667.0
Kenya	11.5	77.0
Mauritius	4.1	---
Morocco	1.8	---
Namibia	---	---
Nigeria	14.8	862.0
South Africa	14.7	796.0
Swaziland	---	---
Tunisia	30.2	148.0
Zambia	29.8	72.0
Zimbabwe	---	290.0
Total		**4,844.0**

Source: World Bank, *World Debt Tables* (Washington, D.C.: World Bank, 1996).

famine, ethnic conflict, education, and the lack of economic opportunity. For much of the post–World War II period the continent has failed to achieve significant forward progress in delivering an improving lifestyle to its citizens.

The most advanced nation, South Africa, suffered from ethnic division under regimes committed to maintaining an apartheid system in spite of world-wide condemnation and isolation. With the 1994 transition to a democratically elected government led by Nelson Mandela, South Africa is reentering the global community. As the richest economy on the continent, South Africa is seen as a potential economic engine for future growth. In addition to

South Africa's transition, Africa has seen a democratic transition unparalleled in the twentieth century.

With the historical precedents and the unfolding democratization, Africa presents itself to the global community for attention. Africa is in transition, with a growing degree of political stability. However, in some nations democracy exists in name only. Elections can be rigged or bought. Only South Africa is a democracy among the big four countries (the others being Nigeria, Sudan, and Congo). Despite the difficulties in achieving forward progress, changes have come to the continent. Thus, the global community is once again examining the opportunities to participate in the transformation of Africa's once stagnant economic environment.

According to the 1996 Heritage Foundation Study on economic freedom, Africa's challenges are great: "As a whole, sub-Saharan Africa remains the most economically unfree, and by far the poorest area in the world. Of the 38 sub-Saharan African countries graded, none received a score of free. Only 10 received a score of mostly free, 22 scored mostly unfree, and six were rated repressed. Morocco, Tunisia, Swaziland, Botswana, and Zambia are the highest-ranking African countries."[5]

STRUCTURAL ADJUSTMENT PROGRAMS

More than two-thirds of African countries are implementing structural reforms that emphasize growth, private-sector development, and greater openness to the global economy. Building stable economies is a vital element in establishing democracies on the continent.

Today, the African continent contains one-fifth of the world's landmass and is home to more than 700 million people. The annual birth rate of 3 percent a year makes Africa one of the world's fastest growing populations. African nations are challenged to make the growth of their population a positive influence on the future rather than a constraint on development. Economic growth must exceed the rate of population growth in order for nations to experience positive real economic growth. To date, many African nations have failed to achieve economic growth rates greater than population growth, making real economic growth elusive. Often, economic measurements reflect a lack of consistent progress and real per capita income is lower or essentially unchanged from the time of independence.

The development of an efficient financial infrastructure is a critical element in the allocation of scarce capital and resources to their most productive uses. Structural Adjustment Programs (SAPs) have played a vital role in Africa's current emergence as a more open economy.

It is difficult for private firms to access bank credit because governments and public enterprises have been given first claim on financial resources, both foreign and domestic. This distorts the efficient allocation of resources. The development of well-functioning capital markets is a critical element in the stimulation of the business environment. While these conditions are rarely fulfilled in African countries, they are important targets to strive for in the interest of development.[6]

Privatization is an area targeted by economic reforms. However, progress is thwarted by the lack of domestic savings within African countries, the absence of aggressive entrepreneurship, and the lack or underdevelopment of stock markets. Thus, despite the advances made in a few countries, for the continent as a whole further efforts are needed to increase investment, accelerate growth, and alleviate poverty. This explains why African economies have made profound reorientation in their approaches to the development challenges.

The reorientation in Africa's approach to development is warranted. Current economic conditions confirm that Africa has not been fully able to translate the newly adopted economic precepts into appreciable rates of growth. In this respect, it is notable that in recent years numerous measures have been taken to encourage the flow of private capital to Africa. Within the context of such reforms, governments have streamlined the regulatory and administrative framework, dismantled systems of import and export licensing, and instituted improved packages of investment incentives. Many of these reforms have been articulated in new investment codes.

Though there are several explanations for the continent's poor economic performance since 1980, the low level of domestic investment is a major causal factor. Gross fixed capital formation has declined in Africa from a total of $76.3 billion in 1980 to $58.9 billion in 1989. Poor performance can also be attributed to inadequate macroeconomic frameworks and irrelevant approaches to structural adjustment. In the majority of African countries, the macroeconomic policy framework is that of the current International Monetary Fund (IMF)/World Bank–induced structural adjustment programs. It is a fact that current SAPs, designed to address Africa's economic problems, have not succeeded in reversing the declining trends in investment, even in relatively stable countries with long histories of adjustment. The World Bank's study on SAPs notes the following:

Investment generally responds slowly to adjustment in Africa and elsewhere. This slow response is understandable. Investments cut capital spending as part of their fiscal stabilization—while the private sector adopts a wait-and-see attitude during the early phases of adjustment due to the irreversibility of investment decisions and reversibility of key policy changes (frequent in previous episodes). The problem is particularly serious where there is no consensus about the importance of private-sector-led growth.[7]

The rate of return on investment in Africa has declined significantly over the years and more precipitously during the past decade. According to the World Bank, rates of return on sub-Saharan Africa have dropped from around 30.7 percent in 1961 to 1973 to around 2.5 percent in 1980 to 1987.

On the other hand, during that period the rate of return in South Asia, for instance, grew from 21.3 to 22.4 percent.[8] However, in the 1990s African project returns have led the world with returns of more than 25 percent annually.

African economic performance has been distorted by government controls on the critical elements of both macroeconomic and microeconomic policy. To transition the economies, international agencies have advocated the adoption of SAPs designed to address the issues of market distortion and weakness. Typically the programs involve policy reforms and development of the economic institutions to support growth. The characteristics of individual SAPs vary from country to country based on specific economic issues and the political environment. Typical elements of the programs include the following:

- Controlling government employment levels and wages.
- Decreasing recurrent government expenditures.
- Restructuring and privatization of public enterprises.
- Strict evaluation of public investment programs (PIPs) to eliminate government waste.
- Developing effective government revenue systems.[9]

At the end of 1993, the World Bank noted, "No African country has achieved a sound macroeconomic policy stance—which in broad terms means inflation under 10 percent, a very low budget deficit, and a competitive exchange rate."[10] This failure highlighted the need for fundamental restructuring of economies to make development possible. The adjustment programs are designed to provide incentives for development and the efficient allocation of resources.

The task ahead is monumental. In evaluating the requirements for African growth, Culagovski and colleagues project that achieving the 5-percent target growth rate for sub-Saharan Africa by 2000 would require $28 to $30 billion annually in gross external financing (in 1988 dollars).[11] Gross financing is defined as the amount needed to meet the net import bill and debt service payments coming due. As a share of GDP, these gross foreign financing requirements fall from 18 percent of GDP at the beginning of the decade to 13 percent at the end. The success of SAPs in creating a stable macroeconomic environment for transition is critical to an improving standard of living. As exchanges evolve, they provide more efficient allocations of resources.

NOTES

1. Keith Marsden and Thérèse Bélot, *Private Enterprise in Africa: Creating a Better Environment* (Washington, D.C.: World Bank, 1987), 23.

2. Huw Pill and Mahmood Pradhan, "Financial Liberalization in Africa and Asia," *Finance & Development*, June 1997, 10.

3. Ibid.

4. *U.S. News & World Report,* 13 October 1997.

5. Kim Holmes, Bryan Johnson, and Melanie Kirkpatrick, *1997 Index of Economic Freedom* (New York: Heritage Foundation and *Wall Street Journal,* 1997).

6. Marsden and Bélot, *Private Enterprise in Africa,* vii.

7. *Adjustment in Africa: Reforms, Results and the Road Ahead* (Washington, D.C.: World Bank, 1994), 124.

8. *Sub-Saharan Africa: From Crisis to Sustainable Growth* (Washington, D.C.: World Bank, 1989).

9. Marsden and Bélot, *Private Enterprise in Africa,* 27.

10. World Bank, *Adjustment in Africa,* 1.

11. Jorge Culagovski, Victor Gabor, Maria Cristina Germany, and Charles Humphreys, "African Financing Needs in the 1990s," in *African External Finance in the 1990s,* ed. Ishrat Husain and John Underwood (Washington, D.C.: World Bank, 1991).

Chapter Two

INVESTMENT FLOWS AND REGIONAL DEVELOPMENT

The African Structural Adjustment Programs are designed to create the proper macroeconomic environment for attracting development capital. Increased capital flows are essential for Africa's future development. Investment flows to Africa remain small and are subject to year-to-year fluctuations. The World Bank estimates that net foreign direct investment flows to sub-Saharan Africa increased from $0.9 billion in 1990 to $3.0 billion in 1994 but fell to $2.2 billion in 1995 and accounted for 2.4 percent of such flows to all developing countries in that year.[1] In 1996 FDI totaled $4.5 billion, double 1995 levels, as U.S. companies invested $1.2 billion. North Africa's figures are similar.

A growing source of foreign investment for Africa has been foreign portfolio investment (FPI). FPI includes bonds issued to international capital markets (portfolio debt flows as well as country funds, depository receipts, and direct purchases of stocks by foreign investors [portfolio equity flows]). Africa's growth in FPI has been due primarily to structural adjustment policies, the establishment and development of stock exchanges in the region, and an interest on the part of foreign investors in portfolio diversification.

Portfolio debt flows to sub-Saharan Africa have been highly concentrated in a few countries. For instance, during 1994–1995 only Congo, a first-time borrower, South Africa, and Mauritius had new bond issues.[2] Most foreign portfolio equity investments in sub-Saharan Africa are in the petroleum, mining, chemicals, and plastics industries. According to the World Bank, portfolio equity investment flows to sub-Saharan Africa increased from $144 million in 1992 to $860 million in 1994, before falling to $465 million in 1995.[3]

The lifting of financial sanctions against South Africa precipitated the launching of several international funds devoted to South Africa, such as

Alliance Capital Management's $100 million Southern African Fund and Morgan Stanley's $230 million Africa Fund, which have encouraged foreign portfolio investment in South Africa.[4]

REGIONAL INTEGRATION

Regional pacts and agreements have been pursued to reduce the barriers to free trade among the member nations. The following provides a brief overview of the membership and organizational goals for each of the major regional agreements. Table 2.1 provides an overview of the development organizations' membership and regional affiliations.[5]

Lome Convention

The Lome IV Convention is an agreement between the fifteen European Union (EU) countries and the seventy African, Caribbean, and Pacific (ACP) countries. The convention provides for export commodities originating from ACP states to enter EU countries free of customs and other duties.

Table 2.1
Sub-Saharan Africa: Selected Regional Integration Groups

Country	COMESA	SACU	SADC	WAEMU	PTC/EAC
Botswana		X	X		
Côte d'Ivoire				X	
Ghana					
Kenya	X				X
Malawi	X		X		
Mauritius	X		X		
Namibia	X	X	X		
Nigeria					
South Africa		X	X		
Swaziland	X	X	X		
Uganda	X				X
Zambia	X		X		
Zimbabwe	X		X		
Total Members	**20**	**5**	**12**	**7**	**3**

Source: U.S.–Africa Trade Flows and Effects of the Uruguay Round Agreements and U.S. Trade and Development Policy, Investigation No. 332-362, Publication 300 (Washington, D.C.: U.S. International Trade Commission, 1996), 5.2.

Common Market for Eastern and Southern Africa (COMESA)

COMESA was established on December 8, 1994, in response to the lack of member countries' success in improving their economies under the COMESA's predecessor organization, the Preferential Trade Area (PTA).[6] COMESA's stated objectives are as follows:

- To attain sustainable growth and development of member states by promoting a more balanced and harmonious development of its production and marketing structure.
- To promote joint development in all fields of economic activity and the joint adoption of macroeconomic policies and programs to raise the standard of living of its peoples to foster closer relations among its member states.
- To cooperate in the creation of an enabling environment for foreign, cross-border, and domestic investment, including the joint promotion of research and the adaptation of science and technology for development.
- To cooperate in the promotion of peace, security, and stability among the member states in order to enhance economic development in the region.
- To cooperate in strengthening the relations between the common market and the rest of the world and the adoption of common positions in international foreign affairs.
- To contribute toward the establishment, progress, and realization of the objectives of the African Economic Community.

Southern African Customs Union (SACU)

SACU provides a common pool of customs, excise, and sales duties according to the relative volume of trade and production in each member country.

West African Economic and Monetary Union (WAEMU)

Seven African countries initiated the WAEMU in 1994.[7] WAEMU was created to help stabilize the financial base of the countries' economies following the devaluation of the Central African franc (CFAF) in January 1994.

Permanent Tripartite Commission for East African Cooperation (PTC/EAC)

The PTC/EAC officially opened on March 14, 1996. It represents a market of approximately 80 million people. Since its formation, the currencies of the three countries have been made convertible. Program priorities include development of transport and communications, trade, and industry, harmonization of fiscal and monetary policies, and security and immigration.[8]

Southern African Development Community (SADC)

The Southern African Development Coordination Conference gave rise to SADC in 1992. SADC is working toward the creation of a 130-million-person southern African common market by the year 2000. SADC's objectives include free trade, free movement of people, a single currency, democracy, and respect for human rights.[9] SADC's primary focus has been on trade reform. On August 24, 1996, the members of SADC signed a trade protocol providing for a free trade agreement to be phased in over the next eight years.[10]

The African Development Bank

The African Development Bank (ADB) represents the main development bank of Africa. The Bank was established in 1963 by the Organization of African Unity (OAU), with start-up capital of $250 million. Subsequently the Bank has grown into a $33 billion, multinational development bank, with fifty-two African and twenty-four other shareholders. ADB provides Africa with developmental capital for financing projects and investments in member states, with a particular emphasis on regional projects. Affiliates of the ADB include the African Development Fund (ADF) and the Nigeria Trust Fund.[11]

The eighteen members of the Board of Governors oversee the ADB. The board consists of representatives from member countries. There is a nine-member Executive Council. The board has the responsibility for the general operation of the bank. Further information can be obtained from the bank headquarters at:

01 Boite Postal 1387
Abidjan 01
Côte d'Ivoire
Tel.: +225-21-44-44
Fax: +225-22-70-04

Organization of African Unity

The Organization of African Unity was founded in 1963. The OAU's primary purpose is to promote unity and solidarity among African countries. In addition, its goals include improving the general living standards in Africa, defending the territorial integrity and independence of African states, and promoting international cooperation. The OAU membership comprises fifty-three of the fifty-four countries of Africa. The only African state that is not a member is the Kingdom of Morocco, which withdrew in 1985 following the admittance of the disputed state of Western Sahara as a member in 1984. Further information concerning the OAU can be obtained:

The Secretariat
P.O. Box 3243
Addis-Ababa
Ethiopia
Tel.: +251–1–51–7700
Fax: +251–1–51–2622

With South Africa's peaceful transition in 1994, expectations were high that South Africa would lead the development of the sub-Saharan regional economic renaissance. No longer isolated by the world community, the richest country on the continent could dismantle trade barriers erected during the apartheid era and move forward. By 1996, the major transition in African trade was evident in that 16 percent of South Africa's total exports were to other African countries, compared with 3 percent in 1990.[12]

Africa's continued economic transition is highly dependent upon access to capital for development. High levels of African debt make accessing global capital difficult. As shown in Table 2.2, external debt has increased at a 6.5 percent annual rate over the 1980 to 1995 period. Long-term debt increased 7.23 percent annually over the period. The high debt levels inhibit further growth by limiting market access to lower-cost debt financing. The debt burden for Africa is particularly difficult when evaluated relative to GDP levels. In 1993 the debt to GDP ratio equaled 73.3 percent for North Africa and 123.1 percent for sub-Saharan Africa. This is reflected in the difficulties African nations have encountered in debt repayments.

Through 1997, Moody's debt rating service has rated four African nations: Mauritius at Baa2, South Africa at Baa3, and Tunisia at Baa3, all investment grade ratings, and Egypt at Ba2, a speculative grade investment rating. In addition, Standard and Poor's has rated three African nations: Egypt, Local Currency Debt: A-/Stable/A-, Foreign Currency Debt: BBB-/Stable/A-3; South Africa: Long-term local currency debt: BBB+, Long-term foreign currency debt: BB+ (a speculative grade investment); Tunisia: Local currency debt: A/Stable/A-1, Foreign currency debt: BBB-/Stable/A-3.[13]

The debt and debt service information in Table 2.2 illustrates the difficulty which Africa's markets have experienced in servicing their debt burdens. In the 1980s, thirty of forty-four sub-Saharan countries ran into debt servicing difficulties, as reflected by arrears and reschedulings. The difficulty is most acute for Côte d'Ivoire, with debt equaling 184.9 percent of GNP. Both Zambia and Nigeria reported 1995 debt burdens greater than 100 percent of GNP. Botswana, which consistently runs a budget surplus, reports a low debt burden of 13.1 percent of GNP. Kenya and Zambia have made improvements compared to 1993 levels. Nigeria's debt service burden reflects the greatest deterioration in its abilities from 1980 to 1995.

Absolute FDI in Africa has increased from the 1980s through 1995 and the trend continues (see Table 2.3). In 1980, both Nigeria and South Africa were

Table 2.2
African Debt Levels

Country	External Debt		Long-Term Debt		Debt Service % GNP
	1980	1995	1980	1995	1995
Botswana	147.0	699.0	143.0	682.0	2.2
Côte d'Ivoire	7,462.0	18,952.0	6,339.0	14,559.0	11.6
Egypt	19,131.0	34,116.0	14,693.0	31,638.0	5.1
Ghana	1,398.0	5,874.0	1,162.0	4,595.0	6.0
Kenya	3,383.0	7,381.0	2,489.0	6,372.0	8.7
Mauritius	467.0	1,801.0	318.0	1,449.0	5.5
Morocco	9,277.0	22,147.0	8,013.0	21,678.0	11.3
Namibia	---	---	---	---	---
Nigeria	8,921.0	35,005.0	5,368.0	29,002.0	6.3
South Africa	---	---	---	---	---
Swaziland	---	---	---	---	---
Tunisia	3,526.0	9,938.0	3,390.0	9,007.0	8.7
Zambia	3,261.0	6,853.0	2,227.0	5,091.0	68.4
Zimbabwe	786.0	4,885.0	696.0	3,741.0	10.5
Total	57,759.0	147,651.0	44,838.0	127,735.0	---

Source: World Bank, World Debt Tables (Washington, D.C.: World Bank, 1996).

experiencing a net divestiture of investments. This trend reversed in 1995 as their economies opened to FDI and barriers to entry came down. In 1995, Ghana and Zambia attracted a significant percentage of their total investment from FDI. However, the hesitation of the foreign investors is reflected by these figures. Increasing both internal and external capital is essential for privatization programs to succeed. The Asian Tigers have been a favored destination of U.S. FDI. This trend may be interrupted by the 1997 currency

Table 2.3
African Foreign Direct Investment (FDI)

Country	FDI Percentage of Gross Domestic Investment		FDI Percentage of Gross National Product	
	1980	1995	1980	1995
Botswana	30.6	6.5	11.5	1.6
Côte d'Ivoire	3.5	1.4	0.9	0.2
Egypt	8.7	7.5	2.4	1.3
Ghana	6.4	19.6	0.4	3.6
Kenya	3.7	1.8	1.1	0.4
Mauritius	0.4	1.5	0.1	0.4
Morocco	2.0	4.3	0.5	0.9
Namibia	0.0	8.9	0.0	1.5
Nigeria	-3.6	---	-0.8	2.4
South Africa	-0.1	0.0	0.0	0.0
Swaziland	---	---	---	---
Tunisia	9.0	6.1	2.7	1.5
Zambia	6.9	13.8	1.6	1.6
Zimbabwe	0.2	2.2	0.0	0.6

Source: World Bank, World Debt Tables (Washington, D.C.: World Bank, 1996).

turmoil. Capital flows to Asia are expected to fall by 25 percent to $107.1 billion in 1997 based on a survey by the Institute of International Finance.[14]

From 1990 through 1995, Africa's FDI increased 14 percent, from $2 billion to $2.3 billion (see Table 2.4). The countries with significant privatization programs—Egypt, Ghana, Morocco, Nigeria, and Tunisia—reflect the greatest degree of FDI. Both Zimbabwe and South Africa have transitioned from net divestiture to positive foreign direct investment as the political climates have changed to favor foreign investment. With the peaceful government

Table 2.4
Foreign Direct Investment ($ Millions)

Country	1990	1995
Botswana	95.0	70.0
Côte d'Ivoire	48.0	19.0
Egypt	734.0	598.0
Ghana	15.0	230.0
Kenya	57.0	32.0
Mauritius	41.0	15.0
Morocco	165.0	290.0
Namibia	29.0	47.0
Nigeria	588.0	650.0
South Africa	-5.0	3.0
Swaziland	---	---
Tunisia	76.0	264.0
Zambia	203.0	66.0
Zimbabwe	-12.0	40.0
Total	**2,034.0**	**2,324.0**

Source: World Bank, World Debt Tables (Washington, D.C.: World Bank, 1996).

transition in South Africa, international investment is beginning to reappear after years of protest. However, the net $3 million in foreign direct investment leaves the South African economy in last place among African nations in attracting FDI. Africa's overall attraction of $2 to $3 billion in FDI is limited when contrasted with Asia's anticipated 1997 estimate of $107 billion.

Double-digit interest rates have slowed the economic growth of African economies, however the real rates of interest are low to negative (see Table 2.5). Both Ghana and Nigeria have reported negative real interest rates. These make equity investments an attractive alternative to debt instruments. The high

Table 2.5
African Interest Rates

Country	Official Forex/$	Deposit	Lending	Real
Botswana	2.8	10.0	14.2	0.6
Côte d'Ivoire	499.1	---	---	---
Egypt	3.4	10.9	16.5	2.4
Ghana	1200.4	28.7	---	-8.0
Kenya	51.4	13.6	28.8	12.7
Mauritius	17.4	12.2	20.8	5.9
Morocco	8.5	---	10.0	---
Namibia	3.6	10.8	18.5	5.8
Nigeria	21.9	13.5	20.2	-54.4
South Africa	3.6	13.5	17.9	3.0
Swaziland	---	---	---	---
Tunisia	0.9	---	---	---
Zambia	857.2	---	113.3	---
Zimbabwe	8.7	25.9	34.7	2.0

Source: World Bank, *World Debt Tables* (Washington, D.C.: World Bank, 1996).

real rate of return in Kenya, 12.7 percent, is necessary to keep inflation under control. The negative real rates of return in Ghana and Nigeria illustrate the difficulties in attracting investment. Investors perceive no advantages in investing with negative interest rates. Stabilizing macroeconomic policy with positive real interest rates is essential to attracting both domestic and foreign development funding.

Inflation continues to be a challenge for African economies (see Table 2.6). In the 1990s, inflation has declined in Botswana, Ghana, Morocco, Namibia, South Africa, and Tunisia. Increases in inflation have occurred in Côte d'Ivoire, Egypt, Kenya, Mauritius, Nigeria, Zambia, and Zimbabwe. The structural

Table 2.6
African Inflation Rates

Country	GDP Implicit Deflator		Percent Change
	1980-90	1990-95	
Botswana	13.1	9.2	-30.0
Côte d'Ivoire	3.4	10.4	206.0
Egypt	11.7	13.3	14.0
Ghana	42.4	23.8	-44.0
Kenya	9.0	18.5	106.0
Mauritius	15.0	30.4	103.0
Morocco	7.2	3.9	-46.0
Namibia	13.6	9.3	-32.0
Nigeria	16.6	47.1	184.0
South Africa	14.8	11.5	-22.0
Swaziland	---	---	---
Tunisia	7.4	5.4	-27.0
Zambia	42.4	107.8	154.0
Zimbabwe	11.5	27.6	140.0

Source: World Bank, *World Debt Tables* (Washington, D.C.: World Bank, 1996).

adjustment programs have as a major priority the reduction of the rate of inflation. Reducing inflation to a single digit is a policy goal. Controlling inflation will also result in higher rates of real growth in the economies. North Africa exhibits the best performance in controlling inflationary pressures.

SUMMARY

Creating the right macroeconomic environment for Africa's economic development has been a challenge. The region's increasing integration presents new opportunities to work toward improving the economic base.

As governments work to open their economies, Western nations must recognize the need for assistance with high debt burdens and financial infrastructure development. Attracting increased levels of FDI is necessary for the economies to move forward. Under appropriate conditions this will be the renaissance, not only for South Africa, but for the entire continent.

NOTES

1. World Bank, *World Debt Tables*, vol. 1 (Washington, D.C.: World Bank, 1996).

2. Ibid., 101.

3. Ibid., 102. According to the World Bank, portfolio equity flows declined globally in 1995 due to higher U.S. interest rates in early 1994 and to the devaluation of the Mexican peso in late 1994, which eroded investor confidence in emerging market investments.

4. U.S. Department of Agriculture, Foreign Agricultural Service, *1996 Country Risk Assessment: South Africa* (Washington, D.C.: U.S. GPO, 1995).

5. A complete organizational overview and listing of members not possessing stock exchanges can be found in *The African Business Handbook: A Comprehensive Guide to Business Resources for African Trade and Investment* (Washington, D.C.: 21st Century Africa, Inc., 1996–1997).

6. Facsimile received by the staff of the U.S. International Trade Commission from the Secretariat of the COMESA, Development, Finance & Technical Cooperation, 29 July 1996. The PTA was the same group of countries as COMESA, with the addition of Djibouti and Seychelles.

7. Also known as the Union Economique et Monétaire Ouest Africaine (UEMOA).

8. "EAC Chief Commends Economic Integration Efforts," *News Edge/LAN*, 9 August 1996.

9. Southern African Development Community profile information web site at *http://www.kent.edu/bus_coll.www/sabos/intro.htm.*

10. Lionel Williams, "South African Trade—Southern Africa Agrees on Establishment of Free Trade Area," *News Edge/LAN*, 9 August 1996.

11. To examine the International Finance Corporation's work in South Africa, see "The IFC in South Africa," at *http://www.ifc.org/PUBLICAT/PRESS/FACTSHEE/africa.HTM.*

12. "Sub-Saharan Africa: Turmoil and Progress," *Rand Focus: The Treasury Financial Newsletter of First National Bank of Southern Africa Limited*, May/June 1997.

13. Standard & Poor's ratings were assigned as follows: Egypt, January 1997; South Africa, local rating, November 1995, foreign currency rating, October 1994; and Tunisia, April 1997.

14. Mark Huband, "North Africa Offers Haven," *Financial Times*, 27 October 1997, p. 24.

CHAPTER THREE

SECURITIES MARKET PROFILES

The following securities market profiles highlight the organizational design and operation of Africa's developing stock exchanges. Profiles include a brief overview of the country, including its political environment and economic background. This section of the book has benefited from the expertise of market participants, however I note that securities markets are dynamic organizations and in a state of continual evolution and change. Consequently, this research provides a view of the markets that will change policies and procedures. To assist the reader in recognizing these changes, each market profile contains numerous internet address connections that can be used to update the material presented.

There are fourteen active securities markets in Africa and three emerging exchanges. Detailed reviews of the fourteen active exchanges are provided along with brief highlights of the emerging markets. Table 3.1 provides an overview of the exchanges' market capitalization.

Overall, African markets declined in their share of the world's emerging securities markets from 16 percent of the total in 1995 to 12.8 percent in 1996. The decline resulted primarily from the South African market, which declined 13.9 percent in 1996. Excluding South African markets reflects an increase in market capitalization for the African exchanges. The dominance of the South African capital markets is clearly seen in the market capitalization figure. In 1990 the other African stock exchanges had a total market capitalization of $8.7 billion, or 5.9 percent of the continent's total capitalization. By 1995 this had increased to $26.9 billion, or 8.8 percent of the continent's market capitalization. The non–South African markets have increased a cumulative 211 percent over the five-year period, for an annual growth rate of 25.5 percent. In contrast, the continent's markets have increased at a cumulative 110 percent, or an annual 16-percent growth rate, when South Africa is included in the population.

Table 3.1
Market Capitalization

Country	1995	Percent	1996	Percent	Change
Botswana	398.0	0.1	326.0	0.1	-18.1
Côte d'Ivoire	866.0	0.3	914.0	0.3	5.5
Egypt	8,088.0	2.6	14,173.0	5.0	75.2
Ghana	1,649.0	0.5	1,492.0	0.5	-9.5
Kenya	1,886.0	0.6	1,846.0	0.6	-2.1
Mauritius	1,331.0	0.4	1,676.0	0.6	25.9
Morocco	5,951.0	1.9	8,705.0	3.1	46.3
Namibia	189.0	0.1	473.0	0.2	150.3
Nigeria	2,033.0	0.7	3560.0	1.3	75.1
South Africa	280,526.0	90.6	241,571.0	84.9	-13.9
Swaziland	339.0	0.1	1,642.0	0.6	384.4
Tunisia	3,927.0	1.3	4,263.0	1.5	8.6
Zambia	435.0	0.1	229.0	0.1	-47.4
Zimbabwe	2,038.0	0.7	3,635.0	1.3	78.4
Total					
w/ South Africa	309,656.0		284,505.0		-8.1
w/o South Africa	29,130.0		42,934.0		47.4
All Emerging Markets					
	1,931,411.0		2,225,957.0		15.3

Source: Emerging Stock Markets Factbook 1997 (Washington, D.C.: International Finance
Corporation, 1997).

The data on the percent of the GDP that the market capitalization represents clearly indicate the undeveloped nature of African securities markets
and their role in the economy. Only South Africa's 206.2 percent of GDP represents a developed market standard. Compared with 1990, the importance
of the markets is increasing as represented by an increasing percent of GDP.

Table 3.2 provides a brief overview of the region's securities markets and
their highlights. By 1997, the markets have opened to foreign investment. A
number of markets retain limits on foreign control and ownership stakes, but
foreign investment restrictions have been lifted in an effort to attract capital.

BOTSWANA

COUNTRY

The Republic of Botswana has an area of 224,607 square miles (581,730 square kilometers) in Southern Africa. For comparative purposes, it is slightly smaller than Texas. Botswana is landlocked in the center of Southern Africa, bordered by South Africa in the south and southeast, Zimbabwe in the northeast, and Namibia in the north and west. The capital is Gaborone.

The region contains sites from the Iron Age that date from A.D. 190. The area was settled during the migration of Bantu-speaking farmers. From the seventh to the thirteenth century, chiefdoms developed. In the eighteenth century, Tswana dynasties moved into the region and established several states. Warfare slowed the Tswana advance in the early nineteenth century.

With the discovery of gold in 1867, Europeans became interested in the region. In 1885 the region was designated by the British as the British Bechuanaland Protectorate. In 1886 the area became a crown colony and was annexed by the Cape Colony a decade later. Bechuanaland was a British protectorate until its independence in 1966.

Botswana's location as a landlocked nation creates a difficult situation, as the nation is economically dependent upon South Africa. This dependence was particularly difficult due to the geo-political environment in Southern Africa in the 1980s. Botswana was a haven for Rhodesian refugees and guerrillas of the Zimbabwe People's Revolutionary Army before Zimbabwe's independence in 1980. This role led to difficult relations with South Africa. Relations were strained as the result of South African raids on Gaborone in 1985 and 1986. The pressures eased with the independence of Namibia in 1990 and the transitions in South Africa's political environment.

Official Religion	None[1]
Religions	Traditional religions, 85%; Christian, 15%. Many traditional religious practices incorporate a strong Christian element, and people may follow both Christian and traditional beliefs. Religion plays an important part in daily life and social relationships.
Population	1,477,630 (July 1996 est.)[2]
	Urban: 26%
	Rural: 74%
	Population under the age of 15: 43%
Ethnic Divisions	Batswana, 95%; Kalanga, Basarwa, and Kgalagadi, 4%; white, 1%
Languages	English (official), Setswana
Education	Population over age 15 who are literate: 74%

Table 3.2
Securities Market Highlights

Country	Exchange	Instruments	Developments	Market Entry
Botswana	Botswana Stock Exchange	12 Equities and government bonds	Strong economic development has caused the market to post strong gains in 1997	Free entry for foreign investment
Cote d'Ivoire	Bourse des Valeurs Abidjan	31 Equities	The market closed December 31, 1997 pending the opening of regional Francophone Market	Free entry for foreign investment
Egypt	Cairo and Alexandria Stock Exchanges	646 Equities	Significant Privatization Program	Free entry for foreign investment
Ghana	The Ghana Stock Exchange	21 Equities	Government Privatization Program	Free entry for foreign investment
Kenya	The Nairobi Stock Exchange	56 Equities	Current weakness of the Kenyan Shilling	Free entry for foreign investment
Mauritius	Stock Exchange of Mauritius	40 Equities	Daily trading started November 1997	Free entry for foreign investment

Morocco	Casablanca Stock Exchange	47 Equities	Mutual funds recently established, significant model privatization program underway	Free entry for foreign investment
Namibia	Namibian Stock Exchange	12 Equities	A number of listings are cross-listed and traded with the Johannesburg Stock Exchange	Free entry for foreign investment
Nigeria	The Nigeria Stock Exchange	183 Equities	Political uncertainty exists for investors entering the market	Free entry for foreign investment
South Africa	The Johannesburg Stock Exchange	626 Equities, Debt and Derivatives	Transition to Electronic Trading Systems. Commercial and Financial Rand consolidated	Free entry for foreign investment
Swaziland	The Swazi Stock Market	6 Equities	The government privatization program is proceeding	Free entry for foreign investment
Tunisia	Bourse des Valeurs Mobilieres	30 Equities	The market has transitioned to an electronic market	Free entry for foreign investment
Zambia	Lusaka Stock Exchange	5 Equities	The market faces the task of privatizing Zambian Copper, the largest firm in the market	Free entry for foreign investment
Zimbabwe	Zimbabwe Stock Exchange	64 Equities	Market capitalization increased dramatically in 1996	Free entry for foreign investors

The Political System

Botswana is a multiparty parliamentary republic. The National Assembly is a unicameral body with forty directly elected members, four indirectly elected members, and two ex officio members (the president and the attorney general). Members of Parliament are elected to five-year terms. In addition, the House of Chiefs, with fifteen members, is an elected body representing the principal tribes and serves as an advisory board to the government. Any legislative matter impacting on tribal affairs must be referred to the House of Chiefs before the National Assembly can pass it. The President is directly elected to a five-year term.

Last election: October 1994

Next election: By October 1999

Head of State: President HE Sir Ketumile Masire (since July 13, 1980)

Political Web Site: http: //www.geocities.com/~derksen/election.htm

Legal System

Botswana's common law is based on Roman–Dutch law, while criminal law is based on English law. There is an independent judiciary with magistrates, courts, high court, and appeal court. In rural areas tribal courts hear customary cases.

Suffrage is at twenty-one years of age and is universal.[3]

The Economy

Botswana's economy is mixed with both private- and public-sector participation.[4] Economic development involves the mining of diamonds, copper, and nickel. Exporting diamonds produces the greatest source of foreign exchange and governmental revenues and accounted for approximately 37 percent of the GDP in 1994. Mining also contributed 80 percent of export earnings and 60 percent of government revenues. The diamonds are mined jointly by the government and De Beers Consolidated Mines of South Africa. In addition to mining, approximately three-fourths of the working population are employed in agricultural activities.

The Government of Botswana believes that positive real interest rates together with a stable financial system, an equitable tax structure, and sound fiscal policy must be established and maintained as a prerequisite for the more complete liberalization of the country's foreign exchange regime. To lessen its dependence on the mining industries, the government targeted services, manufacturing, and tourism for growth in the National Development Plan 7. The plan shifts the focus for development from the government to the private sector. This transition is critical to reducing the unemployment rate, which in November 1995 stood at an estimated 21 percent.

The Cost-of-Living Index for the period 1991 to 1995 shows inflation increasing from 12 percent in 1991 to 16 percent in 1992 and subsequently decreasing to 10–11 percent in 1995, having dropped from a peak of over 17 percent in 1992. In 1997, Botswana's rate of inflation dropped from 8.9 percent in July to 8.5 percent in August, according to the Central Statistics Office. This is its lowest level of inflation since July 1988. The decline is attributed to the reductions in the cost of petrol and diesel during August 1997. The national inflation rate dropped to 7.8 percent at the end of 1997, its lowest level in almost ten years.

On August 4, 1997, the Economist Intelligence Unit (EIU) reported that five out of twenty of the world's fastest growing economies that are likely to grow more than 6 percent in 1997 are in Africa, and include Botswana, Zimbabwe, Angola, Uganda, and Côte d'Ivoire.

Economic Policy Web Site: http://www.businessmonitor.co.uk/bbp_index/botswana/1:1.shtml

Gross Domestic Product[5]

Botswana is classified as a middle-income country, and has the highest ranking in sub-Saharan Africa in the United Nations Development Program (UNDP) Human Development Index, which measures the quality of life. Real per capita GNP growth over the period 1985 to 1994 averaged 6.6 percent per annum.[6]

GDP purchasing power parity	$4.5 billion (1995 est.)
GDP real growth rate	1.0% (1995 est.)
GDP per capita	$3,200 (1995 est.)

Central Bank: The Bank of Botswana[7]

The objectives of the Bank of Botswana, which was established to carry out the central banking functions, are stated in the Bank of Botswana Act of 1975. These included the following:

1. Promotion and maintenance of monetary stability and proper functioning of a soundly based financial system.
2. Fostering of monetary, credit and financial conditions conducive to economic development.
3. Provision of assistance in the attainment of national economic goals.

Postal Address

Bank of Botswana
Private Bag 154
1863 Khama Crescent
Gaborone
Botswana
Tel.: 267–360–600   Fax: 267–372–984

In addition to the Bank of Botswana Act, the Financial Institutions Act and the Exchange Control Act regulate the functions of commercial banks and other financial institutions in Botswana and control the outflow of capital. The Bank of Botswana provides not only all the services of a central bank, but also some which arise because of Botswana's relatively strong financial position. The bank acts as a deposit taker of last resort for commercial banks, parastatal bodies, and any other individual or business that is able to meet certain necessary criteria. In this respect, the bank, in 1991, started to issue Bank of Botswana Certificates; these are regularly auctioned to banks and other authorized entities with excess funds and assist in the market determination of the level of interest rates. The prime lending rate at the start of 1994 was 13 percent, and it increased to 14.5 percent at the end of 1995. At the end of February 1997, the Bank of Botswana reduced its lending rate to financial institutions from 13 percent to 12.5 percent per year. A statement was issued, saying, "The Bank of Botswana feels it is opportune to signal lower nominal interest rates in Botswana because of the inflationary trend. Over the past year Botswana's interest has come down from 10.5 percent in January 1996 to 9.1 percent in January 1997."[8] In the first quarter of 1997 the prime rate was 14 percent.

Credit Rating

Botswana has not been rated for either domestic or foreign currency debt. Due to its surplus budget positions, access to international financial markets has not been essential for economic development.

Commercial Banks

Financial services are offered by commercial banks which provide a wide range of retail banking services, with some boasting an extensive branch network throughout the country. The commercial banks include Barclays Bank of Botswana, Standard Chartered Bank Botswana, First National Bank of Botswana, Zimbank Botswana, and Stanbic Bank Botswana.

Currency

Monetary unit: pula (P) = 100 thebe

The pula was introduced in 1976 when Botswana broke with the South African rand. The pula was initially pegged to the U.S. dollar, and is now pegged to a basket of currencies predominated by the rand (pula means "rain"; one-hundredth of a pula is a thebe, or "shield"). The pula is one of Africa's strongest currencies. A forward market exists for up to three months and, on occasion, to six months. Exchange rates are as follows: pula per US\$1–3.7037 (September 1997), 2.8305 (January 1996), 2.7716 (1995), 2.6831 (1994), 2.4190 (1993), 2.1327 (1992), 2.0173 (1991).[9] There are a number of web sites providing updated currency exchange values. The following is an example:

http://www.bloomberg.com/markets/currency/currcalc.cgi

As of January 1, 1995, for the first time the government permitted the establishment of foreign currency denominated accounts in Botswana (in U.S. dollars, British pounds, German marks, or South African rand). Businesses may open such accounts without prior approval from the Bank of Botswana. In 1996 the government authorized the issuance of foreign currency denominated loans.

The February 1996 relaxation of exchange controls included permitting external borrowing without prior approval from the Bank of Botswana up to prescribed limits, and that excess borrowing requirements must be referred to the Bank of Botswana. Botswana's foreign exchange reserves declined by over P1.0 billion between January and March 1997, to P18.847 million. The central bank does not intervene in the foreign exchange markets, however the bank does determine the level and timing of interest rate changes. Commercial banks are free to make foreign currency readily available up to any amount for current account transactions without consulting the Bank of Botswana.

In 1997 the Botswana Development Corporation (BDC) announced plans to issue the first ever bonds denominated in Botswana pula in a move to create a brand new market in this currency. BDC plans to issue P50 million (\$18.58 million) in bonds maturing between five and seven years. The Bank of Botswana issues short-term pula-denominated money market bills, but the issue would be the first fixed coupon instrument with a long maturity. The deal may establish precedence for other parastatal Botswana borrowers who the government is presently trying to wean off direct public funding.[10]

Pricing the issue in the absence of any kind of long-dated pula yield curve will be a process of discovery with potential investors, with South African debt providing a proxy benchmark. However, there are distinct differences between the two markets. Botswana is debt free, has never had an international credit rating, and has a long history of political stability and relative prosperity. A secondary market will be created in these instruments.

Privatization

The government is engaged in most facets of business through parastatals, equity holdings in mining ventures, and its market regulatory and licensing powers. The government has indicated that it will move forward with privatization of government holdings. It is government policy not to privatize its holdings in Debswana, the diamond mining joint venture with De Beers of South Africa.

THE STOCK EXCHANGE: BOTSWANA STOCK EXCHANGE

The stock market's development has been driven by the government's desire to list companies developed by the Botswana Development Corporation. The local market index increased 6.4 percent in 1995; however, after inflation and currency were factored in the returns were negative in both domestic and U.S.-dollar terms. In 1996 the local index increased 5.8 percent, however due to the depreciation of the pula the market price index declined 20.3 percent in U.S.-dollar terms. Botswana's performance ranked it seventy-first (of seventy-six) in the International Finance Corporation's 1996 World Stock Market Performance ranking.[11] Over the longer term, 1989 to 1996, equities significantly outperformed treasury bills.[12] In 1997, the market increased 91 percent, the second largest increase in the world.

Stockbrokers Botswana Ltd.
Private Bag 00417
Ground Floor, Barclay House
Khama Cresent
Gaborone, Botswana
Tel.: (267) 357 900   Fax: (267) 357 901

Web Sites	http://www.africa.co.uk/exchange/ex-bot.htm
	http://mbendi.co.za/exbo.htm
	http://www.wna.co.za/achill/botswana/busbul/stock.html
Established[13]	Share market established on June 19, 1989.
	Stock Exchange Act passed in 1994.
Stock Exchange Act	Stock Exchange Act was implemented November 1, 1995.
Trading Days	Monday to Friday
Trading Hours	9:00–16:00 Monday to Thursday
	9:00–12:00 Friday
	The international time zone is GMT + 2.

Market Index

The Botswana Share Market (BSM) Index is weighted according to the volume of shares in issue, as well as the current bid price. The index base was set at 100 in June 19, 1989. When the Botswana Stock Exchange (BSE) market opened November 1, 1995, the BSE All Share Index with an initial value of 308.95 replaced the BSM, the closing value of the old index. This is a market capitalization index, which includes all listed shares. The exchange index ended 1997 at 708.49.

STOCK MARKET ACTIVITY

The passage of the Botswana Stock Exchange Bill links the exchange to developments in the rest of the world. The bill facilitates the attraction of new listings, encouraging the inflow of foreign capital and providing Botswana with enhanced access to equities as a form of savings and a means of participating in the benefits of private-sector growth. The Trading Structure is a single price auction floor system.

Performance

The Botswana Stock Exchange listed equities rose 5.8 percent in 1996, but a 22-percent decline in the value of the Botswana pula caused the 1996 market's price index to fall 20 percent in U.S.-dollar terms as of the end of December 1996.[14] Through the end of 1997, the exchange was up 91 percent.

Market Valuation[15]

Year	Price–Earnings Ratio	Dividend Yield
1991	16.02	na
1992	9.01	na
1993	8.04	na
1994	9.33	na
1995	9.97	6.47
1996	7.28	7.50
1997	10.33	4.77

Ownership

Private investment accounts for 8 percent of total market capitalization. Foreign investment accounts for 60 percent of total direct investment and 8 percent of total portfolio investment. Local institutions and investors hold the remaining 24 percent of shares. There are approximately 10,000 shareholders. Foreigners have invested $65 million in the twelve companies listed on the Botswana Stock Exchange. Membership is corporate.

Listing Requirements[16]

Annual listing fees are as follows: A fee of P15,000 minimum/P65,000 maximum per company per annum as determined by market capitalization, or 0.025 percent of the company's market capitalization calculated on the market price of the company's share at its year-end (sustaining fees). The choice depends upon which realizes the greater amount. Fees are payable

annually in advance, calculated on the company's share price as supplied by
the share transfer secretary and confirmed by the Botswana Share Market.

Number of Listed Firms

As the number of listed firms remained constant from 1995 to 1996, the
market capitalization declined 18 percent in U.S.-dollar value. The number
of firms listed increased at an annual compound rate of 6 percent from the
end of 1991. The annual compound growth rate of market capitalization
over this period is 4.5 percent.

Number of Listed Firms and Market Capitalization[17]

Year	Number of Firms	Market Capitalization (US$ Millions)
1991	9	261
1992	11	295
1993	11	261
1994	11	377
1995	12	398
1996	12	326
1997	12	613

Through 1996 there were no foreign firms listed on the exchange.[18] In
December 1996, the government relaxed the capital account exchange controls to make it possible for foreign listed and registered companies to dual
list on the exchange and be regarded as domestic investors. By September
1997, there were six foreign firms trading. These were Johannesburg Stock
Exchange companies Avis, De Beers, Forbes, McCarthy, Profum (SA), and
the Dublin exchange listing RUAAF.

Liquidity

Trading volume has risen since 1989 following the market's opening to
foreign investors, listings of privatizations and foreign firms on the exchange, and corporate restructurings. The concentration of shares in the
hands of major controlling shareholders and some institutional shareholders that do not trade restricts the float in a number of securities.

Around 44.9 million shares traded in 1995, an increase of almost 50 percent on the previous year. Botswana has long had liberal investment policies and continues to encourage foreign investment, notably through the
Industrial Development Act 1993, the Financial Assistance Policy, and a regional development program in Selebi-Phikwe. The International Finance

Corporation ranks Botswana fifty-ninth (of eighty-four) in terms of market turnover. This ranks Botswana fifth in Africa.[19]

Market Turnover Ratio

Year	1992	1993	1994	1995	1996	1997
Turnover Ratio[20]	5.3	7.2	9.9	10.0	9.0	10.4

Market activity slowed 10 percent in 1996 from the earlier levels. In dollar terms the value of trading declined 18 percent to $31 million from 1995. In 1996, the average daily U.S.-dollar trading was approximately $141,000; by 1997 trading had increased to $56.4 million with $256,000 trading daily.

Instruments Traded

Equities and government bonds are traded. Currently there are no derivative products traded on the exchange, and the exchange has no plans to institute them. The bond market deals only in three- to nine-month treasury bills (Bank of Botswana Certificates), which are made available to the public on the exchange. Treasury bills are not for sale to nonresidents. In December 1997, the Botswana Development Corporation issued Botswana's first ever bond—a P50 million bond. The seven-year bond was listed on the Botswana Stock Exchange on December 5, 1997. The issue was nearly 50 percent oversubscribed. The BDC bond issued by a government parastatal demonstrates the Botswana government's desire to reduce the amount of cheap money that is available through Public Debt Service Funds. Botswana's 15 percent withholding tax levied on this issue makes the issue unattractive to international investors.

Brokerage Rates

Amounts up to P50,000	2.0%
P50,000 to P100,000	1.5%
Amounts over P100,000	1.0%

A handling fee of P15 is charged on purchases and P10 on sales.

Margin/Securities Lending

Short sales are permitted. However, there are restrictions that they must be on the "up-tick," the total amount of the sale must be deposited with the broker, and the buyer must be notified that it is a short sale. The broker may not lend the purchaser any part of the purchase price against the security as collateral. A bank may make such a loan, and there are no limitations or regulations on the bank's actions in this regard.

Insider Trading

Trading regulations prohibit insider trading.

Dividends and Capital Gains Taxation

There are no capital gains taxes on listed shares. Taxes on dividends are withheld at 15 percent and paid net. The tax rate on interest payments is 15 percent. The country has double taxation agreements with South Africa, the United Kingdom, and Sweden.

Regulatory Controls

The BSE Committee, with three members appointed by the Ministry of Finance and three members of the stockbroking business, oversees share dealings, listings, takeovers, mergers, and suspensions. Stockbrokers Botswana is currently the sole registered stockbroker in the country. It administers the trading functions of the BSE. Ernst & Young, a professional accountancy firm, administers the compliance of the exchange.

Foreign Investment Restrictions

Nonresidents may invest freely. There are no restriction on the repatriation of capital, dividends, and related earnings. However, exchange control permission is needed for nonresidents wishing to hold more than 5 percent of the capital of a public company. Total foreign holdings may not exceed 49 percent of any company. For exchange control purposes, a foreign investor holding more than 5 percent of the issued capital is categorized as a "direct investor," and capital flows in and out of the country require central bank approval. An investor holding less than 5 percent is a "portfolio investor," and there are no restrictions on capital and dividend flows. Portfolio investors may not collectively own more than 49 percent of a listed company's "free" float (total shares less "direct investors" held shares).

Based on information from the U.S. Department of Commerce National Trade Data Bank in April 1997, precise figures on foreign direct investment are not available. Best estimates are that FDI amounts to over US$1 billion. The U.S. Embassy estimates U.S. direct investment in Botswana at US$60 to 80 million. The total for Europe is probably somewhat higher. The majority of foreign direct investment in Botswana comes from South Africa.[21]

Trading

There are no price limits or daily trading ranges. Trading is conducted in share lots of 100 shares. The market has low market liquidity. In 1996 trading averaged twelve trades a day.

Central Depository

There is no central depository, however there are plans to establish one. Barclays Bank of Botswana Limited and Standard Chartered Bank Botswana Limited both offer custodial services for overseas investors.

Settlement

Settlement for trades is made by book entry and clearance is by transaction. Settlement must be made within ten working days. Delivery of scrip must take place within five working days, against payment within trade plus ten working days. Failed trades do not exist in Botswana, however in about 1 percent of trades settlement is delayed until such time that settlement can occur.

Registration

Nominees names are acceptable for share transfer registration. Several companies operate their own share registers, while others have company secretaries. Shares will be transferred from seller to buyer once the share certificate and transfer documents are tendered to them. The average time for registration is three weeks. Shares may trade even if they are in the registration process.

Corporate Actions

Information concerning corporate actions is published weekly in the Stockbrokers Botswana Ltd. newsletter. Public notification is also made through local newspapers. Corporate actions include flotations, rights issues, bonus shares, share splits, and dividends.

Voting

Proxy voting is allowed. Foreign shareholders are permitted to vote and possess the same rights as domestic shareholder. Minority shareholders rights are protected under the provisions of the Stock Exchange Act, Botswana Stock Exchange Committee, Members' Rule and Listing requirements.

Reporting Requirements

Listed firms must submit final and interim reports (every six months). Reports are publicly available.

Legal Issues

Domestic courts would enforce a governing law clause that provides for New York Law. Botswana's legal system is sufficient to ensure the conduct of secure commercial dealings. Secured and unsecured creditors enjoy the same rights under bankruptcy proceedings as they would in the United States, and foreign and domestic parties have equal recourse to the judicial system. Botswana is a member of the International Center for the Settlement of Investment Disputes (ICSID) and the Multilateral Investment Guarantee Agency (MIGA).

Regional Affiliations

The Southern African Customs Union, linking Botswana with South Africa, Lesotho, Namibia, and Swaziland, is an arrangement which allows the free movement of goods between member countries, enabling each to receive its due share of the customs pool generated by commodities imported from outside. Botswana is also a member of the twelve-country Southern African Development Community.

INTERNET RESOURCES

News

The Panafrican News Agency, at http://www.africanews.org/south/botswana, offers periodic news reports about Botswana.

Business Resources

Botswana Stock Exchange, at http://mbendi.co.za/exbo.htm, provides an overview of the exchange, regulations, market listing, and contact information. Maintained by a private entity, Mbendi Information Services.

Ernst and Young Investment Profile, at http://mbendi.co.za/ernsty/cyboeyip.htm, includes general background information on Botswana, including procedures on how to establish a business, taxation, and incentives. Maintained by a private entity, Mbendi Information Services.

Telecommunications Sector Profile for Botswana at http://rtr.worldweb.net/Textonly/botsp1.htm

United Nations Trade Point Development Center, at http://tradepoint.cs.tut.fi/
untpdc/incubator/africahp/bwa/bw.htm, includes comprehensive information
on Botswana's economy, foreign trade, and investment, and in-depth coverage of
various economic sectors. It is an overview of Botswana's commercial environment (economic, political, and market analysis) from an American perspective.

U.S. Department of Commerce's International Trade Administration 1996
Country Commercial Guide, at http://www.ita.doc.gov/uscs/ccgobots.html, is
an overview of Botswana's commercial environment (economic, political, and
market analysis) from an American perspective.

NOTES

1. CIA Factbook web site at http://www.odci.gov/cia/publications/nsolo/
factbook/bc.htm.

2. Ibid.

3. Ibid.

4. K. R. Jefferis, University of Botswana presents an overview of economic reform
and development in Botswana at web site http://www.unicc.org/untpdc/incubator/
africahp/bwa/bw2.htm. He notes, "In common with many other countries, the past
year has been one of disappointingly slow economic growth in Botswana. Recent estimates are that the economy grew by approximately 2 percent in 1992/93 and 1993/
94, which is not particularly poor by current world standards but significantly below
the 10 percent a year average growth rates experienced in Botswana during the
1980s."

5. CIA Factbook web site.

6. The World Bank's criteria for middle-income classification is a GNP per
capita of $766 to $9,385 in 1995. Botswana's per capita GNP in 1995 was $3,020.

7. Discussion of Central Bank Function and Financial Institutions at web site
http://www.unicc.org/untpdc/incubator/africahp/bwa/bw16.htm.

8. The Central Bank comments are at ibid.

9. CIA Factbook web site.

10. Alister Bull, "World's first Botswanan Pula-bond looms," *Reuters*, 12 September
1997.

11. *Emerging Stock Markets Factbook 1997* (Washington, D.C.: International Finance
Corporation, 1997).

12. Christopher Hartland-Peel, *African Equitites: A Guide to Markets and Companies*
(London: Euromoney, 1996), 79.

13. Market data were obtained from exchange sources and from MBendi, a private company that maintains African data and web sites. See web site http://
mbendi.co.za/exbo.htm. Used with permission.

14. *Emerging Stock Markets Factbook 1997.*

15. Stockbrokers Botswana Limited, 5th Floor, Barclays House, Khama Crescent,
P.O. Box 41015, Gaborone, Botswana.

16. *Going Public, A Guide to Share Market Listings* (Gaborone: Botswana Stock Exchange
Publication, 1990).

17. Stockbrokers Botswana Limited, 5th Floor, Barclays House, Khama Crescent,
P.O. Box 41015, Gaborone, Botswana.

18. *The Botswana Share Market: Procedure for Listing and General Requirements for Listed Companies* (Gaborone: Botswana Stock Exchange Publication, 1990).

19. *Emerging Stock Markets Factbook 1997.*

20. Ibid.

21. Information on the investment climate in Botswana is available at web site http://www.tradeport.org/ts/countries/botswana/climate.html.

CÔTE D'IVOIRE

COUNTRY

Until 1986, Côte d'Ivoire was also known as the Ivory Coast. This West African country covers an area of 123,847 square miles (320,763 square km). The nation's size is comparative to New Mexico. The capital is Yamoussoukro, while Abidjan is the administrative and commercial center. French is the country's official language, though there are more than sixty independent tribes, each with a separate dialect. Dioula is the most widely spoken dialect.

The French established a presence in Côte d'Ivoire at the end of the seventeenth century. Treaties were negotiated with local chiefs during the 1800s, and in 1893 Côte d'Ivoire became a French colony. Between 1908 and 1918 the French military occupied the country. In 1946 the nation became a territory in the French Union. The nation achieved peaceful self-governance in 1958 and independence on August 7, 1960. France and Côte d'Ivoire continue their close economic ties.

Official Religion	None[1]
Religions	Indigenous, 25%; Muslim, 60%; Christian, 12%
Population	14,762,000 (1996 est.)
	Urban: 42%
	Rural: 58%
	Population under the age of 15: 48%
Ethnic Divisions	Baoule, 23%; Bete, 18%; Senoufou, 15%; Malinke, 11%; Agni, 11%; foreign Africans (mostly Burkinabe and Malians, about 3 million), 20%; non-Africans 130,000 to 330,000 (French 30,000 and Lebanese 100,000 to 300,000), 2%
Languages	French (official), sixty native dialects with Dioula the most widely spoken
Education	Population over age 15 who are literate: 40%

The Political System

The country is a multiparty republic governed by the politically moderate Democratic Party of Côte d'Ivoire (PDCI). The country's 1960 constitution provides for a political system led by a president who is elected to a five-year term by popular vote. Côte d'Ivoire enjoys universal adult suffrage. The legislative branch consists of the National Assembly, which is also elected to five-year terms by popular vote. Opposition parties were legalized in 1990.

Felix Houphouet-Boigny, founder of the PDCI, ruled the country from its 1960 independence until his death in 1993. Power was peacefully transferred to the constitutional successor, Henri Konan Bédié, on December 7, 1993. The last presidential election was held on October 22, 1995 and President Bédié was elected with 95 percent of the vote. The next presidential election is scheduled for October 2000. Legislative elections were held on November 27, 1995, and are next scheduled for November 2000. For the presidential election of October 22, 1995, the votes were distributed as follows.[2]

Candidate	Party	Percentage
Konan Bédié	PDCI	95.2
Francis Wodié	PIT	3.8
Laurent Gbagbo	FPI	boycott
Djény Kobina	RDR	boycott

Parliament

The National Assembly has 175 members, elected for a five-year term in single-seat constituencies. Based on elections on November 26, 1995 and December 30, 1996, the distribution of Assembly seats is as follows:

Parti Démocratique de la Côte d'Ivoire	148
(Democratic Party of Ivory Coast, authoritarian)	
Rassemblement des Républicains	14
(Rally of the Republicans, centrist)	
Front Populaire Ivorienne	12
(Ivorian People's Front, social-democratic)	
Vacant	1

Political Web Site   http://www.geocities.com/~derksen/election/country/iv.htm

Legal System

The legal system is based on the French civil law system and customary law; judicial reviews occur in the Constitutional Chamber of the Supreme Court. Côte d'Ivoire has not accepted compulsory ICJ jurisdiction.

Suffrage is at twenty-one years of age and is universal.

The Economy

On August 4, 1997, the Economist Intelligence Unit reported that five out of twenty of the world's fastest growing economies that are likely to grow more than 6 percent in 1997 are in Africa, and include Botswana, Zimbabwe, Angola, Uganda, and Côte d'Ivoire. The country's economic base is primarily agricultural. It leads the world in production of cocoa and is one of the largest coffee producers. The agricultural base was hit hard during the 1980s by falling prices for coffee and cocoa. Subsequently, the economy began to diversify to include the production of bananas, cotton, rubber, and palm products.

The country is heavily indebted with a debt to GNP ratio of over 150 percent. Thus, Côte d'Ivoire fell into arrears on its debt repayments and abandoned its structural adjustment program in 1986. Between 1987 and 1993 the economy contracted at an average rate of 1 percent per year. At the beginning of 1993, however, it devalued its currency and is now trying again with another reform program. In 1994 the economy grew at 1.8 percent and in 1995–1996 it increased at a 7-percent rate.

The economic problems of the 1980s were exacerbated by an overvalued CFAF and low commodity prices. Côte d'Ivoire is among the world's largest producers and exporters of coffee, cocoa beans, and palm-kernel oil. Consequently, the economy is highly sensitive to fluctuations in international prices for coffee and cocoa and to weather conditions. Despite attempts by the government to diversify, the economy is still largely dependent on agriculture and related industries. The Ivorian economy began a comeback in 1994, due to improved prices for cocoa and coffee, growth in nontraditional primary exports such as pineapples and rubber, trade and banking liberalization, offshore oil and gas discoveries, and generous external financing and debt rescheduling by multilateral lenders and France. The 50 percent devaluation of Franc Zone currencies on January 12, 1994 caused a one-time jump in the inflation rate to 26 percent for 1994. Inflation fell to 4.5 percent in 1996.[3] In 1997 inflation increased to 5 percent. Moreover, government adherence to donor-mandated reforms led to a budget surplus in 1994. Real growth of GDP in 1994 was 1.7 percent, a significant improvement following several years of negative growth. In 1995 growth picked up to 5 percent.

When it completes the rescheduling of its outstanding debt, Côte d'Ivoire will be the second African country after Nigeria to issue Brady bonds. As part of the debt accord, the government will buy back a minimum of 30 percent of all eligible debt in cash, at 24 percent of face value.

	1996	1997E	1998E
Real GDP growth	6.2%	6.0%	5.5%
Export growth (year on year)	4.1%	2.3%	10.0%
Average Annual Inflation	7.4% (1990–1996)		
	3.0% (projected 1997–2000)		
Foreign Exchange reserves	US$621.5 million (12/31/96)[4]		

Gross Domestic Product[5]

Côte d'Ivoire is classified as a low-income country under the World Bank's classification of economies.[6] For comparability, Gross Domestic Product is expressed in purchase power parity terms.

GDP purchasing power parity $21.9 billion (1995 est.)
GDP real growth rate   5.0% (1995 est.)
GDP per capita $1,500 (1995 est.)

The per capita GDP fell significantly following the 1994 devaluation of the CFA franc.

Central Bank: The Banque Centrale des Etats de l'Afrique de l'Ouest

The Banque Centrale des Etats de l'Afrique de l'Ouest (Central Bank of West African States; BCEAO), the nation's central bank, was established on November 1, 1962. The eight members using the Central Bank are Benin, Burkina Faso, Côte d'Ivoire, Guinea-Bissau, Mali, Niger, Senegal, and Togo. New statutes for the BCEAO, attached to the West African Monetary Union's Treaty of November 14, 1973, were adopted by the governments of the six countries forming the Union and put into operation in 1975. The headquarters has been located in Dakar, Senegal, since July 1, 1978.[7]

Postal Address
B.P. 1769
Avenue Delafosse et Blvd. B. Roussel
Abidjan 01
Côte d'Ivoire
Tel.: +(225) 21–0466/9070   Fax: +(225) 22–2852
Web Site   http://www.imf.org/external/np/sec/decdo/bceao.htm

There are sixteen commercial banks, including Banque Paribas, Barclays Bank, and Citibank. The country's high debt levels have affected the banking system by creating considerable arrears. Financial institutions began making provisions for bad debts in 1993 and 1994.

Credit Rating

At present, Côte d'Ivoire has not been rated by international rating agencies for either domestic or foreign currency debt.

Currency

Monetary unit: Central African franc = 100 centimes

In January 1994, the CFAF was devalued to CFAF 100 per French franc from CFAF 50 at which it had been fixed since 1948. The devaluation of the currency has helped the country's trade balance.

There are a number of web sites providing updated currency exchange values. The following is an example:

http://www.bloomberg.com/markets/currency/currcalc.cgi

Privatization

Privatization efforts began in 1991 with the privatization of the country's electric company. Privatization proceeds increased from CFAF 6.5 billion in 1991, to CFAF 53.6 billion in 1996. The government seeks to sell between 35 to 51 percent of a firm to a strategic shareholder, sell 10 to 15 percent of the shares on the Abidjan Stock Exchange, reserve 3 to 5 percent for the company's employees, and retain 20 to 30 percent for itself. The Privatization Committee evaluates strategic partners based upon price and technical considerations, with price being given the greatest consideration. To ensure public support and demonstrate the transparency of the process, bids are opened in public.

Under the country's privatization program and economic reforms, the stock exchange mobilized between CFAF 11.5 billion ($24 million) for investment between 1992 and 1995. The privatization of the SIVOM port maintenance authority was oversubscribed by 57 percent. Côte d'Ivoire has privatized about sixty companies through August 1997.

In 1997 the country sold 51 percent of CI-Telecom to France Telecom, realizing CFAF 140 billion from the transfer. France Telecom, taking a strategic share of CI-Telecom, has committed to quadruple the number of phone lines within five years. To ensure competition the government will end CI-Telecom's monopoly rights in seven years. The privatization achieved a price per line of $3,500, or double the emerging market norm.[8] In the March 1997 privatization of CI-Telecom the government raised $193 million. The government plans to retain 35 percent while the remainder will be sold to employees and private investors through an offering on the Abidjan Stock Exchange.

THE STOCK EXCHANGE: BOURSE DES VALEURS D'ABIDJAN (ABIDJAN STOCK EXCHANGE)

The Bourse des Valeurs d'Abidjan is the only stock exchange in francophone West Africa. The exchange is working to transform its operations into a regional stock exchange to serve West African countries. The regional exchange will be called BRVM (Bourse Regionale des Valeurs Mobilieres). The exchange will be launched as soon as its computerization is complete. A Canadian company, EFA Software, was awarded the contract for the project. The computer system will enable all public and private users in the UEMOA zone to access the stock market information directly. The regional exchange's initial target launch date was before the end of 1997.[9] However, the 1997 launch was delayed and the regional exchange is expected to open in the first quarter of 1998. The Abidjan Stock Exchange closed for trading on December 31, 1997, but listed shares are still traded through local banks pending the opening of the regional exchange.

The regional exchange will serve the nations of Benin, Burkina Faso, Guinea-Bissau, Côte d'Ivoire, Mali, Niger, Senegal, and Togo. The region is already united by a common currency, the CFAF, and the nations believe that the regional exchange will facilitate trade and investment under the direction of their Economic and Monetary Union of West Africa. It is intended that the exchange will have a central office in Abidjan and national offices in each country. Shares will be floated in the market simultaneously. The region's traders would be linked by computer to the exchange in Abidjan. The regional exchange will play an important role in the development of capital for economic growth.

Dr. Leon Naka
President and Managing Director
01 BP 1878
Abidjan 01
Côte d'Ivoire
Tel.: 225–21 57 42/83   Fax: 225–22 16 57

Web Sites	http://africa-info.ihost.com/pages/2ci/2eco070.htm (French)
	http://www.mbendi.co.za/exci.htm
	http://www.mbendi.co.za/werksmns/lexaf/busci.htm
	http://www.africa.co.uk.htm
Established	July 24, 1974
	Commenced trading in April 1976
Trading Days	Tuesday to Friday; shares are traded on Tuesday and Thursday, bonds are traded on Wednesday and Friday.
Trading Hours	9:00–10:00
	The international time zone is GMT.

Market Index

There are two indexes, the general index (BVA) and one that tracks the top twelve companies (12VB).

STOCK MARKET ACTIVITY

The trading structure involves bonds on a screen-based quote system, and shares on open outcry.

Performance

In 1995, with a 140.8 percent U.S.-dollar return, the exchange was the leading market in the world. For 1996 the market recorded a 5.3 percent return, ranking it forty-ninth (of seventy-six) in the world. Equity returns have been greater than debt returns, in both nominal and real terms, since 1992. This is not the case from 1976 forward. From the stock exchange's inception in 1976 through 1996, debt instruments outperformed equity instruments by a considerable margin.[10]

Market Valuation

Year	Price–Earnings Ratio	Dividend Yield
1996	13.6	6.9%

As the number of listed firms remained constant from 1995 to 1996, the market capitalization increased 5.5 percent in U.S.-dollar terms. The number of firms listed increased at an annual compound rate of 4.4 percent from the end of 1991. The annual compound growth rate of market capitalization over this period is 11.1 percent.

Number of Listed Firms and Market Capitalization[11]

Year	Number of Firms	Market Capitalization (US$ Millions)
1991	25	541
1992	27	483
1993	24	414
1994	27	428
1995	31	866
1996	31	914

Liquidity

Trading activity on the exchange has increased from 1991, when only 1.4 percent of the market turned over, versus 2.2 percent in 1996. The concentration of shares in the hands of major shareholders that do not trade restricts the float in a number of securities.

Market Turnover Ratio

Year	1991	1992	1993	1994	1995	1996
Turnover Ratio[12]	1.4	0.8	1.3	3.7	2.2	2.2

Around $19.5 million worth of shares traded in 1996. The market's average daily turnover in 1996 was $88,600. The International Finance Corporation ranks the Côte d'Ivoire exchange seventy-fourth (of eighty-four) in terms of market turnover in 1996. This places the exchange in eleventh place in Africa.[13] Foreign investors own about 70 percent of the shares on the Abidjan Stock Exchange.[14]

Instruments Traded

About thirty government bonds are listed on the Abidjan Stock Exchange. In addition, two international bonds issued by the Lome-based BOAD (a regional bank) are listed on the exchange. Local residents are given precedence over foreign investors in the case of oversubscribed primary issues. There are no restrictions on overseas ownership on the secondary market.[15]

Societe Generale developed two mutual funds designed for the Central and West African countries of Cameroon and Côte d'Ivoire. The funds will be denominated in CFAF and sold to local investors. The first fund is designed to invest in unlisted shares in the region's recently privatized companies. The fund is targeted at $10 million in investments. The second fund will trade listed shares on the Abidjan Stock Exchange. The funds will have minimum investments of about $2,000 to attract both international and local investors.[16] There are currently no derivative products traded and the exchange has no plans to institute them.

Brokerage Rates

2% on bonds

3% other securities

Reduced to 1.5% on larger amounts up to CFAF 25 million

Insider Trading

Insider trading is illegal.

Dividend and Capital Gains Taxation

There is a 12 percent withholding tax on dividends but no capital gains tax. There is a 12 percent withholding tax on securities with maturities less than five years, and 6 percent on securities of more than five years.[17]

Regulatory Controls

The Abidjan Stock Exchange is regulated by the Conseil de la Bourse, a ten-person committee that includes the president of the stock exchange and a representative from the Ministry of Finance. No entity regulates acquisitions and takeovers, even where a change of control occurs.

Foreign Investment Restrictions

There are no restrictions on foreign ownership of shares or on the repatriation of capital, as Côte d'Ivoire generally welcomes foreign investments and almost all business activities are open to foreign investors. Exchange controls exist. Côte d'Ivoire belongs to the Franc Zone, and there is no exchange control between the following states: France, Monaco, all the states of the West Africa Economic and Monetary Union (Benin, Burkina Faso, Côte d'Ivoire, Equatorial Guinea, Mali, Niger, Senegal, Togo), and the following members of the Central African Economic and Union (CAEU): Cameroon, Central African Republic, Congo, Gabon, and Chad. Transfers out of WAEMU are subject to a transfer tax of 0.25 percent.

Central Depository

There is a central depository.

Settlement

Settlement is made by accounts, clearing every Monday.

Regional Affiliations

Côte d'Ivoire is a member of the Economic Community of West African States (ECOWAS). The community aims to promote trade and economic growth among member countries. Currently there are sixteen member countries, including Benin, Burkina Faso, Cape Verde, Gambia, Ghana, Guinea, Guinea Bissau, Côte d'Ivoire, Liberia, Mali, Mauritania, Niger, Nigeria, Senegal, Sierra Leone, and Togo.

Economic Community of West African States
Executive Secretariat
6 King George V Rd
Lagos
Nigeria
Tel.: +234 (0)1 63–6841

NOTES

1. CIA Factbook web site at http://www.odci.gov/cia/publications/nsolo/factbook/iv.htm.
2. See web site http://www.agora.stm.it/elections/election/ivorycst.htm.

3. "Country Profile: Côte d'Ivoire," *Emerging Markets Week*, 1 September 1997.

4. Ibid.

5. CIA Factbook web site.

6. The World Bank's criteria for low-income classification is a GNP per capita of less than $765 in 1995. Côte d'Ivoire's per capita GNP in 1995 was $660.

7. See web site at http://www.imf.org/external/np/sec/decdo/bceao.htm.

8. Nicholas Denton, "France Telecom edges ahead in African bid," *Financial Times*, 9 January 1997. Despite the record per-line privatization value accorded to CI-Telecom, all the current African Telecoms privatizations combined have raised less than the partial sale of Telecom Eireann of Ireland.

9. "W. Africa Regional Exchange Nears Launch," *Emerging Markets Week*, 26 January 1998.

10. Christopher Hartland-Peel, "Côte d'Ivoire," in *African Equities: A Guide to Markets and Companies* (London: Euromoney, 1996), 290.

11. *Emerging Stock Markets Factbook 1997* (Washington, D.C.: International Finance Corporation, 1997).

12. Ibid.

13. Ibid.

14. *Emerging Markets Week*.

15. Ibid.

16. "SOCGEN Targets Investors in Central, West Africa," *Emerging Markets Week*, 7 July 1997.

17. Ibid.

EGYPT

COUNTRY

The Arab Republic of Egypt (Jumhuriyat MIsR Al-'Arabiyah, Arabic MISR) has an area of 385,229 square miles (997,739 square kilometers) in the northeastern corner of Africa. The country's area is comparative to slightly more than three times the size of New Mexico. The capital is Cairo.

The nation is primarily concentrated in the Nile River valley, which is between five to ten miles wide before the Nile Delta. The Aswan High Dam (1970) has allowed the annual Nile flood to be totally controlled. The Delta is 100 miles long and 150 miles wide. In contrast to many African nations, the Egyptian population is a fairly homogeneous group.

The nation represents one of the world's oldest civilizations. Upper and Lower Egypt were united around 2925 B.C. The unification began 3,000 years of native leaders. Foreign entities invaded Egypt starting with the Assyrians in seventh century B.C. Alexander III the Great's invasion in 332 B.C. ushered in an era of Hellenism and Semitic learning. Egypt was controlled by the Romans from 30 B.C. to A.D. 395, with control transferred to Constantinople after that date. This control ended in A.D. 642 with an Arab invasion. Subsequently, Egypt developed into an Arabic state with Islam as the dominant religion. The Ottoman Turks conquered Egypt in 1517 and it was ruled from Istanbul. A brief French invasion in 1798 brought Egypt to Europe's attention. In 1882, during a period of civil disturbance, the British occupied the country. Egypt became a British protectorate in 1922, with a constitutional monarchy.

A 1952 coup overthrew the monarchy and saw the emergence of Gamal Abdel Nasser as leader. Nasser orchestrated a nationalization of the Suez Canal and instituted socialist policies. Nasser waged two unsuccessful wars with Israel, in 1956 and 1967, consequently losing the Sinai to Israeli occupation. Nasser was succeeded by Anwar el-Sadat. Sadat also went to war with Israel in 1973, but Sadat also played a leading role in Middle East peace talks. In October 1981 he was assassinated by Muslim fundamentalists. He was succeeded by Hosni Mubarak, who continued the peace initiatives that resulted in the return of the Sinai to Egyptian control. Egypt became the only Arab state to establish relations with Israel, in 1982, and Egypt was subsequently condemned by other Arab nations and began a period of isolation and ostracization. Its position as a leading Arab state was recognized in the Gulf War when it joined other Arab states in opposition to the Iraqi invasion of Kuwait.

Official Religion   Islam, predominantly Sunnite[1]

Religions   Muslim (mostly Sunni) 94% (official estimate), Coptic Christian and other 6% (official estimate). Al-Azhar University, founded in A.D. 970, is a leading center of Islamic and Arabic learning.

Population	63,575,000 (1996 est.)[2]
	Urban 45%
	Rural 55%
	Population under the age of 15: 38%
Ethnic Divisions	Eastern Hamitic stock (Egyptians, Bedouins, and Berbers) 99%, Greek, Nubian, Armenian, other European (primarily Italian and French) 1%
Languages	Arabic (official), English and French widely understood by educated classes
Education	Population over age 15 who are literate: 51.4%

The Political System

The political system consists of a president nominated by the national legislature and confirmed to a six-year term (renewable) by a popular national referendum. The last presidential elections were held in October 1993. The last elections/confirmation was won by President Hosni Mubarak. The next presidential elections are scheduled for October 1999.

The unicameral national legislature has 454 members, with 444 elected by popular vote to five-year terms and ten members appointed by the president. The National Democratic Party, HDW, dominates the political environment, controlling 316 seats outright and an additional ninety-nine seats held by "Independents" joining HDW. The party prohibits communists and Islamic fundamentalist from organizing into political parties. Parliamentary elections were held in November 1995 with President Hosni Mubarak's National Democratic Party winning the elections. Much of the fundamentalist opposition to the regime has been eliminated. A key political agenda for the new term was privatizing government holdings and increasing the ownership base. The next elections are scheduled for November 2000. Egypt's supreme judiciary is the Supreme Constitutional Court.

Political Web Site   http://www.geocities.com/~derksen/election/egypt.htm

Legal System

The Egyptian legal system is based on English common law, Islamic law, and Napoleonic codes. Judicial review is by the Supreme Court and the Council of State (oversees validity of administrative decisions). Egypt accepts compulsory ICJ jurisdiction, with reservations.

Suffrage is at eighteen years of age and is universal and compulsory.

The Economy

Under the nationalization policies of Gamal Abdel Nasser the economic orientation of the country was mainly socialist. Currently there is a reorientation, with a privatization program moving forward in the transition to free enterprise. At the outset of the privatization drive approximately 70 percent of Egypt's industry was nationalized. The GNP originates primarily from industry, followed by agriculture. The cash-only underground economy is estimated at 50 percent of GDP.

From the late 1980s inflation was reduced from 30 percent annually to 8 percent in 1995 and the country built up hard currency reserves of $18 billion. In August 1997, the annualized inflation had declined to 4.7 percent. Egypt's fiscal deficit declined from 20 percent of GDP to 1.1 percent of GDP in 1996, with the assistance of new and improved taxes and lower government subsidies on non-food items.

The government must sustain future GDP growth rates of at least 6.5 percent to keep pace with the population growth. This level of growth will require a significant emphasis on exports. The cheap and abundant labor force will be crucial to the government's efforts to attract manufacturing enterprises. However, there is a significant shortage of skilled labor, as 2.5 million Egyptians work abroad, mostly in Saudi Arabia and the Arab Gulf states (1993 estimate). Unemployment rates in 1995 were estimated at 20 percent; by 1997, the official estimate had fallen to 9.4 percent, though unofficial estimates are 15 to 17 percent.

Gross Domestic Product[3]

Egypt is classified as a middle-income country under the World Bank's classification of economies.[4] For comparability, Gross Domestic Product is expressed in purchase power parity terms.

GDP purchasing power parity: $171 billion (1995 est.)

GDP real growth rate: 5% (1996)

GDP per capita: $2,760 (1995 est.)

As the Egyptian government moves forward with its privatization program it is opening its economy to market forces. The investment grade credit rating by Standard & Poor's opened access to international capital markets for Egyptian enterprises, allowing reduced borrowing costs. In addition, Egyptian capital markets have a long-term, ten-year horizon for lending compared to other emerging African economies that have limited capital market access and one year or less funding. The cost of the long-term, ten-year bond decreased from 11.57 percent in 1995 to 10.8 percent at the end of 1996.

Central Bank: Central Bank of Egypt/Bank al-Markaz al-Misr

The Central Bank of Egypt is constitutionally and operationally independent from the government, but it acts as an agent to the Ministry of Finance and as a banker to the government. The bank's primary responsibilities are to set and implement monetary policy and control interest rate changes. The bank may intervene in foreign exchange markets, and provides supervision and oversight to the banking sector and other financial institutions.

Postal Address

Central Bank of Egypt/Bank al-Markaz al-Misr
31 Kasr el-Nil Street
Cairo
Egypt
Tel.: 20–2–392–6211   Fax: 20–2–392–6361

Credit Rating

Following the Gulf War, Egypt benefited from debt forgiveness totaling $24 billion. Consequently, in 1997 Standard & Poor's rated Egyptian local currency debt A-/stable/A-1 and its foreign currency debt BBB-/Stable/A-3, which is an investment-grade rating.[5] Moody's rated Egypt's long-term currency debt a speculative Ba2 rating in October 1996. This rating was upgraded to Ba2 in November 1997.

Banking Sector

Nationalization of the banking sector occurred in the 1950s and 1960s. The resulting system involved four public-sector banks and some specialized banks. In 1974, President Sadat permitted the establishment of a number of joint ventures and offshore banks. By 1997 the Egyptian banking sector consisted of eighty-one banks. The deregulation of the banking sector transformed a highly regulated industry into a competitive one. The transition involved banks in a significant evolution in terms of assets and liabilities. The Commercial International Bank (CIB) completed an international equity placement through a GDR issue, listed on the London Stock Exchange, in July 1996. The placement was five times oversubscribed and raised more than $490 million in capital for the bank.

A major breakthrough of the Economic Reform and Structural Adjustment Program in Egypt is the strengthening and liberalization of the financial and banking sector, as well as introducing new securities and financial services. The banking sector has become more efficient and many joint-venture banks are in the process of being privatized. The central bank plays a regulatory role through offerings of treasury bills and monetary policies.

There are twenty-five public-sector banks, four commercial banks, four specialized banks, and seventeen agricultural banks. These banks dominate the retail sector with 847 branches, but offer limited products. There are fifty-six private and joint-venture banks, twenty-four commercial banks, eleven business and investment banks, and twenty-one offshore banks. The Commercial International Bank (Egypt) was rated B/C by IBCA, the first such rating in Egypt.

Commercial International Bank
21–23 Guiza Street
Guiza
Greater Cairo
Egypt
Tel.: 20–2–570–2679   Fax: 20–2–571–2362

The U.S. credit ratings agency Moody's Investors Service rated Egypt's four state-owned banks. It rated their long- and short-term deposits at Ba3/Not Price, in line with Moody's sovereign ceiling for Egypt. National Bank of Egypt received a financial strength rating of D, while Banque Misr, Banque du Caire, and Bank of Alexandria all received E.[6]

Currency

Monetary unit: Egyptian pound (LE) = 100 piastres

At the outset of Egyptian economic reform in 1990, the Egyptian pound was overvalued and supported at the official exchange rates by a nonconvertible currency regime. To avoid the massive depreciation of its currency, the government defied IMF advice and increased interest rates to support the currency exchange rates. Rates increased to 21 percent. The subsequent recession reduced inflation to 5.4 percent while exchange rates were stabilized. The pound has been a managed floating currency since November 1991. Central bank foreign currency reserves reached $20.4 billion at the end of 1997.

A forward market exists for up to twelve months, but it can be used only for commercial transactions and full details of the transaction are required. There are a number of web sites providing updated currency exchange values. The following is an example:

http://www.bloomberg.com/markets/currency/currcalc.cgi

Privatization

The government initiated reforms in 1991 and 1992. Law 203 provided for the restructuring of 314 public-sector enterprises in preparation for privatization, while law 230 established new incentives for foreign direct investment. Law 95 revitalized the stock and bond markets to give companies greater flexibility in meeting their financial needs.[7] In the past decade, Egypt has been breaking new ground in establishing a solid and attractive business and investment environment in the country. It has undergone major economic reform policies and a comprehensive structural adjustment program aimed at cutting bureaucracy and red tape, promoting free trade, liberalizing financial markets, restructuring and privatizing public enterprises, facilitating the participation of the private sector, relaxing the regulatory environment, and freeing prices.

In May 1996, the government sold its first majority stake through the stock exchange. The sale of 75 percent of Madinet Nasr Housing represented a major commitment of the government to the transition of the economy to a open economy. In 1996 the government sold majority stakes in sixteen companies and stakes of between 10 to 40 percent in nine other companies. The government's privatization program raised $680 million through the sale of assets in 1996 and was expected to accelerate in 1997, as the government proposed the sale of $1.5 billion of state-owned enterprises. The government indicated that privatization receipts will be treated as a capital item and used to restructure debt and lower the interest rate burden.

In response to Egypt's privatization, the private sector's contribution to the gross domestic product increased from 51 percent to 67 percent. The total investments expected during the fourth five-year plan period (1997–2002) are about 400 billion Egyptian pounds (about $117 billion). At the end of 1997 Egypt will have sold shares in sixty-eight companies with a total value of $1.5 billion. The state has indicated a goal of privatizing 300 state-owned companies. In January 1997 the first privately owned Egyptian holding company was floated on the Cairo Exchange. The Olympic Group Financial Investment (OGFI) offering was oversubscribed by 11.4 times in January 1997. In August the firm was issuing shares worth $22 million in its subsidiary, Cairo Precision Industries. The firm sold 7.5 million shares of the family-owned Olympic Group Financial Investment in the sale.[8]

THE STOCK EXCHANGE: CAIRO STOCK EXCHANGE

After performing strongly in 1994, the Egyptian stock market lost ground in 1995, with the index dropping by 11.8 percent, but the market surged in 1996 recording a yearly gain of 38.8 percent. The market performance ranked Egypt as the fourteenth best performing market in 1996 based on the IFC price indexes ranking in U.S.-dollar terms.[9]

Mr. Sherif Rafat
Chairman
Cairo Stock Exchange
4 (A) El Sherifeen Street
Cairo, Egypt

Tel.:   (202) 392–1447, (202) 392–8698, (202) 392–1402, (202) 393–3864
Fax: (202) 392–8526, (202) 392–4214

Founded   1883
First Established   1903

Stock market activity in Egypt goes back as far as 1883. The Alexandria Stock Exchange was the fifth oldest in the world. The Cairo Stock Exchange was later established in 1903. Since their inception, the two exchanges were active in truly reflecting the performance of the Egyptian economy, which was led by the private sector.During the late 1950s, the economy was based on privately owned companies, many of which were publicly held and constituted the core of the Egyptian capital market. The market was then the predominant source of funding for business. As a result of nationalization in 1959, however, the market dwarfed and stagnated. In 1994 the two exchanges were unified into a single market and are now electronically linked for real-time trading.

The stock exchange in Alexandria is a satellite of the Cairo exchange, and is linked by a network. The Alexandria market represents 15 percent of the total number of investors (165,000) and 8 percent of the total value of transactions.[10] Alexandria accounts for 25 percent of the small and medium-size investors (i.e., up to $3 million). Market reporters indicate that it is easier to deal from Alexandria than directly through Cairo, as stockbrokers in Alexandria are not fully loaded, direct contact between brokers and executors in the dealing room is possible, and customer service is more efficient, particularly with the transfer of share titles.[11]

The Alexandria Stock Exchange
11 Talat Harb Street
El Menshia, Alexandria

Tel.:   (20–3) 482 7966/1842/2979   Fax: (20–3) 482 3039

Established   1883

Trading Days   Sunday to Thursday

Trading Hours   10:30–12:30
                    The international time zone is GMT + 2.

STOCK MARKET ACTIVITY

The Trading Structure is open outcry, computer-based screen trading, with an automated OTC system.

The Lebanese, Kuwaiti, and Egyptian stock exchanges began cross-trading shares on January 6, 1997, according to Beirut Stock Exchange President Gaby Sehnaoui.[12] The stock exchanges of Kuwait, Egypt, and Lebanon began a cross-listing link-up to enable investors to conduct easier and faster share transactions on those markets. Share prices from each bourse are listed on the three markets. The electronic link-up comes under a cross-listing agreement initially signed in April 1996 between Kuwait's exchange and Egypt's official Capital Markets Agency. Lebanon entered the accord in September.[13] Law 95/1992 and its amendment in 1996 promulgated the rules for trading on the Egyptian exchange. The law identifies three types of securities: blue chips, bonds, and mutual fund certificates. The law provides for regulations governing mutual funds. In 1994, there were only two mutual funds in the market; this had increased to fifteen local funds and five offshore funds by mid-1997. The funds have an estimated total capital of $1 billion.[14]

There are 117 brokerage firms trading on the Egyptian Stock Exchange, but each is only allowed one computer screen on the exchange. There is an eleven-member board that oversees the exchange's daily operation under the auspices of the Capital Market Authority (CMA).[15]

Institutional reforms of the stock exchange have been essential to market development. The Capital Market Authority is determined to improve internal checks within the sales system to provide real-time records and install constant observation of trade from within the Cairo and Alexandria Stock Exchanges. Thirteen mutual funds are investing in Egyptian stock, creating transparency by publishing quarterly statements, lists of fund holdings, and, in the case of one fund manager, daily redemption.[16]

Performance

The International Finance Corporation ranked Egypt's 1996 market performance, based upon change in price indexes in U.S. dollars, as fourteenth of seventy-six markets. In 1996 the price index increased 38.8 percent, with the index increasing 28 percent in the fourth quarter. The market rerated mainly as a result of increasing investment by foreign institutional investors and greater research coverage by global brokerage houses. The market currently sells at a prospective multiple of eleven times earnings supported by a 5.5 percent dividend yield. GDP growth of 4.5 percent is expected with inflation declining to 6 percent in 1997. President Mubarak is committed to rapid privatization and recently announced that all remaining government-owned shares in joint-venture companies will be privatized in 1997.[17]

To support market development and provide liquidity to local markets, the Egyptian government has decided to invest part of the $25 billion state pension fund surplus in equities.

Market Valuation

Year	Price–Earnings Ratio	Dividend Yield
1995	19.3	na
1996	13.0	4.9%

The Cairo Stock Exchange was once the sixth largest exchange in the world. However, due to nationalization and socialist government policies, the exchange lost its status as a leading world market. Some 646 companies are listed on the exchange, but most are there solely for tax purposes and do not trade. Foreigners are allowed to own shares in only a few stocks.

Listing Requirements

For public offering, disclosure begins with the publication of a prospectus in two nationwide Egyptian newspapers of which at least one must be an Arabic language newspaper. The prospectus must contain, among other things, the following information:[18]

1. Objects of the company, its name, duration, and legal form
2. The issued and paid-in capital of the company
3. Information about the offered stocks, the nominal value and class of each stock, its advantages, and terms of offer
4. Names of the founders, the value of their participation, and information about the capital in kind if any
5. The investment policy of the company with respect to the proceeds of the public offering and its expectations as to the prospectus of such policy
6. The amount required to be paid up at subscription, which may not be less than 25 percent of the nominal value of the stock
7. The auditors of the company
8. An estimate of the incorporation costs
9. Details of dividends
10. Any contracts concluded by the founders within five years preceding incorporation which the founders intend to assign to the company
11. Names of the chairman, directors, and managers

As an incentive to list, joint stock companies that are listed on the exchange are exempt from corporate tax to an amount equal to a percentage of the paid-in capital determined by the central bank discount rate.[19]

Number of Listed Firms and Market Capitalization[20]

Year	Number of Firms	Market Capitalization (LE Millions)
1991	627	8,845
1992	656	10,845
1993	674	12,807
1994	700	14,480
1995	746	27,420
1996	646	48,086

Listings on the Cairo Stock Exchange have included a large number of firms that are infrequently traded.[21] This involves a number of family-owned Egyptian firms, which are listed on the exchange for tax reasons and do not trade. In fact, the trading of the exchange's largest listed firms was so infrequent as to make early attempts to calculate a daily index of trading impossible. From 1995 to 1996, the number of listed firms decreased 13.4 percent, from 746 to 646. This occurred as the CMA delisted firms that traded infrequently. By mid-1997 the number of listed companies had increased to 666.[22]

In 1997 there were eighteen registered mutual funds with total assets of $1 billion. Two companies, the Commercial International Bank and Al-Abram Beverages, have floated securities as Global Depository Receipts on the London Stock Exchange.

Liquidity

Despite the increase in trading volume and value the Egyptian markets, the IFC ranked Egypt forty-sixth in the world for market turnover in 1996. The market's turnover ration was 22.1 percent. However, this places Egypt in first place in terms of turnover among its African peers. As liquidity increases, the turnover in the first four months of 1997 was almost equal to the entire ten-year period from 1986 to 1996.[23]

The number of investors involved in the exchange has increased from 200,000 in 1995 to 1.1 million in 1997.[24] In the first half of 1997 Egyptian stock market turnover increased threefold over the same period in 1996, $3.6 billion versus $970 million. Foreign investors were involved in 31 percent of transactions in the first six months of 1997. Foreign portfolio investment now stands at $1.5 billion, or 7.5 percent of the stock market capitalization. There are six mutual funds that are restricted to overseas subscribers that have capital totaling $650 million.[25]

Market Turnover Ratio

Year	1990	1991	1992	1993	1994	1995	1996
Turnover Ratio[26]	4.1	4.1	3.4	2.3	8.9	10.9	22.2

Turnover of listed shares increased 263 percent from 1995 to 1996. Average daily turnover was valued at $11.2 million. The government's privatization program and the inflow of foreign investment capital enhanced liquidity. The International Finance Corporation rated Egypt's market turnover as forty-sixth (of eighty-four), ranking it first in Africa for market liquidity.[27] The 1997 market activity increased due to the growth in domestic mutual funds, foreign portfolio investment, increased research coverage by international emerging market firms, and Egyptian inclusion in the IFC's Emerging Market Indices.

Trading volume increased 188 percent from 1995 to 1996, with a 185-percent increase in the value of shares traded over the same period. Increased trading also reflects the privatization efforts of the government in listing firms on the exchange. The enthusiasm of individual investors has been evident in the trading volumes, however the Egyptian market still lacks the depth of financial market participation provided by institutional investors, such as pension funds and insurance companies.

Plans in Egypt are to increase daily trades from 15,000 to 100,000. Shares in family-owned companies have become increasingly active as they come to see the benefit of share issues as a source of investment finance. The flotation of 30 percent of Olympic Group, Egypt's leading manufacturer of electric heaters, was eleven-times oversubscribed in July 1997, and signaled that initial public offerings present a real opportunity.[28]

On August 10, 1997, the exchange instituted an automated control system on daily transactions and eliminated the daily 5 percent price movement limitation. Closing prices are to be calculated on an average of all prices according to the highest quantity, not less than 100 units.[29] In September 1997 the volume of transactions on the stock exchange reached 5,000 daily transactions valued at LE90 million.[30] The market chairman expects the volume to increase to 10,000 transactions a day over the next five years.

Instruments Traded

Equities, preference shares, corporate debentures, and government bonds are traded. The bond market began to develop in 1995 with the issuance of five-year government bonds. There are currently no derivative products traded and the exchange has no plans to institute them.

In 1994 the market increased 167 percent in U.S.-dollar terms. The number of investors attracted to the Egyptian market privatizations has increased from 20,000 to over one million and $1 billion of foreign capital has flowed into the exchange, both from foreign investors and in the repatriation of flight capital. In 1996 the market experienced approximately $700 million in foreign portfolio inflows. There are 150 international mutual funds operating in the Egyptian market. The funds own 25 percent of shares of public-sector firms offered for privatization. Foreign firms concentrate in trading the shares of sixty highly liquid companies from the total number of listed firms. Of the transactions on the exchange, 35 percent are for individuals while the balance are handled by financial institutions.

Brokerage Rates

Brokerage commissions became negotiable in October 1994. However, for smaller transactions of up to LE10,000, rates may not exceed the following percentage:

Bonds: 0.2%

Shares: 0.5%

There is a minimum of LE2 per transaction.

As signatory to the GATT agreement of 1994 resulting from the Uruguay Round of multilateral trade negotiations, Egypt allows foreign securities' intermediaries to operate on the same nondiscriminatory basis as national firms, with no limitation on capital mobility and no restrictions on foreign exchange. The market currently does not have brokerage functions, such as margin accounts and short selling. For a list of brokers dealing on the Cairo Stock Exchange, check web site http://www.egyptianstocks.com/brokidx1.htm.

Insider Trading

Insider trading is illegal in Egypt, however the rules against insider trading have not been used yet. Current law allows for the suspension of the brokerage firm from the Capital Market Authority register for insider trading. However, current exchange regulations permit trading "under cover," that is, with the identification of the trader concealed. The exchange is examining the issue of requiring real identification of traders to prevent insiders from trading unknown to market regulators.

Dividends and Capital Gains Taxation

The 1992 Securities Law provides for shares to be free of stamp duty and dividends to be exempt from tax. As an incentive to use the equity markets, the law also provides that listed companies with at least 150 shareholders and raising over 30 percent from the public receive a corporate tax break and do not pay taxes on dividends. There are no capital gains taxes, and the 40-percent income tax on mutual funds' profits was abolished in 1996. All taxes on the repatriation of capital have been removed.

Regulatory Controls

The CMA regulates the exchange under the measures provided by the Capital Markets Law. Companies engaged in securities activities must apply to the CMA for a license and register with the stock exchange. In May 1997 a new board for the Cairo Stock Exchange was elected. The system, set by presidential decree, calls for an eleven-member board with six elected members and five appointed by the government, including the chairman.[31]

Capital Markets Authority (Egypt)
Abdel Hamid Ibrahim, Director
20 Emad El-Din St.
Cairo, Egypt
Tel.: (20–2) 578–3901/578–7470   Fax: (20–2) 575–5339

Foreign Investment Restrictions

All restrictions on capital mobility and repatriation have been removed. Exchange rates and interest rates are now market driven rather than administratively controlled. Share ownership restrictions have been lifted. Nonresidents may invest freely in stocks listed on the stock exchange. No restrictions on repatriation of capital, dividends, and related earnings exist. Egyptians must be offered 49 percent of public offerings in joint stock companies.

In addition to a liberal investment climate, the new cabinet appointed in January 1996 initiated its efforts with a determination to further enhance the investment climate in Egypt. As a result, the following measures were adopted: granting automatic approval upon notification regardless of invested capital in all kinds of activities in designated industrial parks and remote areas, repatriation of profits upon investors' request at the highest declared rate of exchange, issuing articles of incorporation for simple partnership companies without requesting a paid-in capital, right of foreigners and foreign-owned projects to own lands, no discrimination between Egyptian and non-Egyptian investors, abolishing the annual levies or stamp taxes on companies' share capital, reducing notarization fees by 50 percent of what was due on all kinds of contracts to be authenticated, allowing foreign participation to exceed 49 percent in authorized capital of private and joint-venture banks following the Central Bank's approval, and streamlining and extending foreign investors' residence permits from three to five years.

Figures that relate to Investment Law 230 in Egypt include the following: Egyptian (i.e., national) investments projects paid in capital in Egypt in 1996 reached LE7,888 million compared to LE4,550 million in 1995. Arab investments in Egypt in 1996 reached LE1,104 million compared to LE393 million in 1995. Foreign investments in Egypt in 1996 reached LE948 million against LE361 million in 1995. Total investments in Egypt in 1996 therefore reached LE9,940 million compared to a total of LE5,304 in 1995. Total investment volume in the free zones in 1996 reached LE2,779 million against LE331 million in 1995. Total investment volume inside the country and free zones in 1996 hit LE12,719 million against LE5,635 million in 1995. By July 1996, foreign investment accounted for about 35 percent of the total value of trading, up from 6 percent in 1995, with over 126 overseas institutional investors participating in the market.

Central Depository

In October 1996 the Egyptian CMA installed a computerized depository, clearing, and settlement system. The market is moving toward a paperless system. This will be critical to the exchange's effort to increase liquidity and trading.

Settlement

Settlement is physical. The vendor surrenders securities on the third business day following the transaction date, and delivery is against payment. All transactions are settled on a cash basis.

Reporting Requirements

Firms must disclose activities and financial positions in a quarterly filing with the CMA. The CMA is to receive copies of the firm's annual report and financial statements at least one month before the annual meeting. Failure to file reports has resulted in the delisting of a number of firms. In addition, any material information must be immediately disclosed if it would affect the firm's financial position or activities. The disclosure must include publication in two nationwide newspapers. The exchange's press coverage has improved, and the state-controlled Cairo daily Akhbar el-Yom now prints a regular page of data on stocks and mutual funds.

NOTES

1. CIA Factbook web site at http://www.odci.gov/cia/publications/nsolo/factbook/eg.htm.
2. Ibid.
3. Ibid.

4. The World Bank's criteria for middle-income classification is a GNP per capita of $766 to $9,385 in 1995. Egypt's per capita GNP in 1995 was $790.

5. Cem Karacadag and David T. Beers, *Standard & Poor's Sovereign Reports Service: Arab Republic of Egypt* (New York: Standard & Poor's, 1997). Rating assigned January 1997.

6. "Finance: In Brief," *Middle East Economic Digest*, 13 June 1997, 4.

7. David Shelby, "The Cairo Stock Exchange? It Has Its Ups & Downs," *Arab Business & Investment Journal* 1 (1997).

8. "Olympic Float Set for Success," *Financial Times*, 29 July 1997, 19.

9. *Emerging Stock Markets Factbook 1997* (Washington, D.C.: International Finance Corporation, 1997).

10. U.S. and Foreign Commercial Service, "Egypt Stock Exchange and Market Overview," *International Market Insight Reports*, 20 June 1997.

11. Ibid.

12. "Beirut, Kuwait, Cairo Stock Exchanges Begin Cross-Trading." International News Section, Agence France Presse, 6 January 1997.

13. While Egypt's market is open to all investors worldwide, Lebanon permits Arab investors to trade freely, and non-Arabs on specialized listings. Only citizens of the six Gulf Cooperation Council (GCC) states—Saudi Arabia, Kuwait, Bahrain, Oman, Qatar, and the United Arab Emirates—may trade on the Kuwait Exchange, with the exception of three mutual funds open to all nationalities. "Beirut, Kuwait, Cairo Stock Exchanges Begin Cross-Trading," Agence France Presse Release, 6 January 1997.

14. "Egypt: Stock Market Overview," *International Market Insight Reports*, 1 October 1997.

15. "Coping with a Successful Bourse," *Middle East Economic Digest*, 30 May 1997.

16. "Booming Cairo Looks Ahead," *Financial Times*, 10 October 1997, 44.

17. Morgan Stanley Africa Fund, *1996 Annual Report*, 1997 (New York: Morgan Stanley, Inc., 1998).

18. David Rathborne, Jacqueline Grosch, and David Galloway, *The LGT Guide to World Equity Markets 1997* (London: Euromoney, 1997), 160.

19. "Egypt: New Rules for Investors," *Middle East Economic Digest*, 29 August 1997, 25.

20. Capital Market Authority, *Exchange Reports* (Cairo, 1997).

21. "Egypt Stock Market Turnover Triples," *United Press International*, 2 July 1997. Note that the number of traded companies in the first half of 1996 was 262. This increased to 289 in the first half of 1997.

22. "Egypt: Stock Market Overview."

23. "Egypt Unveils Stock Market Plans," *United Press International*, 28 July 1997.

24. "Egypt: Stock Market Overview."

25. "Egypt Market," *United Press International*, 3 July 1997.

26. *Emerging Stock Markets Factbook 1997.*

27. *Emerging Stock Markets Factbook 1997.*

28. "Booming Cairo Looks Ahead."

29. "Egypt: Stock Market Overview."

30. "Volume of Dealing in Securities in Stock Exchange," Info-Prod Research (Middle East) Ltd., *Middle East News*, 29 September 1997.

31. "New Board Elected for Bourse," Info-Prod Research (Middle East) Ltd., *Middle East News*, 18 June 1997.

GHANA

COUNTRY

The Republic of Ghana has an area of 92,098 square miles (238,533 square kilometers) in West Africa. The country's landmass is slightly smaller than Oregon. The capital is Accra. The official language is English, however the nation has seventy-five different tribes with distinctive languages.

Archaeological records indicate that the earliest human habitation within modern Ghana was around 10,000 B.C. at a site on the Oti River. As the region's civilization developed, the Guan began their migrations down the Volta Basin from Gonja toward the Gulf of Guinea around A.D. 1200. The Akan kingdom of Bono was founded in 1298.

The first Europeans arrived in the area between 1471 and 1482. From 1500 to 1807, the region was beset with slave raids and wars as states formed on the Gold Coast. The Asante Empire was consolidated from 1697 to 1745. The British established the Gold Coast Colony in 1874. Cocoa was introduced to Ghana in 1878, and in 1902 the Northern Territories were also proclaimed a British protectorate. In 1956 the Convention People's Party won 68 percent of the seats in the legislature and passed an independence motion, which was approved by the British Parliament. Independence was granted on March 6, 1957. After voter approval, a republic was created on July 1, 1960 with Nkrumah as president.

In 1966, the army staged a widely popular coup and the National Liberation Council came to power. An unstable political environment existed in the 1970s. On June 4, 1979 junior officers staged Ghana's first violent coup and the Armed Forces Revolutionary Council formed under Flight Lieutenant Jerry John Rawlings. Hilla Limann was elected president in July. On December 31, 1981 Rawlings staged his second coup and became the chairman of the Provisional National Defense Council. Through the 1980s the country began pursuing an economic adjustment program. Restoration of some democratic rights occurred in 1988 and 1989, as elections for new district assemblies were held. In May 1991, the Provisional National Defense Council agreed to a multiparty system. Political parties were restored in May 1992. Jerry Rawlings was elected president November 3, 1992 in a national presidential election.

Official Religion[1]   None

Religions   Indigenous beliefs, 38%; Muslim, 30%; Christian, 24%; other, 8%

Population   17,698,271 (July 1996 est.)[2]

                        Population under the age of 15: 43%

Ethnic Divisions	Black African, 99.8% (major tribes—Akan 44%, Moshi-Dagomba 16%, Ewe 13%, Ga 8%); European and other, 0.2%
Languages	English (official), African languages (including Akan, Moshi-Dagomba, Ewe, and Ga)
Education	Population over age 15 who are literate: 65%

The Political System

Following periods of military control, the government transitioned to civilian rule in 1992 with the approval of a new constitution and multiparty elections. The new constitution was approved April 28, 1992. In the presidential elections held December 8, 1996, votes were distributed as follows:[3]

Candidate	Party	Percentage
Jerry Rawlings	NDC	57.4
John Kufuor	Great Alliance: NPP/PCP	39.6
Edward Mahama	PNC	3.0

The legislative branch of government consists of a unicameral parliament made up of 200 members. Members are elected to four-year terms in single-seat constituencies. In the December 8, 1996 elections, the National Democratic Congress (NDC) party won 132 seats and the New Patriotic Party (NPP) won sixty seats.[4]

Political Web Site   http://www.geocities.com/~derksen/election.htm

Legal System

The legal system is based on English common law and customary law. Ghana has not accepted compulsory ICJ jurisdiction.

Suffrage is at eighteen years of age and is universal.

The Economy

Ghana is well endowed with natural resources. Consequently, Ghana has twice the per capita output of the poorer countries in West Africa. Ghana has made steady progress in liberalizing its economy since 1983, and growth continued at a rate of 5 percent in 1995 due to increased gold, timber, and cocoa production—major sources of foreign exchange. Gold and cocoa dominate the economy. Ghana was formerly known as the Gold Coast. Gold production increased from 285,000 ounces in 1983 to over 1 million ounces in 1996. Ghana is Africa's second largest gold producer after South Africa.

Similarly, cocoa plays an important role in export earnings at 25 percent of the total. Ghana is the world's fourth largest cocoa producer after Côte d'Ivoire, Brazil, and Indonesia.

The economy continues to revolve around subsistence agriculture, which accounts for almost half of GDP and employs 55 percent of the workforce. With the introduction of an economic recovery plan development has proceeded in a market-oriented approach. The central elements of the recovery plan are exchange rate, privatization, and trade reforms.

Inflation rate (consumer prices)	29.2% (March 1995)
Unemployment rate	10.0% (1993 est.)

Gross Domestic Product[5]

Ghana is classified as a low-income country under the World Bank's classification of economies.[6] For comparability, Gross Domestic Product is expressed in purchase power parity terms.

GDP purchasing power parity	$25.1 billion (1995 est.)
GDP real growth rate	5.0% (1995 est.)
GDP per capita	$1,400 (1995 est.)

Central Bank: Bank of Ghana

The Bank of Ghana implements the government's monetary policy through the use of open-market operations and interest rate policy, provides supervision for the banking sector, and regulates other financial institutions. The central bank can intervene in the foreign exchange market and acts independently of the government but in consultation with the Ministry of Finance.

Postal Address
Bank of Ghana
P.O. Box 2674
Thorpe Road
Accra
Ghana
Tel.: +233–21–666902   Fax: +233–21–662996
Web Site   http://www.ghana-embassy.org/trade/gateway/financial.html

Credit Rating

Ghana has not been rated by international rating agencies for either domestic or foreign currency debt.

Currency

Monetary unit: 1 new cedi (C) = 100 pesewas

Exchange rates are as follows: new cedis per US$1–1,246.11 (September 1995), 956.71 (1994), 649.06 (1993), 437.09 (1992), 367.83 (1991). The exchange rate of the country's currency is determined by market forces, as Ghana operates a floating rate exchange system. The existence of public banks and privately owned forex bureaus allow easy conversion. The present financial regime is relatively flexible and allows the easy transfer of foreign currency in and out of Ghana. A foreign investor may, subject to approval, operate a foreign currency account with banks in Ghana. Investments to which the GIPC Act applies are assured of unconditional transferability through authorized dealer banks in freely convertible currency of the following: dividends or net profits attributable to their investment, payments in respect of loan servicing where foreign loans have been obtained, fees and charges in respect of any technology transfer agreements registered under the GPIC Act, and remittance of proceeds (net of all taxes and other obligations) in the event of the sale or liquidation of the enterprise or any interest attributable to the investment.

There are a number of web sites providing updated currency exchange values. The following is an example:

http://www.bloomberg.com/markets/currency/currcalc.cgi

Privatization

The government seeks to privatize government holdings through the development of the stock exchange. In 1995 the government divested approximately $25 million worth of equities through an international placement program. Economic reforms in Ghana, which has large mineral deposits, tropical hardwoods, and export crops, have been widely praised and have encouraged foreign investment.[7]

Ashanti Goldfields

The Ghanaian government's largest privatization has been the gradual privatization of its ownership stake in the Ashanti Goldfields Company. As the company's name implies, the firm's primary operations are in the mining field with the extraction of gold being its primary source of revenues. The company operates the richest goldfield in the world in Obuasi, Ghana. Recognizing the limitations of the local exchange to absorb the shares of Ashanti, the government floated shares on the London Stock Exchange.[8]

On February 21, 1996, it became the first African security to be listed on the New York Stock Exchange. Subsequently, the firm has listed its shares on the Toronto Stock Exchange, the Australian Stock Exchange, and the Zimbabwe Stock Exchange. Despite its innovative privatization, the firm has proven a disappointing investment for U.S. investors.

"Ghana's successful sale of a 30 per cent stake in its national telecom company to an overseas buyer, announced last week, is a sign of the growing number of international offers coming out of Africa. Volta Communications, a company controlled by Telekom Malaysia, bought the holding in Ghana Telecom. Volta will assume the management of GT. The international contest of prospective buyers included Deutsche Telekom, KPN of the Netherlands, Western Wireless and Lightcom, both from the US, and Telkom of South Africa."[9] Several other state-owned enterprises are presently being divested through the Divestiture Implementation Committee (DIC).[10]

THE STOCK EXCHANGE: THE GHANA STOCK EXCHANGE

The Ghana Stock Exchange was formed on July 25, 1989 and superseded the Accra Stock Exchange Company. The exchange opened for trading on November 12, 1990. The exchange was established to assist with the country's economic recovery program by mobilizing funds for long-term capital development by the corporate sectors. In addition, the exchange would ease pressure on bank credit.[11]

In 1994, the Ghana Stock Exchange was one of the top ten stock exchanges in the world's emerging markets. From 1990 through 1996 the exchange raised a total of C140 billion ($69 million) for the government and some listed companies. Total market capitalization as of the end of March 1997 was C2.76 trillion ($1.35 billion). On the performance of equities in the first quarter of 1997, officials say the total number of shares traded was 38.57 million valued at C40.18 billion. This compares with 10.67 million shares valued at C10.87 billion for the same period last year. Despite the successes, the market is still confronted with an economic environment of high inflation, high interest rates, and attractive rates for treasury bills. Treasury bill rates for ninety-day instruments are approximately 33 percent with inflation of 29.2 percent in March 1997.

Mr. Yeboa Amoa
Managing Director
Ghana Stock Exchange
5th Floor, Cedi House
Liberia Road
Accra, Ghana
Tel.: (233) 21 669–908, (233) 21 669–914, (233) 21 669–935
Fax: (233) 21 669–913

E-Mail:	stockex@ncs.com.gh
Web Sites	http://www.ghana.com/stockex/ http://www.ghana.com/republic/stockexc.html http://mbendi.co.za/exgh.htm
Established	November 12, 1990
Stock Exchange Act	1971
Trading Days	Mondays, Wednesdays, and Fridays
Trading Hours	10:00–17:30 The international time zone is GMT.

Market Index

There is currently one index on the Ghana Share Market, which is the Data Bank Stock Index. This is a market capitalization-weighted index. It is calculated after every trading session. Base period market capitalization is an average of November 1990 to December 1993.

Exchange History[12]

A 1968 report on an investigation into the establishment of a stock exchange in Ghana named the "Pearl report" by the Commonwealth Finance Development Company Limited recommended to the government of Ghana the setting up of a stock exchange within two years and suggested ways of achieving it. Since then, activities directed at setting up a stock exchange have taken place in four phases.

A steering committee was appointed in 1970. Its work led to the formation of the Accra Stock Exchange Company in 1971 and the passing of the Stock Exchange Act, 1971 by Parliament. However, the Accra Stock Exchange Company failed to get off the ground.

In 1981, a working committee comprising representatives of the Ministry of Finance and Economic Planning, the central bank, the commercial banks, and National Trust Holding Company Limited was set up on the initiative of the Ministry. Its recommendations were never implemented. A five-man committee was formed in 1986. In March 1987 the committee adopted with some modifications its technical sub-committee's report and thereafter no further progress was made. In February 1989 a nine-member committee was set up. The committee's terms of reference were to take charge and consolidate all previous work connected with the stock exchange project as well as take the necessary measures towards the exchange's actual establishment.

The committee was able to draw up a successful program that culminated in the formation of the Ghana Stock Exchange on July 25, 1989, which supersedes the now defunct Accra Stock Exchange Company. The exchange has been incorporated as a private company limited by guarantee and its floor was open for business on November 12, 1990. The exchange is expected to lend support to a reformed and revitalized financial sector under the ongoing Economic Recovery Program by mobilizing funds for the long-term capital requirements of the corporate sector as well as encouraging foreign invest- ment and easing pressure on bank credit.

The exchange has two categories of members. They are Licensed Deal- ing Members who can operate as stockbrokers on its floor, and Ordinary Members who cannot operate on the floor. Only corporate bodies can be Licensed Dealing Members and such corporate bodies should have stockbroking business as their sole business.

Trading on the Over-the-Counter (OTC) Market[13]

After the public offering, an issue can trade on the over-the-counter market (i.e., trading outside the floor of a stock exchange) through stockbrokers. Going public and trading on the OTC market is normally seen as a stepping stone to seeking a stock exchange listing. What it accomplishes is the rais- ing of equity or debt capital, but normally not in large amounts. It enables the shares to trade and to establish a market value, but usually on the basis of narrow trading. Often the OTC market is not as large or as disciplined as the stock exchange.

STOCK MARKET ACTIVITY

Trading Structure[14]

Trading in approved securities on the floor of the exchange is conducted under the call-over system with a limited auction arrangement. The autho- rized dealing officers of the stockbroking companies assemble every trade made on the floor of the exchange and a designated official of the ex- change presides over the transactions and directs the conduct of business. As he calls out the securities in alphabetical order, the brokers shout their offers and they are recorded on a trading board. Bids are also made simulta- neously and similarly recorded. The highest bidder gets his allocation first before the next levels of bidders are considered. The closing price, which attracts a deal, is then marked on the board. Continuous markings are made of bargains done during the time the floor remains open for trading. Only the last prices marked are considered to be the official prices for the day.

When trading is completed, the transactions are recorded on a bargain slip approved by the exchange in triplicate and signed by both the selling and buying dealing brokers. The original slip is given to the buying broker, the duplicate goes to the presiding officer, and the selling broker keeps the triplicate. The broker's transfer forms are then endorsed by the exchange to indicate that the security concerned has been duly traded.

Within two days after completing a transaction on behalf of a client, every Licensed Dealing Member must forward to the client a contract note settling out the date of the transaction, the number of units of the security bought and sold, the price, and the amount of commission charged. All contract notes must bear the words, "Subject to the Rules and Regulations of the Ghana Stock Exchange." The brokers thereafter dispatch the completed transfer forms to the appropriate registrars to effect the transfers and issue the share certificates to them for onward delivery to their clients. The minimum board lots are in units of 100, with the exception of Ashanti Goldfields Company, which has a board lot of ten.

Performance

Prior to 1993 the returns on equities were negative in both nominal and inflation adjusted terms. The Ghana Stock Exchange price index of listed equities declined 21.4 percent in U.S.-dollar terms in 1996. The IFC ranked the market seventy-second in terms of performance (from a population of seventy-six markets).[15] In 1994 the exchange ranked in the top ten markets in the world, sixth, with a 69 percent U.S.-dollar return.

Market Valuation[16]

Year	Price–Earnings Ratio	Dividend Yield
1991	---	3.3
1992	0.3	7.7
1993	6.7	6.5
1994	11.7	3.9
1995	8.1	5.0
1996	7.6	7.0

Listing Requirements

Applications for listing need to be sponsored by a Licensed Dealing Member of GSE. The company must also comply with the Companies Code, 1963. The company will also have to meet the requirements contained in the listing regulations of GSE. There are three lists available for listing on the exchange, the 1st, 2nd, and 3rd lists. Companies must have a minimum stated capital of C100 million ($85,000) to be on the 1st list, C50 million to qualify for the 2nd list, and C20 million to be on the 3rd list. For the company to be on the 1st list the market value of its floated shares must be at least C30 million, for the 2nd list the market value must be at least C15 million, and for the 3rd list at least C5 million. In addition, a company must have filed audited accounts for at least five years in the case of the 1st list, three years for the 2nd list, and at least one year (which may be waived) for the 3rd list.[17]

Number of Listed Firms[18]

From 1995 to 1996 the number of listed firms increased 10.5 percent, from nineteen to twenty-one, while market capitalization decline 9.5 percent in U.S.-dollar terms over the period.

Number of Listed Firms and Market Capitalization[19]

Year	Number of Firms	Market Capitalization (US$ Millions)
1991	13	76
1992	15	84
1993	15	118
1994	17	1,873
1995	19	1,649
1996	21	1,493

Market capitalization has increased at an average compound growth rate of 81 percent from the end of 1991. The greatest increase came in 1994 with the government's partial sale of its holdings in Ashanti Goldfields. The Ashanti Goldfields capitalization dominates the market at almost 90 percent of total market capitalization.

Liquidity

The International Finance Corporation ranks Ghana's market turnover seventy-seventh (of eighty-four) in the world in 1996. This places Ghana as twelfth in Africa in terms of market liquidity. However, it should be noted that this does not include the significant number of shares in Ashanti Goldfields, which are traded in other markets where it is also listed (Ashanti Goldfields is listed on five foreign exchanges).

Market Turnover Ratio

Year	1992	1993	1994	1995	1996
Turnover Ratio[20]	0.5	4.5	7.1	1.3	1.1

Market activity slowed 15 percent in 1996 from a year earlier. In dollar terms, the value of trading declined 23.8 percent to $17 million from 1995 levels.[21] Average daily trades are valued at $77,275.

Ownership

The exchange has fifty-one members, including forty associate members and eleven Licensed Dealing Members.

Instruments Traded

Equities and bonds are traded. There are currently no derivative products traded and the exchange has no plans to institute them.

Brokerage Rates

Brokerage rates are fixed. A minimum of C850 is charged on trades worth less than C10,000. For trades in excess of C50,000 a declining scale rate from 2.5 percent to 1 percent applies.

Margin/Securities Lending

Short trading is prohibited and at present there is no stock borrowing/lending mechanism.

Insider Trading

In Ghana both the Securities Industry Law 1993 and the Ghana Stock Exchange Listing regulations make provisions for full disclosure. Insider trading, false trading, market rigging, and manipulations and deceptive devices are illegal.

Dividend and Capital Gains Taxation

There is a 10-percent withholding tax on dividend income for all investors. This is a final tax, which excludes dividends from any further taxes. Capital gains are exempt from tax.

Regulatory Controls

A council governs the exchange with representation from Licensed Dealing Members, listed companies, the banks, insurance companies, money markets, and the general public. The Managing Director of the exchange is an ex-officio member. The council sets the policies of the exchange and its functions include preventing frauds and malpractice, maintaining good order among members, regulating stock market business, and granting listings. The exchange has a well-qualified and experienced management team headed by the Managing Director with responsibility for the day-to-day operations of the exchange.

Under the Securities Industry Law, the highest regulatory body will be a Securities Regulatory Commission. Some of its functions will be as follows:

- To advise the Secretary for Finance and Economic Planning on all matters relating to the securities industry.
- To maintain surveillance over securities to ensure orderly, fair, and equitable dealings in securities.
- To protect the integrity of the securities market against any abuses arising from the practice of insider trading.
- To create the necessary atmosphere for the orderly growth and development of the capital market.

Other supervisory bodies of the exchange include the minister of finance and the governor of the Bank of Ghana, who, in the interim, is the sole securities regulatory commissioner.

Foreign Investment Restrictions

Under the Exchange Control Act 1961, foreign investors can deal in securities listed on the exchange without any exchange restrictions and there is no longer a need to obtain government approval prior to initial investment through the Ghana Investments Center. Access to nonresident portfolios was denied until 1993, and prohibitions on foreign investment have now been largely relaxed. External portfolio, corporate, or individual investors can invest in listed companies provided the holding by any one investor does not exceed 10 percent of a company's listed shares and total foreign investment in that company does not exceed 74 percent. Resident foreigners and Ghanaians (both resident and nonresident) may hold any percentage of the shares of listed companies. Security transfers to foreign investors attract a stamp duty of 2 percent.

Exchange control permission has been given to nonresident Ghanaians and foreigners to invest through the exchange without any prior approval. There is free and full foreign exchange remittability for the original capital plus all capital gains, returns, and related earnings. Capital gains on listed securities are exempt from tax until November 2000 and this exemption period may be extended.

There are currently two banks providing custodial services—Barclays Bank of Ghana Ltd. and Merchant Bank of Ghana Ltd. Barclays Bank of Ghana Ltd. provides custodial service for nonresident investors.

Head Office

P.O. Box 2949
Accra
Tel.: 223–21–664901/4

Trading

Securities are bought and sold on the stock exchange through Licensed
Dealing Members also known as stockbrokers.[22] A Licensed Dealing Member
is a firm which buys and sells securities on behalf of investors for a brokerage
fee or commission. When trading is in listed securities, the stockbroker must
be a Licensed Dealing Member of the GSE. An investor cannot personally
come to the stock exchange to buy shares, stocks, and so on, but can only
buy them through the stockbrokers. Stockbrokers, apart from buying and
selling securities on behalf of clients, also advise clients on the mix or portfolio of investments (shares, stocks) and provide functional services such as
a vault for the safekeeping of securities for clients. They also give up-to-date
information about securities to their clients.

To buy securities, the potential investor must first contact a stockbroker.
Once a stockbroker is chosen, the potential investor must decide on the kinds
of securities that are of interest to him. The stockbroker will then recommend
the shares and stocks which are suitable for his needs, assuming the stockbroker is given the option to make recommendations. After making a decision
on the securities at the most advantageous price obtainable at the time of
dealing on the trading floor of the GSE the broker makes a purchase.

On completion of the deal, the stockbroker sends to the buyer a contract
note showing the date of the transaction, the number of shares purchased, the
price per share, the commission chargeable, and a stamp, if any. The final figure will show how much is payable to the stockbroker on receipt of the contract
note. When the transaction is completed, a share certificate is issued to the
buyer.

The procedure for selling securities is similar to buying, but the total
amount on the contract note shows the sale proceeds payable by the stockbroker to the seller excluding commissions and any charges.

Central Depository

There is no central depository in Ghana.

Settlement

The settlement period has been reduced from ten days to five days. The
abridged settlement period applies to all securities traded on the GSE floor
on or after November 1, 1996. It covers any over-the-counter trades permitted

by the Exchange.[23] The change formed part of measures implemented by the council of the GSE to meet standards recommended by the Group of Thirty and accepted by the International Federation of Stock Exchanges (Federation Internationale Des Bourses De Valeurs; FIBV). Securities Clearing and Settlement House Rules embodying the foregoing changes were adopted by the Council of GSE on September 25, 1996 and approved by the Securities Regulatory Commission on October 24, 1996.[24]

Registration

Brokers dispatch the completed transfer forms to the appropriate registrars to effect the transfer and issue the share certificates to them for onward delivery to their clients. No time limit is set for registration but the process can take some time.

Buy-Ins

Buy-ins exist in Ghana and the procedures are as follows:

1. When a member fails within fourteen days to carry out an exchange contract, a purchasing member is entitled to the completion of the relevant trade. After giving the member a notice of the default in writing and having filed with the exchange a report on the unsettled transaction, the trade will be closed out on the next trading day.
2. The notice to "buy-in" or "sell-out" shall be on a form prescribed by the exchange.
3. Any notice to "buy-in" or "sell-out" may be withdrawn by the buyer or seller if it has not been executed.
4. Before each trading session the Managing Director of the exchange posts a list of instructions received from a member who wishes to buy-in, naming the stock, number to be bought, the buyer, the seller at risk, and the price at which it is prepared to bid for immediate delivery. Also, a member who wrote to sell-out, naming the stock, the buyer at risk, and the price at which it is prepared to sell-out for immediate delivery.
5. The buy-in must be for cash.
6. The entitled member shall notify the member in default of the amount of difference if any between the amount paid on the buy-in and the price specified in the original contract. The difference becomes an obligation of the defaulting member. Payment of difference shall be made within twenty-four hours after notice to a defaulting member.

Corporate Actions

Public companies are required by law to disclose all material and relevant information about their performance, operations, and accounts. Giving false or misleading information is punishable by law. In addition, banks are obliged by law to publish their accounts in a daily newspaper circulated in Ghana not later than three months after the end of their financial year.

Voting

Annual general meetings are usually announced in the local newspapers. Proxy voting is legal, but not common. Foreign investors enjoy the same legal voting rights as domestic shareholders.

Regional Affiliations

Ghana belongs to the Economic Community of West African States. The community aims to promote trade and economic growth among member countries. Currently there are sixteen member countries, including Benin, Burkina Faso, Cape Verde, Gambia, Ghana, Guinea, Guinea Bissau, Côte d'Ivoire, Liberia, Mali, Mauritania, Niger, Nigeria, Senegal, Sierra Leone, and Togo.

Economic Community of West African States
Executive Secretariat
6 King George V Rd
Lagos
Nigeria
Tel.: +234 (0)1 63–6841

INTERNET RESOURCES

Doing business in Ghana	http://mbendi.co.za/werksmns/lexaf/busgh.htm
General information	http://www.ghana.com.gh/republic/index.html

NOTES

1. CIA Factbook web site at http://www.odci.gov/cia/publications/nsolo/factbook/gh.htm.

2. Ibid.

3. Panafrican News Agency. Electoral web site at http://www.geocities.com/~derksen/election/country/gh.htm.

4. Ibid.

5. CIA Factbook web site.

6. The World Bank's criteria for low-income classification is a GNP per capita of less than $765 in 1995. Ghana's per capita GNP in 1995 was $390.

7. U.S. Department of Commerce, ITA, *1996 Country Commercial Guide for Ghana* (Washington, D.C.: National Trade Data Bank, 1995).

8. As a result of the privatization of the Ashanti Goldfields, the Ghanaian Stock

Exchange increased its market capitalization from approximately $100 million to $1.8 billion.

9. Joel Kibazo, "Enticement Comes Out of Africa International Equities," *Financial Times*, 23 December 1996, 4.

10. For additional information, see the Divestiture Program web site at http://www.ghana.com/republic/divestit.html.

11. Exchange regulations and organization have been taken from the *Handbook* (Accra: Ghana Stock Exchange, 1992, 1993, 1994, 1995, 1996).

12. Ibid.

13. Ibid.

14. Ibid.

15. *Emerging Stock Markets Factbook 1997* (Washington, D.C.: International Finance Corporation, 1997).

16. Ghana Stock Exchange *Handbook*, 1996.

17. Ibid.

18. *Emerging Stock Markets Factbook 1997.*

19. Ibid.

20. Ibid.

21. Ibid.

22. *Handbook*, 1996.

23. Yeboa Amoa, "Clearing & Sttlement Period Reduced to 5 (Five) Working Days—New Clearing and Settlement Rules Published," issued at Accra this 31st day of October, 1996. Web site at http://ourworld.compuserve.com/homepages/Khaganu/stockex2.htm.

24. Ibid.

KENYA

COUNTRY

The Republic of Kenya (in Swahili, Jamhuri ya Kenya) has an area of 224,961 square miles (582,646 square kilometers) in East Africa. For comparison, the country's landmass is approximately twice the size of Nevada. The capital is Nairobi.

Kenya's early history is focused on its contacts along the coast with outside traders. The Masai entered Kenya from the North in the eighteenth century. The Kikuyu expanded from their territories in the nineteenth century. The Masai raided their neighbors and made it difficult to explore the interior. The area became a British protectorate in 1890 and a crown colony in 1920. The British East Africa Company held commercial control.

The East Africa High Commission formed in 1948 to administer services in Kenya. In the 1950s the Mau Mau Rebellion of the Kikuyu against Europeans resulted in a declaration of state emergency. The emergency was lifted in the early 1960s. Following independence in 1963, the ethnically diverse citizenry recognized the need to develop a strong national identity. The government has fostered the national identity with the motto "Harambee," or "Pulling Together." In 1964 Jomo Kenyatta was elected as the first president. Upon his death in 1978, Daniel arap Moi became president and leader of the ruling party. The years of uncontested rule has lead to government corruption and subsequent unrest. Moi permitted the first multiparty elections for the presidency and National Assembly in 1992, which his party won amid a split opposition. As the uncertainty of 1997 elections increased, popular unrest escalated. Because of a splintered opposition, Daniel arap Moi was reelected in voting on December 29–30, 1997.

Official Religion	None[1]
Religions	Protestant (including Anglican), 38%; Roman Catholic, 28%; indigenous beliefs, 26%; other, 8%
Population	28,176,686 (July 1996 est.)[2]
	Urban: 20%
	Rural: 80%
	Population under the age of 15: 51%
Ethnic Divisions	Kikuyu 22%, Luhya 14%, Luo 13%, Kalenjin 12%, Kamba 11%, Kisii 6%, Meru 6%, Asian, European, and Arab 1%, other 15%
Languages	English (official), Swahili (official), and numerous indigenous languages
Education	Population over age 15 who are literate: 78.1%

The Political System

The nation is governed under a unitary multiparty republic with one leg-islative house, the National Assembly. The President serves as the head of state. The Parliament has 202 members; 188 members are elected for a five-year term in single-seat constituencies, 12 members appointed, and there are 2 ex-officio members.

Kenya held its first multiparty elections on December 29, 1992, maintaining the ruling Kenya African National Union (KANU) party's control and domi-nance. Daniel arap Moi was reelected with 36.4 percent of the vote. President Moi was reelected to a fifth term with 40.1 percent of the vote in 1997.

The IMF put a $220 million loan to Kenya on hold on July 31, 1997, cit-ing insufficient efforts against corruption. In addition, the World Bank said recently that it was withholding a key multimillion-dollar credit and putting investment projects on hold until Kenya demonstrates sincerity in fighting against corruption. The suspension emboldened the opposition and the growing unrest has created political instability.

Political Web Site   http://www.geocities.com/~derksen/election/kenya.htm

Legal System

The Kenyan legal system is based on English common law, tribal law, and Islamic law. Judicial review is in a High Court, and Kenya accepts compul-sory ICJ jurisdiction, with reservations. The constitutional amendment of 1982 making Kenya a de jure one-party state was repealed in 1991.

Suffrage is at eighteen years of age and is universal.

The Economy

Kenya's developing market economy is based upon agriculture. Kenya's agricultural base was hit hard by a drought during the first seven months of 1997. This was particularly damaging to the country's tea exports. Because of the young age of Kenya's bushes—forty years—they do not have the drought resistance of India's Assam tea bushes, which are over one-hundred years old. The exchange rate for the shilling appreciated in 1994 because of the high interest rates offered as the government moved to positive real interest rates to curb inflation. Inflation fell from 55 percent in 1993 to 4 percent in 1994. The consumer price inflation rate in 1995 was 1.51 percent. In 1996 the rate increased to 4.5 percent. Agriculture earns the country 60 percent of total foreign exchange earnings.

Between 1995 and 1996 Kenya's economy was able to grow at a real rate of 4.6 percent. This level of growth was possible due to the stabilization of macroeconomic variables like inflation, exchange, and interest rates. Interest over this period declined from 40 percent in 1993 and 1994 to 20 percent in 1997. The economic progress reported was the result of economic liberalization undertaken in the early 1990s. Price controls were lifted and other restricting legislation was removed.

On July 31, 1997, the IMF suspended a $205 million Enhanced Structural Adjustment Facility (SAF) between the government and the International Monetary Fund. The suspension led foreign investors to liquidate positions in treasury bills and stock exchange company holdings. The Kenyan shilling depreciated as the suspension's impact was felt in the economy. The political uncertainty, civil unrest, strikes, and ethnic conflicts have influenced foreign and domestic investors. The political uncertainty created questions concerning the state of the Kenyan economy. To reinstate international donor aid, the country must hold general elections and establish strong anticorruption mechanisms. In response to the political instability and IMF loan suspension action, the Kenyan market capitalization declined by $50 million in July and August 1997. In addition, the number and value of shares traded declined by 18.4 percent and 23.7 percent, respectively, while the number of deals and average value per deal declined by 20.5 percent and 3.1 percent, respectively.[3] The negative impact of the suspension on the local exchange resulted in the market capitalization on the Nairobi Stock Exchange falling by $50 million.

The current economic difficulties have the potential to limit the economic recovery as interest rates increased from 20 percent to 25 percent in August 1997 to defend the shilling. The shilling dropped 20 percent in value in reaction to the suspension of the IMF loan. Real GDP growth was expected to be 3.2 percent.

Gross Domestic Product[4]

Kenya is classified as a low-income country under the World Bank's classification of economies.[5] For comparability GDP is expressed in purchase power parity terms.

GDP purchasing power parity	$36.8 billion (1995 est.)
GDP real growth rate	4.6% (1996)
GDP per capita	$1,300 (1995 est.)

The growth momentum that started in 1994 slowed down in 1996 mainly because of severe drought in the second half of the year in most parts of the country. In 1996 real GDP growth declined to 4.6 percent. The growth was below the 5.5-percent target, but higher than the 0.2 percent and 3 percent in 1993 and 1994, respectively.[6]

Unemployment Rate   35% urban (1994 est.)[7]

Central Bank: Central Bank of Kenya/Banki Kuu ya Kenya

The Central Bank of Kenya (CBK) is the government's banker, and retains the power to regulate the movement of currency.

Central Bank of Kenya
P.O. Box 60000
Hail Sleaze Avenue
Nairobi
Kenya
Tel.: +254–2–226431/32/ or +254–2–330500/01   Fax: +254–2–340192
Web Site http://www.africaonline.co.ke/cbk/index.html

Objectives of the Central Bank of Kenya[8]

The Central Bank of Kenya's objectives are laid down in the Central Bank of Kenya (Amendment) Act, 1996, as follows:

PRINCIPAL OBJECTIVES

1. The first principal objective shall be to formulate and implement monetary policy directed to achieving and maintaining stability in the general level of prices.
2. The second principal objective shall be to foster the liquidity, solvency and proper functioning of a stable market based financial system.

SECONDARY OBJECTIVES

Without prejudice to the generality of the above two principal objectives, the Bank's secondary objectives shall be to:

1. Formulate and implement foreign exchange policy
2. Hold and manage its foreign exchange reserves
3. License and supervise authorized dealers in the money market
4. Promote the smooth operation of payments, clearing and settlement systems
5. Act as a banker and adviser to, and as fiscal agent of the Government; and
6. Issue currency notes and coins

In 1996, for the third year, the Central Bank of Kenya pursued price stability as the principal monetary policy objective. The pursuit of this policy facilitated the reduction of inflation from three digits in mid-1993 to a single digit in November 1994 and has since helped contain it at low levels. An incipient upward pressure on prices in the later part of the year pushed the three-months-annualized inflation beyond the single digit. It also pushed the month-on-month and the average annual inflation up to higher single-digit levels. The month-on-month, three-months-annualized, and average annual inflation accelerated from 0.2 percent, 2.5 percent, and 6.6 percent, respectively, at the beginning of the financial year to 9.7 percent, 15.3 percent, and 5.2 percent by June 1996.[9] The Central Bank of Kenya's monthly report indicates that in August 1997 inflation declined to 7.7 percent from 8.9 percent in July 1997; but by the end of December 1997, the three-months-annualized rate had increased to 12.3 percent.

Interest Rates[10]

A one-year floating rate bond was introduced in January 1997.

Government Issues	End 1995	End 1996	End 1997
Short term 3 month	21.7%	22.6%	26.4%
Long term 5 year	17.0%	17.5%	---

Commercial loan rates at the end of 1997 were 30 to 35 percent. Short-term treasury bills represent 80.2 percent of the outstanding stock of domestic debt.

Banking Developments

At the end of 1997, Kenya's banking system was comprised of fifty-three commercial banks, sixteen non-bank financial institutions (NBFIs), four building societies, and two mortgage finance companies. There were thirty-seven registered foreign exchange bureaus.

Credit Rating

Kenya has not been rated by international rating agencies for either domestic or foreign currency debt. Kenya's Capital Markets Authority (CMA) is assisting with the launch of a rating agency to evaluate local market debt issuers. The agency will develop as a partnership between a Kenyan brokerage house, bank, or fund manager and either the Rating Agency of Malaysia, or the South African Office of IBCA, the London-based rating agency.[11]

Currency

Monetary unit   Kenya shilling (K Sh) = 100 cents

The Exchange Control Act was repealed effective December 27, 1995. Prior to the repeal, from 1993 to 1995 the shilling went from a low of 35 shillings to the dollar to a high of 82 shillings to the dollar. An overvalued shilling made paying off foreign debt easier, however it was a significant negative for Kenya's export segments. Consequently, industries such as tourism lost their competitive posture as Kenya became an expensive destination. In addition, coffee and tea exporters saw their profits decline. As a result, corporate profits declined as much as 50 percent. The balance between a weaker shilling and the economic stimulation is an increase in inflation as the higher prices of imports get passed on to consumers. A forward market for the shilling exists up to three months, which may extend up to six months.

From July 1, 1995 to June 30, 1996, the trade weighted average of the shilling exchange rate depreciated by 4.4 percent. The overall depreciation mainly reflected the weakening of the shilling against the U.S. dollar and the sterling pound, in which over 60 percent of Kenya's external trade is carried out. In real terms—that is, taking into account the differences in inflation between Kenya and her major trading partners—the shilling exchange rate remained more or less constant, unlike in the previous year when it appreciated by 5 percent.[12]

The Central Bank worked to ensure a free foreign exchange market environment in which the general level and direction of the exchange rate remained market determined. Thus, the Central Bank intervened indirectly through monetary operations during the year only to counteract any speculative behavior that would threaten competitive market determination of the shilling exchange rate. This policy ensured that market forces remained the main determinants of the exchange rate.[13]

In 1997, economic conditions deteriorated as political unrest lead to the suspension of IMF support, and the shilling exchange rate declined from an end-of-year 1996 rate of K Sh55.000 to K Sh63.1 to the dollar in December 1997. Exchange rates are as follows: Kenyan shillings per US$1–56.715 (January 1996), 51.430 (1995), 56.051 (1994), 58.001 (1993), 32.217 (1992), 27.508 (1991).

The sudden depreciation of the Kenya shilling by 30 percent following the suspension of financial assistance by the International Monetary Fund under the Enhanced Structural Adjustment Facility will impact on nearly all aspects of the economy in the months ahead. While some markets, such as those for goods and services, will be adversely affected in terms of price increases, the impact on the foreign exchange and domestic money markets will be a mix of gains and losses. There are a number of web sites providing updated currency exchange values. The following is an example:

http://www.bloomberg.com/markets/currency/currcalc.cgi

Inflation Rate

Consumer prices   1.7% (1995 est.)[14]

The effect of the recent weakening of the shilling has started showing in increased inflation. Underlying inflation that had been declining since January

1997 reversed in August 1997 and continued to increase through December 1997.

Privatization

The stock exchange has served as a major vehicle in Kenya's privatization program. The government initiated its privatization programs in 1992 with the government selling of stakes in National Bank of Kenya, HFCK, and Uchumi Supermarkets. Privatization issues have attracted institutional investor interest. Between 1992 and 1995, the government of Kenya privatized 67 out of a possible 212 public-sector enterprises.[15]

Kenya Airways represents one of Kenya's major successes in privatization.[16] After careful restructuring, the government offered to the public a major stake in the national air carrier. Losses in 1991 and 1992 had reached $50 million, due primarily to its poor reliability and flying unprofitable routes. The government, under pressure from the World Bank, began to restructure the airline in 1991 and prepare it for privatization. New management reduced losses to $30 million in 1993 and in 1994 the airline reported a profit of $7 million. In 1994, to clean up the balance sheet, the government assumed responsibility for the airline's external debt arrears up to the end of 1993, approximately $82 million, and converted around $33 million owed into equity. These actions reduced long-term debt to $49 million and net worth increased to $33 million. The government converted the airline to private ownership.

KLM Royal Dutch Airlines acquired a 26-percent holding in the Kenyan national carrier, Kenya Airways.[17] The continent of Africa is an international air travel growth market, leading KLM to seek to strengthen its position through a strategic alliance with an African national airline. KLM and its Kenyan partner will initiate cooperation by coordinating schedules to offer their passengers seamless connections between their route networks. They envisage further-reaching commercial cooperation in the future.

THE STOCK EXCHANGE: NAIROBI STOCK EXCHANGE

The Nairobi Stock Exchange (NSE) was founded in 1954. The first trading floor was opened in 1991. The exchange is now sub-Saharan Africa's fourth largest, with a market capitalization of around $1.8 billion at the end of 1996. The market's 1996 turnover ratio was 3.6 percent, ranking it ninth among African exchanges in terms of market turnover. There were fifty-six listed firms at the end of 1996, unchanged from the end of 1995. The exchange has twenty member firms.

In July 1994, the NSE acquired a new trading floor with a capacity to accommodate one-hundred dealers and twenty brokers. The facility is fitted with computer terminals and twenty boards catering to about 400 companies. The new facility has a 200-seat public gallery and boards able to take 800 listings.

The Nairobi Stock Exchange is a source of funds for industry through both rights issues and new share issues. In the early 1990s the Nairobi Stock Exchange performed poorly, with negative inflation-adjusted domestic and U.S.-dollar returns in 1991 and 1992. However, following multiparty elections and the economic liberalization, the market returned positive inflation-adjusted domestic and U.S.-dollar returns. In 1994 Kenya was the best performing emerging equity market in the world, with a U.S.-dollar return of 173.9 percent. Economic conditions in 1996 caused a slight deterioration in market performance, with a 9.9 percent U.S.-dollar return.[18]

Mr. J. K. Kihumba
Chief Executive
Nairobi Stock Exchange Limited
P.O. Box 43633, Nairobi
1st Floor, Nation Centre, Kimathi Street
Tel.: (254–2) 230 692   Fax: (254–2) 224 200

Web Sites	http://mbendi.co.za/mbendi/exna.htm
	http://www.africa.co.uk/exchange/ex-ken.htm
	http://www.africa.co.uk/exchange/ex-afric.htm
	http://www.kenyaweb.com/equity/nse.html
	http://www.africaonline.co.ke/stockexchange/bin/index.html
	http://www.arcc.or.ke/nse/nse.htm
Established	1954
Trading Days	Monday to Friday
Trading Hours	10:00–12:00
	The international time zone is GMT +3.

Market Index

The Kenya market index is composed of twenty equally-weighted companies. This results in large capitalization stocks being underweighted. The market movements of small shares can impact the market, however the overall market impact is mitigated by the high correlation between securities listed on the exchange.

STOCK MARKET ACTIVITY

Trading Structure

The opening of the trading floor in 1991 permitted the exchange to transition from the call-over trading system to a more transparent open outcry floor-based continuous auction system.

Performance

The International Finance Corporation price index in U.S. dollars ranks the Kenya Stock Exchange as sixty-fifth (of seventy-six) in the world for performance in 1996. The market declined by 9.9 percent in U.S.-dollar returns.[19] In 1994 the Kenyan market ranked number one in the world with a 179 percent U.S.-dollar return.

Market Valuation[20]

Year	Price–Earnings Ratio	Dividend Yield
1991	5.2	15.7
1992	5.8	11.1
1993	9.4	6.0
1994	9.8	4.2
1995	12.4	4.3
1996	27.8	4.4

Companies generally undertake asset revaluation and thus fixed assets are not undervalued and the depreciation charges are realistic. The price earnings ratio has increased 435 percent from 1991 through 1996. The market now carries a multiple that is higher than that of neighboring exchanges.

Listing Requirements

An applicant for listing on the exchange must do the following:

1. Appoint a member of the exchange to sponsor its application. The sponsor is responsible for ensuring the compliance with exchange listing requirements.
2. Submit to the exchange its memorandum and articles of association, a prospectus or offer for sale document approved by the CMA, along with the Companies Act and other supporting documents.
3. Seek the agreement of the NSE Committee and the approval of the CMA to the advertising of any issue.
4. Publish any prospectus at the time and for a period specified by the CMA.

The Capital Markets Authority must approve any listing. The value of listed shares declined 4.3 percent from 1995 to 1996, while the number of firms listed increased 3.6 percent. However, from 1991 to 1996 the market capitalization increased 179.7 percent in U.S.-dollar terms. The market capitalization peaked in 1994 at $3.10 billion, as investors anticipated the opening of the market to foreign investors. The expected demand did not materialize and market capitalization fell 39.7 percent from 1994 to 1995. There are forty-two domestic firms listed and sixteen foreign companies listed.

Number of Listed Firms and Market Capitalization[21]

Year	Number Firms	Market Capitalization (U.S. Billions)
1991	56	0.64
1992	57	0.61
1993	54	1.42
1994	56	3.10
1995	56	1.87
1996	58	1.79

Liquidity

The International Finance Corporation ranks the exchange number sixty-ninth (of eighty-four) in terms of market turnover for 1996. This places the Nairobi Exchange ninth among African exchanges in terms of liquidity as measured by the market turnover ratio.[22]

Market Turnover Ratio

Year	1991	1992	1993	1994	1995	1996
Turnover Ratio[23]	2.49	1.99	3.06	2.70	3.45	4.00

The turnover ratio reflects the market value of shares traded into the market capitalization. Based on the exchange's turnover ratio, the liquidity of shares has increased approximately 61 percent from 1991 through 1996. Average daily turnover in 1995 was $296,000. This increased to $305,000 in 1996. Despite the difficulties with the IMF, FPIs accounted for 39.8 percent of the Nairobi Exchange's turnover in July 1997.

Insurance companies hold approximately 9 to 10 percent of the outstanding shares, most of which are not traded because of the capital gains tax (that the government plans to eliminate). At present 3 to 7 percent of the listed stocks are actively traded.

Ownership

Institutional Investors	70%
Individuals	30%

Instruments Traded

There are two share types, ordinary and preference. In addition, corporate bonds and debenture stocks trade. In 1996, bonds issued by the East African Development Bank were the first bonds specifically listed on the Nairobi Stock Exchange. There is only the East African Development Bank with a listing on the exchange, along with three companies with commercial paper listed.[24]

On April 1, 1997, the Kenyan government initiated quarterly issuance of one-year floating rate treasury bonds on the exchange. Foreigners pay a 12.5-percent withholding tax on interest earned (local investors pay 15%). There are seven market makers for the treasury bonds. To encourage corporations to obtain credit ratings, the government passed a law to exempt them from taxes on the costs associated with the rating.[25] There are currently no derivative products traded and the exchange has no plans to institute them.

Brokerage Rates

Equities	Sliding fee from 2% to 1.1%
Fixed interest	5% for all fixed income securities

Margin/Securities Lending

There are no facilities for stock lending. However, there are no regulations in the NSE Rules, the CMA Act, or the CMA Regulations prohibiting a broker from lending the purchase price or any part of the purchase price against a security as collateral.

Insider Trading

Insider trading is illegal. Insiders are not allowed to deal in any securities if they have acquired information which is not publicly known and that would have a material effect on the value of the securities. In addition, insiders should refrain from trading for a period of fourteen days after the release of material information to ensure that the information is disseminated and that market participants have had an opportunity to respond. Insider trading/dealing is dealt with under provisions of Sections 33(1) to 33(4) of the CMA Act.

Dividends and Capital Gains Taxation

Tax incentives exist for foreign and local investors. There is no capital gains tax (as of June 14, 1985), stamp duty on transfers, or value-added tax on market transactions. Kenya has double taxation treaties with the following countries: Zambia, Denmark, Norway, Sweden, the United Kingdom, Germany, Canada, and India.

To encourage market participation, the government of Kenya's 1997 budget removed a 35-percent capital gains tax on local insurance companies and exempt private equity funds from paying taxes for ten years on dividends and capital gains from the holding or sale of shares in qualified venture companies.[26] The tax restricted liquidity, with insurers making long-term investments without recognizing gains. It is estimated that as much as US$600 million in stock could be freed for trading.

Regulatory Controls

The Capital Markets Authority, which was established in 1990, regulates the exchange.

Foreign Investment Restrictions

The Exchange Control Act was repealed in 1995 to allow the free flow of foreign exchange. Foreign investors may participate in local companies up to a limit of 40 percent and an individual limit of 5 percent. Once the 40-percent limit has been reached, foreigners may only purchase shares from other foreign shareholders. An informal foreign board has been established to monitor shareholding limits. In a move to encourage domestic investors, foreigners are restricted from investing in the local subsidiaries of foreign-controlled companies.

Despite the market opening to foreigners, investment is restricted to about half the market, as many of the companies, such as Barclays and Brooke Bond, already have majority stakes held by foreign investors. For example, Barclays is not open to foreign investment, as it is 68-percent controlled by Barclays of the United Kingdom. Nevertheless, according to the IFC the regulatory changes resulted in foreign investor capital flows increasing from $3.3 million in 1995 to $11 million in 1996. In 1995 foreign investors accounted for 7 percent of the exchange's turnover, in 1996 participation of foreign investors increased to 19 percent, and the trend in 1997 was upward. In 1997 the establishment of the Africa Online web site facilitated American investors receiving information on results on the NSE three hours before the start of the business day.

In June 1997, the Securities Commission of Malaysia and the Capital Markets Authority of Kenya signed a memorandum of understanding to establish a framework for mutual assistance and cooperation. There is an Investment Promotion Center to assist local and foreign enterprises in their investment in Kenya (tel.: 221 401–4).

Central Depository

There is no central depository, however market plans call for the initiation of one in 1997. Physical delivery of the share certificates is necessary in order to transfer ownership of a listed security under exchange rules. Domestic commercial banks and trust companies can act as custodians. The banks are not required to carry coverage against the loss of securities held in custody, but most do.

Settlement

Delivery takes place on T+7 with settlement occurring on D+7. Settlement and delivery systems were computerized in 1995. Previously there was no set settlement date; however, T+4 to 5 were accepted practice. This enabled cleared funds to be remitted from overseas to settle purchases. The NSE operates as a clearinghouse for the brokers. It can take up to two months to be issued a certificate allowing resale.

Buy-Ins

There are exchange penalties for nondelivery or late deliveries, with the NSE instituting buy-in procedures against defaulting brokers. On the settlement date, unless otherwise agreed to in writing, the buying broker is bound to effect payment within seven days of receiving the properly executed transfer and share certificate or certificates from the selling broker under Rule 89 (a) of the NSE Rules. In the event of nonpayment by the purchaser or nondelivery of the seller of the necessary documents within sixty days after the date of the transaction, Rules 89(b) and (c), 90, and 92 of the NSE come into effect. If the purchaser fails to pay for the shares within ninety days of the date of the sale the buying broker can sell off the securities and seek payment of any loss occasioned. If the seller fails to deliver the transfer and certificate within sixty days of the date of the transaction the buyer can give ten days notice to the seller to deliver the documents. If the seller still fails to deliver the documents he is deemed to have rescinded the transaction. Neither the NSE nor the CMA has the power to void any contract of sale.

Voting

Proxy voting is permitted and foreign shareholders enjoy the same rights as domestic shareholders.

Reporting Requirements

Exchange policy requires prompt and full public disclosure of material development. The exchange requires that it be given information not later than twenty-four hours after a corporate decision has been made concerning the following:

- A proposed distribution of dividends, a change in capital structure, or any moves that would affect the price of the company's shares on the market.

- Any proposed alteration of the memorandum and articles of association.
- Details of any change in substantial shareholding received by the company.
- Any application filed with a court to wind up the company or any of its subsidiaries or associated companies.
- Any acquisition of shares of another company or any transaction resulting in such a company becoming a subsidiary or associated company.
- Any major change of business policy or operations.

Listed companies must report results semiannually, not later than three months after the end of the first half of the year. Annual results must be reported not later than three months after the end of the financial year. Printed annual reports must be submitted to the exchange and stockholders not later than six months after the year end. Annual report contents are established in exchange rules.

Actual financial reporting and disclosure is average for sub-Saharan Africa. Failure to comply with public disclosure requirements may result in a firm's delisting from the exchange. For example, in September 1997 Kenya's leading tourism company, African Tours and Hotels was suspended from the Nairobi Stock Exchange after failing to furnish its quarterly and annual reports.[27]

Legal Issues

Domestic courts would enforce a governing law clause in a subcustody agreement that provides for New York law. A judgment of a United States or New York court is not enforceable in the domestic courts without relitigating the matter. Much of Kenya's common law is the same as in England.

NOTES

1. CIA Factbook web site at http://www.odci.gov/cia/publications/nsolo/factbook/ke.htm.

2. Ibid.

3. "Stock Market Registers Dismal Performance," *Agence France Presse*, 15 October 1997.

4. CIA Factbook web site.

5. The World Bank's criteria for low-income classification is a GNP per capita of less than $765 in 1995. Kenya's per capita GNP in 1995 was $280.

6. *Annual Report* (Nairobi: Central Bank of Kenya, 1997).

7. CIA Factbook web site.

8. *Annual Report*, 1997. As reported at web site: www.africaonline.co.ke/cbk/objectives.html.

9. *Annual Report* (Nairobi: Central Bank of Kenya, 1996).

10. Investors interested in investing in Kenya should consult Ernst & Young's Guide to Investing in Africa, Kenya at web site http://mbendi.co.za/ernsty/eycyprof.htm. The Ernst & Young Africa Group consists of forty-nine offices across Africa.

11. "Kenyan Authority Promotes Rating Agency," *Emerging Markets Debt Report* 10, 27 (July 7, 1997): 1.

12. *Annual Report*, 1996.

13. Ibid.

14. CIA Factbook web site.

15. U.S. Department of Commerce, ITA, *1996 Country Commercial Guide for Kenya* (Washington, D.C.: National Trade Data Bank, 1995).

16. KLM press release, 6 December 1995.

17. KLM Royal Dutch Airlines web site news at http://www.klm.nl/About/default.htm.

18. *Emerging Stock Markets Factbook 1997* (Washington, D.C.: International Finance Corporation, 1997).

19. Ibid.

20. Nairobi Stock Exchange, *Exchange Reports*, Nairobi, 1997.

21. Ibid.

22. *Emerging Stock Markets Factbook 1997*.

23. Nairobi Stock Exchange, *Exchange Reports*.

24. "Kenyan Authority Promotes Rating Agency," 1.

25. Ibid.

26. "New Kenya Rules to Boost Liquidity, Private Equity," *Emerging Markets Week*, 30 June 1997, 5.

27. "Leading Tourism State Firm Delisted from Stock Exchange," *Agence France Presse*, 9 September 1997.

MAURITIUS

COUNTRY

The Republic of Mauritius has an area of 788 square miles (2,040 square kilometers) and is a volcanic island in the Indian Ocean 800 km east of Madagascar. The capital is Port Louis. The official language is English.

Mauritius remained uninhabited until the end of the sixteenth century. The island was visited by the Portuguese, but it was not until the Dutch landed a party in 1598 that the island was claimed and settled. The Dutch colonial period saw the introduction of sugar cane and the importation of slaves to harvest it. The Dutch abandoned their settlements in 1710. In 1721 the French claimed the island and imported large numbers of slaves to cultivate plantations of sugar, cotton, indigo, cloves, nutmeg, and other spices.

At the end of the Napoleonic Wars the island was ceded to Britain, though under the terms of the treaty the French way of life was preserved. Slavery was abolished in 1835. Politics in the nineteenth century centered mainly on the struggle of the Franco-Mauritian plantation owners for more representations in the colonial government. The island was granted its independence in 1968.

Official Religion	None[1]
Religions	Hindu, 52%; Roman Catholic, 26%; Protestant, 2.3%; Muslim, 16.6%; other, 3.1%[2]
Population	1,140,256 (July 1996 est.)[3]
	Urban: 41%
	Rural: 59%
	Population under the age of 15: 27%
Ethnic Divisions	Indo-Mauritian 68%, Creole 27%, Sino-Mauritian 3%, Franco-Mauritian 2%
Languages	English (official), Creole, French, Hindi, Urdu, Hakka, Bojpoori
Education	Population over age 15 who are literate: 80%

The Political System

Mauritius gained independence in 1968. For the first fourteen years a Labor government led by the late Sir Seewoosagur Ramgoolam, the "Father of the Nation," ruled. In 1982 the MMM (Mouvement Militant Mauricien) took over, but this party split in 1983 into the MMM represented by Paul Berenger and the MSM (Mouvement Socialiste Mauricien) represented by

Sir Aneerood Jugnauth. The two parties coexisted for eight years. In 1991 general elections were held and the MSM gained power in 1992 and the nation became a republic. The latest elections were held in December 1995, and a coalition of Labor and MMM parties was elected under the leadership of Dr. Navin Ramgoolam.

Political Web Site   http://www.geocities.com/~derksen/election.htm

Legal System

The Mauritian legal system is based on the French civil law system with elements of English common law in certain areas.
Suffrage is universal at age eighteen.

The Economy

The economy has made a significant structural transformation since the 1970s from a dependence on the sugar crop to a diversified economy based upon export manufacturing and tourism. This economic transformation has resulted in significant challenges as the economy reached its productive limits.

Economic Indicators[4]

Year	Real GDP Growth	Consumer Prices
1990	7.1	13.5
1991	4.5	7.0
1992	6.0	4.6
1993	5.5	9.0
1994	5.0	15.0
1995	5.3	na
1996	5.7	na

The nation made effective use of export processing zones to stimulate its export growth, and enjoys quasi-full employment. For more information concerning the export processing zones, see http://www.mweb.co.za/nibs/maur/epfront.html.

Gross Domestic Product[5]

Mauritius is classified as an upper middle-income country under the World Bank's classification of economies.[6] For comparability, GDP is expressed in purchase power parity terms.

GDP purchasing power parity	$10.9 billion (1995 est.)
GDP real growth rate	2.7% (1995 est.)
GDP per capita	$9,600 (1995 est.)

Privatization

Privatization of state-owned assets has increased investment activities. Through mid-1996 two state-owned enterprises—the State Bank of Mauritius and Air Mauritius—were privatized and listed on the stock exchange. Through 1998 major privatization plans include Mauritius Telecom and New Mauritius Hotels.[7] The listing requirements are the same for companies under the privatization program as for regular listings.

Central Bank: Bank of Mauritius[8]

The Bank of Mauritius is the main regulator of the country's financial markets. As a central bank, it must ensure the financial health of the country's economy and enforce financial discipline. The Bank of Mauritius Act 1966 (as amended) lays down the purposes of the bank. The bank's goal is to "safeguard the internal and external value of the currency of Mauritius and its internal convertibility [and to] direct its policy towards achieving monetary conditions conducive to strengthening the economic activity and prosperity of Mauritius."

The bank is the regulatory authority for the country's monetary and financial system. The bank also seeks to promote economic development consistent with the need to protect the value of the currency. Against this broad concern of the bank, some of the main functions are the following:

1. to issue currency
2. to promote the development of a sound banking system
3. to act as banker and financial adviser to the government
4. to act as bankers' bank
5. to formulate and conduct monetary policy
6. to manage exchange rate and foreign exchange reserves
7. to manage public debt

In a free enterprise economy with a liberalized financial system, central bank supervision of commercial banking institutions is indispensable. Commercial banks in Mauritius are regulated and supervised by the Bank of Mauritius under the Banking Act of 1988. This act replaced the 1971 act in January 1989 with a view to strengthening and modernizing the regulatory and supervisory system as well as providing for the legal framework for the establishment and operation of offshore banks domiciled in Mauritius.

The basic objectives of the Banking Act are to maintain a sound banking system in Mauritius and to protect the interests of depositors. It incorporates the following principles of prudential regulation and supervision of banks:

1. Licensing of banks
2. Capital adequacy
3. Quality of management
4. Liquidity control
5. Concentration of risk
6. Role of external auditors
7. On-site examinations
8. Off-site surveillance
9. Control of advertisements
10. Confidentiality of information
11. Identity of customers

Commercial banks, like any other private enterprise, are profit maximizers. In the pursuit of profit making they may become less cautious and take greater risk in their lending operations. This may endanger the safety of depositors' money. From the supervisory angle, one of the most important concerns of the Bank of Mauritius is therefore to ensure the maintenance of a sound commercial banking structure.

Since the establishment of the Bank of Mauritius, the Mauritian economy and the financial landscape of Mauritius have undergone considerable changes. Exchange control was completely abolished in July 1994. The exchange rate of the rupee and interest rates are freely determined by the market. The Bank of Mauritius is strongly committed to enhancing competition and efficiency in the financial system and ensuring its total integrity.

Bank of Mauritius
P.O. Box 29
Sir Willam Newton Street
Port Louis
Mauritius
Tel.: +230–208 4164 or + 230–211–1355
Telex: 4253MAUBNKIW, 4253 B MAUBNKIW
Fax: +230–208 9204
Web Site http://www.bankofmauritius.co.uk/mdls.htm

Credit Rating

Mauritian debt has received an investment grade rating from Moody's Investment Service, a U.S. debt-rating service. The country's rating is Baa2.

Currency

Monetary unit: Mauritian rupee (Mau Re; plural Mau Rs) = 100 cents

From 1992, exchange controls have been removed to permit the free flow of investment capital. There are a number of web sites providing updated currency exchange values. The following is an example:

http://www.bloomberg.com/markets/currency/currcalc.cgi

THE STOCK EXCHANGE: STOCK EXCHANGE
OF MAURITIUS (SEM)

The stock exchange has played a critical role in the transition of the Mauritian economy, serving as a means of converting savings into long-term capital for industry. The market provides support for Mauritius's role as a regional financial center.

Mr. Sydney Bathfield, Chairman
Stock Exchange of Mauritius Ltd.
6th Floor, Les Cascades Building
33 Bis. Edith Cavell Street
Port Louis, Mauritius
Tel.: (230) 212–9541/2/3
Fax: (230) 208–8409, (230) 208–8351
E-Mail: stockex@bow.intnet.mu
Web Site http://www.mweb.co.za/nibs/maur/stock/cover.html

Established	July 5, 1989.
Stock Exchange Act	Stock Exchange Act of 1988 and the Companies Act
Trading Days	Official Market: Monday, Wednesday, Friday OTC Market: Tuesday and Thursday
Trading Hours	11:00–12:00 The international time zone is GMT +4 hours.

The SEM operates two markets, the official market for dealing in listed securities and the OTC market for unlisted securities. The OTC market began operations in April 1990 and at the end of 1996 the shares of sixty-five companies were traded.

Index

The SEMDEX price index includes all listed shares.

Membership

The SEM has eleven stockbroking companies as members. Each contributed one share of Rs300,000. Each stockbroking company is required to have at least two licensed stockbrokers, each furnishing a guarantee for Rs250,000 as capital for the company.

STOCK MARKET ACTIVITY

Trading Structure

Until the end of 1993 there were two trading systems operating on the exchange, open outcry and box. Open outcry was used for trading in listed shares on the official market and the box method was used for trading on the OTC market. Since January 1994, trading is carried out by the open outcry method for spot transactions in both markets. Nevertheless, the box method is still in use for cases of extreme disequilibrium, when a price quotation cannot be reached by the outcry method. In such cases, buy and sell orders are matched by the computer to determine the quoted price.

Performance

In 1996 the International Finance Corporation ranked the Mauritius market price index U.S.-dollar performance as sixty-third (of seventy-six) in the world. The index declined 6.9 percent from the year earlier.[9]

Market Valuation[10]

Year	Price–Earnings Ratio	Dividend Yield
1991	7.0	6.1
1992	11.6	6.0
1993	12.0	4.2
1994	16.5	3.3
1995	11.1	5.1
1996	11.4	4.0
1997	14.1	4.3

Market price–earnings ratios peaked in 1994 and have subsequently declined to attractive emerging market levels.

Listing Requirements

The 1993 Finance Act established a listing committee to deal with listing applications and to recommend the listing of a company. In addition to having an adequate trading record with published or filed accounts for the three years preceding the request for listing, there are two conditions to be satisfied for admission to the official list: a market capitalization of at least Rs20 million, and public shareholdings of at least 15 percent initially, 20 percent within three years, and 25 percent within five years of listing, with a minimum of 200 shareholders, or the listing application should relate to shares with a minimum nominal value of Rs2 million.

The government offers firms a series of incentives to list their shares on the exchange. These include the following:

1. a tax credit of 30 percent on corporate tax for companies listed on the stock exchange
2. exemption from income tax on dividends for listed companies
3. exemption from registration and stamp duty charges on the transfer of shares
4. exemption from income tax on interest received on bonds
5. an investment tax credit allowance (30 percent over three years) of Rs75,000 in the case of an individual or an associate in a listed company, or Rs300,000 per income year in any other cases
6. a tax rate of 15 percent is granted to unit trusts and approved investment trust companies
7. a tax credit of 10 percent on purchases of newly issued shares of approved investment trust companies listed on the stock exchange to a maximum of Rs8,000

Number of Listed Firms and Market Capitalization[11]

Year	Number of Firms	Market Capitalization (Rs Millions)	U.S. Dollars
1991	20	4,862.48	310.7
1992	21	6,598.88	424.1
1993	30	14,768.15	832.0
1994	35	28,536.06	1,482.4
1995	41	27,817.76	1,517.3
1996	45	33,376.74	1,693.1
1997	46	36,934.88	1,677.3

As an offshore financial center, Mauritius has attracted an estimated $4 billion in offshore funds.[12] The number of listed firms has more than doubled since the end of 1991. This reflects the structural transitions in the economy and the government's goal to privatize state-owned enterprises. Domestic currency market capitalization increased 586 percent from 1991 to 1996, an annual growth rate of 47 percent. There are no restrictions on cross-listing shares of other nations. There are two foreign firms listed on the exchange. There are sixty-five firms listed on the over-the-counter market.

Liquidity

The average turnover per trading session is $538,311. Market information is disseminated widely through local and international networks, such as Bloomberg, Datastream, and FT Extel. A regular publication of the Stock Exchange of Mauritius, the "SEM Newsletter," available on subscription, periodically disseminates data on both markets. The exchange launched a campaign in 1993 aimed at attracting more investors and interest from the large group of companies on the island. The increasing number of privatizations indicates a greater supply of shares and improved liquidity.

Market Turnover Ratio

Year	1992	1993	1994	1995	1996
Turnover Ratio (Official List)[13]	2.7	4.7	5.3	4.4	4.8

The International Finance Corporation ranked the Mauritian market turnover ratio as sixty-eighth (of eighty-four) in the world. The market ranked eighth in Africa in terms of turnover.[14] The over-the-counter market had turnover of Rs175.8 million in 1996, down 24 percent from 1995. Foreigners accounted for 45 percent of the total trading in 1996 and provided net portfolio inflows estimated at Rs650 million ($32 million). In 1997 foreign investors accounted for 14 percent of the exchange's annual turnover. In 1997 the average turnover per session was $850,638.

Instruments Traded

There are two types of shares on the SEM, ordinary and preference. In addition, corporate debentures and government bonds are traded. The government has stated a desire to develop an active bond market. There are currently no derivative products traded and the exchange has no plans to institute them. Market trades are conducted in the local currency, the Mauritian rupee, except for two dual-listed funds quoted in U.S. dollars.

Brokerage Rates

Less than Rs3 million	1.25%
More than Rs3 million, but less than Rs6 million	1.15%
More than Rs6 million, but less than Rs10 million	1.05%
More than Rs10 million	0.90%

Margin/Securities Lending

There is no stock lending in the market. Short sales are not permitted.

Insider Trading

Mauritian insiders must disclose their interest to the Stock Exchange Commission through the Registrar of Interest for securities. Section 46 to 50 of the Stock Exchange Act 1988 prohibits insider trading, fraudulent inducement to invest, and stock market manipulation.

Dividends and Capital Gains Taxation

There are no capital gains taxes or withholding taxes. There are no stamp duties or registration duties on dealings in securities listed on the exchange. Tax treaties exist with France, Germany, the United Kingdom, Italy, Sweden, India, Zimbabwe, Malaysia, Swaziland, Pakistan, China, and Madagascar.

Regulatory Controls

The exchange operates under the control and supervision of the Stock Exchange Commission. The Stock Exchange Commission (the supervisory body) is managed by an Executive Committee of twelve members (nine stockbroking company representatives and three members appointed by the Ministry of Finance).

Foreign Investment Restrictions

The stock exchange opened to foreign investors in 1994. The government has abolished all restrictions on foreign investors and eliminated exchange controls. Foreign and local investors are treated on an equal footing as far as fiscal incentives are concerned. Foreign investment accounted for 44 percent of turnover in 1996, compared to 15.8 percent in 1995.[15]

Mutual Funds

The Mauritius Fund Ltd. is traded on the London Exchange and is managed by the Mauritius Fund Management Company (Reuters Code: SOWI). The Fund has gross assets of approximately $28 million as of September 17, 1997. The Fund traded at a discount to net asset value of –20.6 percent. The one-year price total-return performance in British pounds was +0.4 percent; three years was –33.1 percent. As measured in British pounds, the Fund's one-year NAV increase was +11.5 percent, three years was –20.3 percent. The Fund seeks long-term capital appreciation through investment in a diversified portfolio of shares listed in Mauritius, new issues, and unlisted securities of Mauritian companies. Pending equity investments in Mauritius, the assets of the fund will be invested in liquid, low-risk money market instruments or deposits with financial institutions on or offshore. The Fund may also invest up to 10 percent in equities outside Mauritius. The Fund's largest investments are the Mauritius Commercial Bank, State Bank of Mauritius, Rogers & Co., and Caudan Development Ltd. (Tel.: 230 208 2801, Fax: 230 208 8484).

Central Depository

In the second half of 1996 a central depository system and an automated clearing and share settlement system were set up. The depository opened February 14, 1997.

Settlement

A five-day clearing and settlement system is in place. The Bank of Mauritius acts as a clearing bank and the depository ensures strict delivery versus payment. The Central Depository and Settlement Co. is a private company that was established to provide centralized depository, clearing, and settlement services. The firm is 51-percent owned by the Stock Exchange of Mauritius and its board of directors consists of representatives from the exchange, listed companies, insurance companies, company secretaries, the Ministry of Finance, and the Bank of Mauritius. The depository is designed based upon the G30 recommendations. The system is based on the technology used at the Colombo Stock Exchange and was built by Millennium Information Technologies and Colombo Stock Exchange & State Information.[16] The Bank of Mauritius acts as clearing bank and the depository ensures delivery versus payment. Settlement is guaranteed through a fund to which all brokers contribute. Participants in the system have until noon on T+2 to make trade corrections. On settlement day, T+5, funds settlement occurs between participants' settlement banks through a transfer directly at the Bank of Mauritius. If a participant does not have the securities in its account on T+5, the trade is temporarily suspended and a buy-in procedure is immediately initiated. The participant is required to make a cash deposit to the depository and a daily penalty is imposed on the participant until the buy-in is completed or the situation is corrected. If after five trading sessions the buy-in is unsuccessful, the depository will give the cash deposit to the buyer and cancel the trade. The participant bears all losses and expenses associated with the buy-in.

Voting

Shareholders are allowed to vote by proxy.

Reporting Requirements

Companies must notify the SEM of any major developments, including the following:

1. any decision to pay a dividend or other distribution in listed securities, or to fail to pay a dividend or interest payment
2. a preliminary announcement of profits or losses on a half-yearly basis together with copies of the half-yearly interim report
3. any proposed change in capital structure, issues, and redemption of securities
4. change in the rights attached to any class of listed security
5. details of major acquisitions or realizations of assets
6. any change in the directorate or in senior executive officers
7. any proposed alteration of the memorandum and articles of association of the company
8. copies of the audited annual accounts and source and application of funds statement
9. any notice of changes to substantial shareholdings and details thereof
10. any acquisition of shares of another company or transaction resulting in such a company becoming a subsidiary of the listed company

Provisional financial statements must be made public within three months of the financial year end.

Legal Issues

The Companies Act 1984 provides for the protection of minority shareholders. Mergers and acquisitions regulations are not current established, though the government is presently working on an Act of Parliament to deal with this issue.

INTERNET RESOURCES

Business

Mauritius Chamber of Commerce and Industry at http://mns.intnet.mu/mcci.htm

Export Processing Zone Development Authority at http://epzda.intnet.mu/ mcci.htm, is sponsored by the EPZDA (Export Processing Zones Development Authority), a parastatal organization operating under the aegis of the Ministry of Industry and Commerce in Mauritius. EPZDA distributes information on various sectors of the Mauritian economy.

Ministry of Finance at http://www.intnet.mu/ncb/finance.mof.htm

Mauritius Offshore Business Activities Authority at http://www.intnet.mu/ncb/finance/mobaa.home.htm

Mauritius Information Website at http://www.mauritius-info.com, includes News and Events (l'Express); Mauritius E-mail Directory (e-mail addresses of Mauritians in the United States); Business Directory (list of companies by Economic Sector, economic data, setting up a business, import/export, services, banks and finance, Mauritius Freeport Authority, Port Louis Harbor); Government & Political System of Mauritius; Travel & Tourism Information; History; and Art and Culture.

Mauritius Online at http://www.mauritius-online.com, is a collaboration of Coopers & Lybrand and Ad Venture in Mauritius, and provides up-to-the-minute news and information about Mauritius and the region. It includes links to the home pages of the leading Mauritian and Indian Ocean region companies and services.

NOTES

1. CIA Factbook web site at http://www.odci.gov/cia/publications/nsolo/factbook/mp.htm.

2. Ibid.

3. Ibid.

4. Web site http://www.mauritius-info.com/bus-info/eco-data.htm.

5. CIA Factbook web site.

6. The World Bank's criteria for middle-income classification is a GNP per capita of $766 to $9,385 in 1995. Mauritius's per capita GNP in 1995 was $3,380.

7. "Country Profile: Mauritius," *Institutional Investor, Inc. Operations Management* 3 (1997): 7.

8. Bank of Mauritius web site statement at http://www.bankofmauritius.co.uk/about.htm.

9. *Emerging Stock Markets Factbook 1997* (Washington, D.C.: International Finance Corporation, 1997).

10. Stock Exchange of Mauritius, *Exchange Reports* (Port Louis: The Exchange, 1997).

11. Ibid.

12. A critical element of the offshore financial center is Mauritius's double taxation treaty with India. The reciprocal agreement reduces capital gains taxes by about 10 percent on average. Mauritius has also entered into taxation agreements with Pakistan and China. "Country Profile: Mauritius," 7.

13. Stock Exchange of Mauritius, *Exchange Reports.*

14. *Emerging Stock Markets Factbook 1997.*

15. "Stock Exchange Share Prices Rebound," *Institutional Investor,* July 1997, S10.

16. "Country Profile: Mauritius," 7.

MOROCCO

COUNTRY

The Kingdom of Morocco (in Arabic al-Maghrib, or al-Mamlakah al-Maghribiyah) has an area of 177,117 square miles (458,730 square kilometers). For comparison, the area is slightly larger than California. The capital is Rabat. The official language is Arabic.

Berbers came to Morocco at the end of the second millennium B.C. In the twelfth century B.C. the Phoenician traders established trading outposts. Carthage had settlements along the Atlantic in the fifth century B.C., and Morocco allied itself with Rome with the fall of Carthage. The Muslim invasion of North Africa reached Morocco in the late seventh century. The Berbers revolted against Damascus's rule in 740 and gained their independence, and a Berber confederation conquered all of Morocco in the middle of the eleventh century, eventually extending their control to southern Spain. They were driven from Spain in 1492.

European nations increased their intervention in North Africa in 1830. Great Britain gained favorable trading rights in 1856, and the Spanish increased their North African territories at Morocco's expense in 1859. In 1912 Morocco accepted status as a French protectorate. Morocco gained independence from France in 1956. King Hassan II ascended the throne in 1961. Elections were held in 1977.

Official Religion	None[1]
Religions	Muslim, 98.7%; Christian, 1.1%; Jewish, 0.2%[2]
Population	29,779,156 (July 1996 est.)[3]
	Population under the age of 15: 38%
Ethnic Divisions	Arab-Berber 99.1%, other 0.7%, Jewish 0.2%
Languages	Arabic (official), Berber dialects, French often the language of business, government, and diplomacy
Education	Population over age 15 who are literate: 43.7%

The Political System

Morocco is governed by a constitutional monarchy.[4] The supreme executive power is vested in the hereditary king who appoints a Prime Minister. The legislative power rests with a bicameral House of Representatives. For the first chamber of representatives, the constitution calls all the members to be elected directly and for the second chosen by an Electoral College.

Their terms of office are six years. The independent judiciary is lead by the Supreme Count appointed by the King.

The second Chamber of Representatives (Majlis Nawab) is elected by an electoral college of government, professional, and labor representatives; direct, popular elections were last held November 14, 1997 and December 5, 1997.

Political Web Site   http://www.geocities.com/~derksen/election.htm

Legal System

The Moroccan legal system is based on Islamic law and French and Spanish civil law systems. There is a judicial review of legislative acts in the Constitutional Chamber of the Supreme Court.

Suffrage is at twenty-one years of age and is universal.

The Economy

Morocco's economy is a mixed one based on services, agriculture, and mineral industries. To encourage development of industries outside Casablanca, the government developed liberal foreign investment regulations. Morocco has opted for a market-led approach to modernizing its economy. The manufacturing sector contributes 16 percent of GNP and is significantly larger than in other African nations. The manufacturing sector was hampered in 1994 and 1995 by the appreciation of the dirham, especially in relationship to the Spanish peseta. Inflation has been moderate, at a 3.9 percent annual rate over the 1990 to 1995 period, the best performance on the continent.

Morocco has pursued an economic structural adjustment program with the support of the IMF, the World Bank, and the Paris Club of creditors. The economy has substantial assets, the world's largest phosphate reserves, diverse agricultural and fishing resources, a sizable tourist industry, a growing manufacturing sector, and remittances from Moroccans working abroad. In 1995, Morocco suffered a drought which negatively impacted on economic growth. Real GDP growth rate in 1995 was estimated at a –6.5 percent. The unemployment rate is estimated to be 16 percent. The economy boasts a well-developed corporate finance sector with adequate legal, accounting, and professional services.

Gross Domestic Product[5]

Morocco is classified as a middle-income country under the World Bank's classification of economies.[6] For comparability, GDP is expressed in purchase power parity terms.

GDP purchasing power parity $87.4 billion (1995 est.)
GDP real growth rate   –6.5% (1995 est.)
GDP per capita $3,000 (1995 est.)

Central Bank: Bank al-Maghrib

The monetary authorities comprise the Ministry of Finance and the central bank, Bank al-Maghrib. The central bank was established on June 30, 1959. In addition to its essential task of monetary policy regulation (in charge of refinancing mechanisms, limitation of credit distribution, etc.), the country's financial and exchange reserves management agent, Bank al-Maghrib is also a private bank and can effect all operations like a commercial bank. Moreover, it is entrusted with the very large task of controlling banking activity and monitoring specialized financial bodies and, at the control level, is the sole effective authority to which the banks are subjected. As a central bank, it holds the privilege of issuing currency, which it manufactures itself. Bank al-Maghrib is represented in seventeen cities throughout the kingdom. The banking system comprises two categories of institutions: commercial banks and specialized financing bodies.

Bank al-Maghrib is located in seventeen cities: Agadir, Laâyoune, Marrakech, Safi, Beni Mellal, Casablanca, El Jadida, Kénitra, Larache, Rabat, Tanger, Tétouan, Al Hoceïma, Fès, Nador, Oujda, and Meknès.

Credit Rating

Moody's Investors Services rated the kingdom's foreign currency bonds and notes Ba1 in its inaugural rating assigned in March 1998. For foreign currency long-term bank deposits, the rating was Ba2 and Not Prime for ratings of short-term foreign currency obligations of issuers in Morocco. In assigning its ratings, Moody noted the country's sound economic policy and progress on structural reforms.

Standard & Poor's is concerned about the economy's vulnerability to agricultural output and the high level of public sector and external debt. S&P assigned a BBB long-term and an A-3 short-term sovereign credit rating to local currency obligations. It gave a BB to long-term and B to short-term ratings to Morocco's foreign currency obligations.[7]

Currency

Monetary unit   1 Moroccan dirham (DH) = 100 centimes

The Central Bank (Banque du Maroc) ended currency fixing on May 2, 1996, authorizing a domestic foreign exchange market. The Bank al-Maghrib authorized banks and designated dealers to quote buy-and-sell rates for the

Moroccan dirham within a band specified by the central bank. Prior to this the bank fixed the value of the dirham daily against a basket of currencies which reflected Morocco's trade positions. Exchange rates are as follows: Moroccan dirhams per US$1–8.607 (January 1996), 8.540 (1995), 9.203 (1994), 9.299 (1993), 8.538 (1992), 8.707 (1991).[8]

There are a number of web sites providing updated currency exchange values. The following is an example:

http://www.bloomberg.com/markets/currency/currcalc.cgi

Privatization

Privatization has been essential to recent growth of the stock exchange. Since Parliament passed privatization legislation in 1989, market capitalization increased fourteenfold through 1996. During the same period, average daily share volume grew over 175-fold from DH0.5 million to DH87.1 million. In 1995 the privatization ministry issued nearly DH1.8 billion ($200 million) in privatization bonds that could be exchanged for shares in companies sold by the state. There were four public offerings in 1996 and all were heavily oversubscribed. The consumer credit firm, CREDOR, was floated in December 1996. It was the first floatation of a private firm since the market was deregulated in 1993. The floatation was oversubscribed 17.5 times. Twenty-eight companies and eighteen hotels have been transferred to the private sector.

Cumulative revenue	DH9.7 billion	($1.1 billion)
Cumulative investment	DH2.3 billion	($260 million)

Privatization has been carried out through open and transparent means; 38.7 percent of the revenue was generated through tenders, and a further 35 percent came from public offerings on the Casablanca Stock Exchange (CSE). Of the twenty-eight companies and eighteen hotels privatized, ten and four respectively were sold in whole or in part to foreign buyers. Industrial operators and financial investors have provided 30 percent of privatization revenue so far. Four types of private placement have been employed:

For the workers' shares	1.6% of revenue
After an unsuccessful tender	11.5% of revenue
To satisfy a right of first refusal	9.7% of revenue
To meet certain social goals set in the law	3.5% of revenue

Moroccan firms generally have a direct foreign investor to increase efficiency and productivity.

Typical Steps For a Privatization[9]

1. Decision. A feasibility study is undertaken by the Ministry from the list of firms and hotels. A background and options report is prepared for the Transfer Commission on the possibility and options of sales. The Transfer Commission evaluates the proposals and makes a decision on whether to proceed with the sale. During this phase there is no final choice as to options for sale.

2. Preparation. A private firm is selected to carry out an audit of the firm targeted for privatization and evaluates the need by law for the transfer. The firm develops additional options for sale. During this phase the firm targeted for privatization begins to prepare for the transition. The evaluation firm works with management, the supervisory Ministry, any holding companies, and employees. The Transfer Commission finalizes the conditions for sale after receiving a final audit and evaluation report. Final preparations are made per the Transfer Commission decision, if necessary, to proceed with any pre-sale adjustments. Then the Valuation Authority sets the price for shares to be sold under each option retained by the Transfer Commission.

3. Sale. For each transfer method, several steps are followed before the sale:

1. *Stock Market.* Moroccan or other bank and brokers advisors are selected for sale via the stock exchange. They set conditions for sale, finalize the prospectus, and launch an advertising campaign. The subscription period is closely monitored. Shares are allotted to subscribers.

2. *Tender.* For sale via tender, Moroccan or other merchant banks are selected. The set terms of reference and the final information memorandum are determined. The tender is advertised. The technical bids and financial bids are examined. The shares are awarded and payment received.

3. *Direct Negotiation.* Ministry officials start to negotiate with potential buyers. Upon the conclusion of the negotiations, the Transfer Commission grants formal approval and prepares it for publication. The sale contract and payment are processed.

4. Finish. A press conference is held or an announcement is released to the press. The legal certification is prepared for signature by the Prime Minister. The transfer of property from public sector to private sector is completed.

THE STOCK EXCHANGE: CASABLANCA STOCK EXCHANGE

The Casablanca Stock Exchange has been instrumental in the liberalization of the economy as the government moves forward with an active privatization program. The market has been instrumental in corporate restructuring and fundraising for the development of indigenous companies. The International Finance Corporation ranks the 1996 market price index performance in U.S. dollars as +38.4 percent.[10]

Mr. L. Abderrazak
Director General
Casablanca Stock Exchange
98, Bd Mohamed V-2000
Casablanca, Morocco
Tel.: (212) 2 20–0366, (212) 2 27–9354, (212) 2 47–1246, (212
Fax: (212) 2 20–0365, (212) 2 20–4110

Web Site	http://mbendi.co.za/exmo.htm
Established	1929
Trading Days	Monday to Friday
Trading Hours	11:00–12:15 Open Outcry
	8:30–12:45 OTC
	The international time zone is GMT.

Founded in 1929, the exchange is one of the oldest in Africa. New securities laws creating a Securities Exchange Commission were passed in July 1993.

Market Index

All share listings are included in the exchange's index, the Index de la Bourse des Valeurs de Casablanca.

STOCK MARKET ACTIVITY

Trading Structure

The market has three trading systems, an open outcry market operating for one-and-a-quarter hours daily; electronic quotation, which operates for two hours; and an OTC market on which all transactions must be reported to the CSE before 12:45 P.M. The electronic system began trading on March 4, 1997. The exchange plans to phase out open outcry when all firms are listed in the electronic system. Block trades on the electronic quotation system will replace the OTC.

Performance

Based on the 1996 change in price indexes in U.S.-dollar terms, the International Finance Corporation ranks the Moroccan market fifteenth (of seventy-six) in the world. The price index increased 38.4 percent over the year.[11] Except for 1992, equity returns in both domestic inflation adjusted and U.S.-dollar terms have outperformed treasury bill returns by a large margin.[12]

Market Valuation[13]

Year	Price–Earnings Ratio	Dividend Yield
1994	16.6	3.33
1995	16.5	3.42
1996	15.1	3.14

As the exchange instituted increased supervision of listing requirements, the number of listed firms declined from 1991; however, from 1995 the number increased 6.8 percent to forty-seven firms, while local currency market capitalization increased 48.7 percent over the same period. Total local currency market capitalization has grown at a 33-percent annual compound rate over the period from 1991 to 1996.

Number of Listed Firms and Market Capitalization[14]

Year	Number of Firms	Market Capitalization (DH Millions)
1991	68	18,143
1992	68	22,900
1993	65	31,754
1994	61	48,463
1995	44	50,827
1996	47	75,583 ($8.6 billion)

Four firms were listed in 1996 and one firm was delisted for noncompliance with reporting requirements. The number of firms listed has declined from 1991 as industry consolidation takes place. Dirham market capitalization increased 48.7 percent in 1996. Market capitalization increased at an annual compound rate of 33 percent from the end of 1991.

Market Turnover Ratio

Year	1991	1992	1993	1994	1995	1996
Turnover Ratio[15]	4.2	4.1	21.7	22.1	45.9	5.9

Official market turnover declined in 1996, reflecting the large privatizations in 1995. However, including the over-the-counter market trades, total market turnover increased 4 percent in 1996. Excluding public offerings and privatization bonds, trading increased 60 percent year to year. Average daily trading value was $6 million. Most trading occurs over the counter. In 1996 the exchange reported 45 percent of the country's total trading, up from 11 percent in 1995. The International Finance Corporation ranked the Moroccan market's 1996 turnover as sixty-sixth (of eighty-four) in the world and seventh in Africa.[16]

In 1996, trading activity on the floor of the stock exchange registered 45 percent of the country's total trading, up from 11 percent in 1995.[17] Trading volume on the over-the-counter market is two to three times higher than on the official market, as operating hours are longer and commission rates are different. All trades are reported to the stock exchange. Trading volumes increased significantly in 1994 because of the privatization of several firms and the market entrance of foreign investors.

Instruments Traded

Equities, government bonds, and other securities trade. Markets have benefited from the introduction of domestic mutual funds.

Brokerage Rates

Official rates are a maximum of 0.35 percent charged by the stock exchange and 0.6 percent by the brokers. A further 0.7 percent value-added tax is charged. However, unofficial rates of between 0.8 percent and 1.0 percent may be negotiated.

Margin/Securities Lending

Short selling is prohibited.

Insider Trading

Insider trading is illegal.

Dividends and Capital Gains Taxation

There are no taxes on nonresident shareholders, including no capital gains tax. A 10-percent withholding tax on dividends is levied on all investors. Neither individuals nor companies (nonresidents) pay taxes on fixed income yields. There is a tax of 0.5 percent on each trade based on the value of the trade. In July 1997, the exchange regulatory agency began imposing a 0.04-percent tax on share trading and a 0.02-percent tax on bond transactions.

Regulatory Controls

The September 1993 legislation involved establishing the Securities Commission or stock exchange watchdog, called the Conseil Déontologique des Valeurs Mobiliéres (CDVM).

Foreign Investment Restrictions

There are no foreign exchange controls for nonresidents. Remittance of capital and related income to nonresidents is guaranteed. No limitations are imposed on the time or amount of profit remitted. Foreign investors have invested more than $300 million in the market.

Central Depository

There is no central depository. Individual commercial banks handle the depository functions, however the exchange is moving toward a central depository. The Moroccan Central Bank is in charge of the cash clearing system on a daily basis. The Bourse is responsible for the securities clearing system. A law was enacted at the end of 1996 that approved establishing a depository, and it is anticipated that the central depository will be established by April 1998.

Settlement

Settlement and cash movements take place between T+5 and T+9. However, the physical transfer of securities from one bank to another takes place twice a month. On that day all shares are gathered at the stock market, where the clearing takes place for the trades of the previous two weeks (i.e., shares exchanged between the first and fifteenth of the month would be physically delivered on the thirtieth of the same month). T+3 is used for settlements on the over-the-counter market.

One local market practice that creates difficulties in the settlement of transactions is a tendency to settle against IOU notes. Stocks are often traded several times against an IOU without changes being entered in the share register. Thus, custodial records do not always match the title on the original share certificate. Market participants are working to transfer stock onto a book-entry system operated by a local clearinghouse (Maroclear). However, some more-liquid stocks continue to be settled physically against IOUs.[18] Ninety percent of foreign investors clear with Banques Commerciale du Maroc.

Registration

Most trading is done in shares in bearer form. The registration of shares takes place by sending a registration form to the company along with a complete identification of the buyer, plus a transfer statement signed by the seller. Nevertheless, most of the shares trading on the Casablanca Bourse are in a bearer form. As soon as purchased, the securities become available and can be sold.

Buy-Ins

There are no rules governing buy-ins.

Voting

Proxy voting is only allowed if the beneficiary is a shareholder in the same company. This is a statutory rule, and power of attorney or proxy is of their choice.

INTERNET RESOURCES

Overview at http://www.arab.net/morocco/morocco_contents.html

Government at http://infoweb.magi.com/~morocco/hassanii.html

Official Government web site at http://www.mincom.gov.ma/

NOTES

1. The constitution guarantees freedom of religion and describes the nation as Muslim and the king as the "Amir El Mouminin," or commander of the faithful. See web site at http://www.sas.upenn.edu/African_Studies/Country_Specific/ Morco_relgn.html.

2. CIA Factbook web site at http://www.odci.gov/cia/publications/nsolo/ factbook/mo.htm.

3. Ibid.

4. The sanction of religious authority and the King's position as the leading figure of the "Shurfa," the descendants of the prophet Mohammed, have been significant in maintaining loyalty to the central government. As the embodiment of Islam, this is probably the single institution commanding the loyalty of virtually all elements of society. See web site at http://www.sas.upenn.edu/African_Studies/ Country_Specific/Morco_relgn.html.

5. CIA Factbook web site.

6. The World Bank's criteria for middle-income classification is a GNP per capita of $766 to $9,385 in 1995. Morocco's per capita GNP in 1995 was $1,110.

7. "Morocco's Inaugural Rating," *The North Africa Journal,* 7 March 1998. See web site at http://www.north-africa.com/ratings.htm.

8. CIA Factbook web site.

9. Moroccan Ministry of Privatization Guidelines. Web site at http:// www.minpriv.gov.ma/english/steps.htm.

10. *Emerging Stock Markets Factbook 1997* (Washington, D.C.: International Finance Corporation, 1997).

11. Ibid.

12. Christopher Hartland-Peel, *African Equities: A Guide to Markets and Companies* (London: Euromoney Publications, 1996), 451.

13. Casablanca Stock Exchange, *Exchange Reports* (Casablanca, 1997).

14. Ibid.

15. *Emerging Stock Markets Factbook 1997.*

16. Ibid.

17. "45% of Trading Activity Now on Floor," Info-Prod Research (Middle East) Ltd., *Middle East News,* 7 October 1997.

18. "Citibank Tries Again with Moroccan Custody Service," *Institutional Investor, Inc. Operations Management,* 3 (1997): 5.

NAMIBIA

COUNTRY

The Republic of Namibia has an area of 318,580 square miles (825,418 square kilometers). For comparison, the landmass is approximately half the size of Alaska. The capital is Windhoek. The country borders the southern Atlantic Ocean, between Angola and South Africa.

Khoikhoi and San peoples and the Bantu-speaking Herero inhabited the country prior to the arrival of European explorers. The Portuguese explored the coastal region in the 1480s, and were followed by the Dutch and English in the seventeenth, eighteenth, and nineteenth centuries. A German missionary group, the Rhenish Missionary Society, arrived in the 1840s. Because of tribal conflicts, the British were asked to take territorial sovereignty to provide protection for the region. In 1876 the Cape Colony brought the territory under British rule after securing treaties with the region's tribal chiefs. However, the British only offered protection for a limited area. In 1884 the region was annexed by Germany and received full German protection.[1]

Tribal conflicts marked the end of the nineteenth century. During World War I, Union of South Africa troops defeated German troops. The League of Nations mandated the region to South Africa. South Africa administered the region as a colony with limited local control. In 1964, the United Nations voted to end South Africa's mandate and in 1968 recognized the name "Namibia." After years of conflict, South Africa agreed to grant independence in 1988. In 1989, elections were held for an assembly to draft a new constitution and in 1990 Namibia gained full independence.

Official Religion	None[2]
Religions	Christian, 80% to 90%; Lutheran, at least 50%; other Christian denominations, 30%; native religions, 10% to 20%
Population	1,677,243 (July 1996 est.)[3]
	Urban 33%
	Rural 67%
	Population under the age of 15: 44%
Ethnic Divisions	black 86%, white 6.6%, mixed 7.4%; about 50% of the population belong to the Ovambo tribe and 9% to the Kavangos tribe; other ethnic groups are Herero 7%, Damara 7%, Nama 5%, Caprivian 4%, Bushmen 3%, Baster 2%, Tswana 0.5%
Languages	English 7% (official), Afrikaans common language of most of the population and about 60% of the white population German 32%, indigenous languages (Oshivambo, Herero, Nama)

The Political System

The country's multiparty political system is dominated by the South West Africa People's Organization (SWAPO). SWAPO was the group of black Namibians who used guerrilla warfare tactics against South Africa to gain independence. Since March 21, 1990, the chief of state and head of government has been President Sam Nujoma who was elected for a five-year term. The last election was held December 7–8, 1994. The next election is scheduled to be held in December 1999.

The legislative branch is a bicameral legislature. The National Council last held elections in November and December 1992 (next to be held by December 1998); the twenty-six total seats were divided SWAPO 19, DTA 6, UDF 1. The National Assembly last held elections in December 1994 (next to be held in December 1999); the seventy-two total seats were divided SWAPO 53, DTA 15, UDF 2, MAG 1, DCN 1.

Political Web Site   http://www.geocities.com/~derksen/election.htm

Legal System

The Namibian legal system is based on Roman–Dutch law and the 1990 constitution.

Suffrage is at eighteen years of age and is universal.

The Economy

The economy is heavily dependent on the extraction and processing of minerals for export. Mining accounts for almost 25 percent of GDP. Namibia is the fourth-largest exporter of nonfuel minerals in Africa and the world's fifth-largest producer of uranium. Rich alluvial diamond deposits make Namibia a primary source for gem-quality diamonds. Namibia also produces large quantities of lead, zinc, tin, silver, and tungsten. More than half the population depends on agriculture (largely subsistence agriculture) for its livelihood.[4]

Inflation Rate (consumer prices)   8% (1996)[5]

The 1996 inflation rate declined to 8.01 percent from the 10.01 percent inflation rate reported for 1995. The 1997 inflation rate averaged 8.82 percent. An economic analysis is provided by the Namibian Economic Policy Research Unit (NEPRU).[6]

P.O. Box 40219

Windhoek/Namibia

Tel.: +61–228284   Fax: +61–231496

Unemployment Rate   21–30% with 50% of the employed underemployed[7]

Gross Domestic Product[8]

Namibia is classified as a middle-income country under the World Bank's classification of economies.[9] For comparability, GDP is expressed in purchase power parity terms.

GDP purchasing power parity $5.8 billion (1994 est.)

GDP real growth rate   6.6% (1994 est.)

GDP per capita $3,600 (1994 est.)

Reflecting its rich mineral base, the Namibian economy is one of the strongest in Africa in terms of GDP per capita.

Central Bank: Bank of Namibia

The gross foreign reserves of the Bank of Namibia at the end of October 1996 were N$919 million compared to N$824 million at the end of 1995. This level of foreign reserves covers about six weeks of imports, which is low by international standards.[10]

Credit Rating

Namibia has not been rated by international rating agencies for either domestic or foreign currency debt.

Currency

Monetary unit   The Namibian dollar (N) is linked 1 to 1 with the South African rand 1 South African rand (R) = 100 cents

The forward market in the South African rand is free of any South African Reserve Bank controls, and is liquid up to twelve months. A currency option market in the South African rand is developing in the Johannesburg market. Exchange rates are as follows: South African rand per US$1–3.6417 (January 1996), 3.6266 (1995), 3.5490 (1994), 3.2636 (1993), 2.8497 (1992), 2.7653 (1991).

In July 1997, the South African Reserve Bank announced further measures relaxing exchange controls, including the approval of foreign currency accounts for individuals resident in South Africa. In contrast to previous steps, the Bank of Namibia decided not to implement this measure due to the low level of foreign reserves (equal to six weeks of imports).[11] This incident also indicates that the objective of small countries to have an independent currency is not without costs—in this case one cost is the apparently necessary delay in the implementation of the stated objective of liberalization, which results in a temporary comparative disadvantage relative to South Africa.[12] There are a number of web sites providing updated currency exchange values. The following is an example:

http://www.bloomberg.com/markets/currency/currcalc.cgi

Privatization

Namibia has been slow to develop and execute a privatization program. Through 1997, Namibia's parastatal companies had contributed little to government revenue, while the twenty-nine parastatals drew a total of N$313,349 million from state coffers in the 1997–1998 budget, 5 percent of the total budget.

THE STOCK EXCHANGE: NAMIBIAN STOCK EXCHANGE

The Namibian Stock Exchange (NSE) was modeled on the legislation and regulations of the Johannesburg Stock Exchange in the Republic of South Africa.[13] However, because of the difference in size and market sophistication there are some amendments to the main act and a reduction of the regulations. Namibia has no over-the-counter market. From its inception, the exchange itself acted as agent and dealer. The U.S.-dollar price index return was 36 percent in 1996.[14]

Mr. Tom Minney
General Manager
The Namibian Stock Exchange
P.O. Box 2401
Windhoek
Namibia
Tel.: 264 61 227647   Fax: 264 61 248531

Web Site	http://www.worldnet.co.za/achill/namibia/busbul/nsenews.html
Established	1992
Stock Exchange Act	Amendments to a 1985 Stock Exchanges Control Act were made to facilitate a September 30, 1992 launch with trading starting October 1, 1992.
Trading Days	Monday to Friday
Trading Hours	10:00–12:00 and 14:00 to 16:00 The international time zone is GMT +2.

STOCK MARKET ACTIVITY

Trading Structure

No principal trading is allowed. The Namibian Stock Exchange is the only dealer and acts as agent in all transactions. The NSE as agent records two separate transactions. Currently no netting is being practiced. The operation of the Namibian Stock Exchange is a continuous auction market system operating on the concept of best execution thus price driven. Commissions are fixed by the stock exchange rules. Should a foreign broker forward a matched buying and selling order, the NSE will share the commission with the broker. If foreign natural persons are admitted as broking members of the NSE, they will in all respects be subject to the rules of the NSE in all transactions effected on the NSE in which they are involved. Section 3 of the Stock Exchange Control Amendment Act No. 26 1992 prohibits over-the-counter transactions. There are no price limits or daily trading ranges.

Performance

The International Finance Corporation ranks the Namibian market's 1996 price index change in U.S. dollars as nineteenth (of seventy-six) in the world. The price index recorded a 36-percent return for the year.[15] In 1997 the NSE overall index increased 3 percent over 1996.

Market Valuation[16]

Year	Price–Earnings Ratio	Dividend Yield
1993	12.3	5.1%
1994	15.4	3.3%
1995	11.0	3.6%
1996	23.8	1.5%
1997	14.3	2.5%

The method of calculating the market price–earnings ratio (PE) became effective September 15, 1997 in order to bring the NSE more in line with practice on other stock markets. The PE is a ratio between the share price and a company's earnings per share, and is used as a way of valuing stocks. The change is that companies which have made losses (negative earnings) are no longer counted in the ratio; that is, neither their market capitalization (share price times number of shares) nor their earnings (earnings per share times number of shares) are included. Previously, negative earnings on fishing companies and mineral exploration companies had affected the ratio.

In April 1997 the average price–earnings ratio for the overall market was 13.9, with some financial shares having a PE between 22 and 44. For August 1997, PE figures had increased for local stocks to 29.86 and the PE of the overall market increased to 14.48. At the end of 1997, the market PE was 14.3. The total value of Namibian-owned and operating shares listed on the NSE at the end of 1997 rose 56 percent to N$3.4 billion.

Dual Listings

The exchange lists a number of Namibian companies that are also listed on the Johannesburg Stock Exchange. If the dual listing securities are included, the exchange is Africa's second largest market capitalization exchange after South Africa. The first Namibian-only listings and capital raising were in 1994. In 1997, the Namibian Stock Exchange signed an agreement for information sharing between the NSE and the Johannesburg Stock Exchange. The agreement is expected to increase the security of investment in the NSE and thus its activities. At the end of 1997, a total of thirty-three companies were listed.

Number of Listed Firms and Market Capitalization[17]

Year	Number of Firms	Market Capitalization (U.S. Millions)
1993	4	28
1994	8	174
1995	10	189
1996	12	473

In 1996 the number of firms listed increased 20 percent from 1995 levels. The annual compound listing growth rate is 44 percent from the end of 1993. The market capitalization increased 150 percent in 1996, and the annual U.S.-dollar market capitalization value has grown at a compound rate of 157 percent since the end of 1993. These figures do not include cross-listed South African companies.

Liquidity

Market liquidity increased significantly from 1995 to 1996. The market activity turnover ratio ranks Namibia fifty-first (of eighty-four) in International Finance Corporation rankings, but second in Africa.[18] The average daily U.S.-dollar value traded in 1996 was approximately $172,275.

Market Turnover Ratio

Year	1993	1994	1995	1996
Turnover Ratio[19]	0.2	16.2	1.6	11.5

In 1997, the number of deals totaled 3,587, up 83 percent over the 1,957 deals done in 1996. The total value of trades was N$942 million.

Instruments Traded

In addition to equity shares, bonds are also listed and traded on the exchange. Listed bonds are issued by the government in the form of Internal Registered Stock and the remainder of the issues are issued by parastatals and backed by government guarantees. In August 1997, the maturity dates for bonds traded extended to the year 2002 for government bonds and 2006 for an Agribank issue. There are currently no derivative products traded and the exchange has no plans to institute them.

Brokerage Rates

Shares are traded in round lots of 100 shares. Besides a stock exchange handling fee of N$15 per transaction, the following brokerage commissions are charged:

Up to N$10,000	1%
Over N$10,000 to N$20,000	0.85% on excess over N$10,000
Over N$20,000 to N$100,000	0.65% on excess over N$20,000
Over N$100,000 to N$500,000	0.55% on excess over N$100,000
Over N$500,000 to N$5,000,000	0.40% on excess over N$500,000
Over N$5,000,000	0.35% on excess over N$5,000,000

A general sales tax of 11 percent is added to the handling charge and commission.

Insider Trading

Namibian markets have extensive regulatory restrictions providing severe penalties for insider trading. The Companies Act 73/1993 and the Stock Exchange Control Act restrict share dealings and insider trading by directors and other officers of a company.

Dividends and Capital Gains Taxation

Dividends are taxed at a 10-percent rate for nonresidents. There are no capital gains taxes. The only difference is in respect of a 10-percent withholding of N.R.S.T. (Non-Residents Shareholder Tax) on dividends paid by the company to a foreign shareholder. However, if the foreigner trades or invests via a locally registered company, no N.R.S.T. will be deductible. Unless a foreigner is classified as a speculator by the tax authorities, there will not be any other liabilities, as there are no capital gains taxes. A speculator is distinct from the ordinary term investor in equities, who over medium and longer terms has a capital gain on the shares he has invested in. The latter is tax free. Income from investments in other entities may attract tax depending on the nature of the income.

Regulatory Controls

Compliance with the Stock Exchange Control Act is overseen by the Registrar of Stock Exchanges who is the Permanent Secretary at the Ministry of Finance, assisted by the Department of Financial Institutions Supervision. The exchange is controlled by the government through the Stock Exchange Control Amendment Act and Regulations and internally by the Rules of the Stock Exchange. There is a code of ethics which is applicable to all stock exchange staff.

Foreign Investment Restrictions

In general, there are no limitations on foreigners purchasing and owning shares in domestic corporations. However, the Namibian Banks Act No. 23 of 1965 restricts foreign equity participation in a local bank to 10 percent of the total nominal value of the issued capital (sec. 28). Upon application to the Minister of Finance, permission may be granted to exceed the limitations. As far as the Namibian fishing industry is concerned, it is explicit government policy to "Namibianize" the industry, which in practice means they require a 51-percent Namibian equity control. Nevertheless, there are exceptions to this policy.

Foreigners are not required to notify any government agency of an intended purchase or sale. Since foreign buying of equities is transacted through the medium of the financial rand (i.e., the foreign investors instrument to invest in the South African common monetary area of which Namibia—with its Namibian dollar—is a member), such deals have to comply with the foreign exchange regulations and directives devised by the S.A. Reserve Bank and supervised in turn by the central bank, the Bank of Namibia. Any local bank as "authorized dealer" can assist in the buying or selling of financial rand to facilitate the buying or selling of shares or securities and to comply with regulatory requirements.

Currency Issues

Legally, the buyer or seller must comply with foreign exchange regulations, but in practice the banks take it upon themselves to comply with any regulatory requirements. Except for the provisions of the Banks Act there are no restrictions. The type of foreign investor is irrelevant.

Central Depository

The exchange is developing a central depository, scheduled for operation in 1998. Currently, all securities are represented by certificates, which may be issued in any denomination. The certificate in respect of the shares to be transferred plus a signed securities transfer form, called Form CM 42 or CM 41, are a broker's transfer form. Physical possession would not be required as long as proof of ownership is beyond doubt.

It is not required but it may be permitted to have different certificates for foreign and domestic holders. A foreign investor who made his acquisition through means of the financial rand will be required to have his certificate endorsed "Non-resident." In the event of a domestic listing which has also been listed on an exchange outside the common monetary area, it will be required to have different certificates issued. The Namibian Central Depository is registered as a subsidiary of the Namibian Stock Exchange. Another subsidiary of the NSE, Namibian Transfer Secretaries, conducts transfer business. The services of these two subsidiaries are available to companies listed on the NSE. Both entities are registered under the Companies Act 61/1973 and are supervised by the NSE.

Currently, the central depository requires that a foreigner, such as Cedel S.A., maintain an account with the central depository. The central depository has no insurance coverage in place but intends to procure coverage. The terms and conditions of the central depository exclude liability on the part of the depository where losses occurred in good faith.

Settlement

Sales and purchases are effected at the stock exchange, preferably by immediate settlement. However, under certain circumstances trade plus seven days occurs and transactions may be executed outside the exchange, in which event a 1-percent stamp duty tax becomes payable.

The affected party may repudiate the transaction or call on the Namibian Stock Exchange to make good a "fail." The broker introducing the transaction that has failed is liable to the other broker. Payment may be requested against delivery of brokers' note—which is mostly the case. Section 22 of the act covers the payment and delivery of securities. Section 36 of the act deals with untraded securities in the possession of a stockbroker and Section 23 deals with securities delivered otherwise than for payment against off of delivery.

Custodian/Registration

Commercial banks have the authority to act as custodian and most have the facility to act as such. Securities may be recovered at any time by the holder/principal or anyone so authorized. In all likelihood such securities would be registered in the name of a nominee entity of the custodian. This is the general practice by banks. Should the custodian hold such securities in his own name without supporting documentation verifying the fact of trusteeship and beneficial ownership, this may prove problematic in the event of insolvency or the like.

Trust funds or securities should always be kept and accounted for separately from the agent's own. Hence, the general practice is to keep such funds either in the principal's name or in a separately registered entity like a nominee company. The principal may of course prescribe the manner in which funds or securities should be dealt with. There is no legal or regulatory limitation on the ability of the security holder to recover the full market value of such lost securities, unless of course the parties have agreed on such limitation or the like. There is no legal or regulatory restriction preventing the custodian from indemnifying the owner of such securities. As this could amount to a contingent liability undertaken in favor of a nonresident, outside the common monetary area, central bank approval may have to be procured. Issuers may be required to replace securities, provided the holder convinces on oath the whereabouts or otherwise of such certificates, and the holder indemnifies the issuer.

Custodians are required by law to keep assets safe, but there is no legal obligation to insure against such risks. Customarily, banks and reputable trust companies do insure. There is no legal restriction preventing receipt of payment in terms of such policy abroad. Beneficial ownership is freely transferable, provided that foreign exchange regulations are complied with, if and when applicable.

Voting

For the purposes of voting there is no distinction between a foreign or national shareholder. The Namibian Stock Exchange allows no securities to be listed with limited voting powers.

Legal Issues

Parties are at liberty to agree that a contract entered into in Namibia shall be governed by the laws of another country subject only to the reservations placed thereon by the tenets of private international law. There is no clear legal precedent on this issue; however, the courts would probably apply the same principals applied by the English courts (e.g., *Ragazzoni vs. Sethia*, 1958 AC 301 [HC]; i.e., that the parties to the contract cannot agree to perform an act which is a crime under the legislation prevailing in a foreign and friendly country).

An authenticated judgment of a U.S. or New York court could be enforceable as a liquid document on which provisional sentence proceedings could be instituted. This procedure would normally entitle the plaintiff to obtain judgment without the necessity of leading any evidence.

INTERNET RESOURCES

Contacts

http://www.sadc-usa.net/members/namibia/key.html

Government

The government's official web site at http://www.republicofnamibia.com

Business Resources

Export Processing Zone at http://www.republicofnamibia.com/export.htm, offers Namibia's exportation and taxation information and a list of useful contacts from the government's official web site.

Business and Investment Opportunities at http://www.republicofnamibia.com/eco.htm, gives investment information from the government's official web site.

Ernst and Young Investment Profile, at http://mbendi.co.za/ernsty/cynaeyip.htm, includes general background information on Namibia, including procedures on how to establish a business, taxation, and incentives; it is maintained by a private entity—Mbendi Information Services.

Namibia Stock Exchange at http://mbendi.co.za/exna.htm, provides an overview, structure, trading conditions, market listing, and market prices; it is maintained by a private entity—Mbendi Information Services.

Telecommunications Sector Profile for Namibia at http://rtr.worldweb.net/Textonly/nampr1.htm, gives general information on the network, regulatory, and competitive developments

U.S. Department of Commerce's International Trade Administration: 1997 Country Commercial Guide at http://www.ita.doc.gov/uscs/ccgonami.html, offers an overview of Namibia's commercial environment (economic, political, and market analysis) from an American perspective.

News

News summaries at http://www.republicofnamibia.com/news/htm, offers news from the government's official web site.

The Panafrican News Agency at http://www.africanews.org/south/namibia, gives periodic news reports about Namibia.

NOTES

1. Germany's Chancellor, Otto Von Bismarck, offered full German protection. See *Encyclopaedia Britannica, Britannica Online*, s.v. "Namibia."

2. CIA Factbook web site at http://www.odci.gov/cia/publications/nsolo/factbook/wa.htm.

3. Ibid.

4. Ibid.

5. The Namibian Economy: Quarterly Economic Review (September 1997), at NEPRU Viewpoint web site, http://www.worldnet.co.za/achill/namibia/busbul/reports.html#nepruq3.

6. Ibid.

7. Ministry of Labor Information. Employment growth at 2.3 percent a year has not been keeping pace with an annual 3.2 percent population growth rate. See NEPRU Viewpoint web site at http://www.worldnet.co.za/achill/namibia/busi a/reports. html#nepruq3.

8. CIA Factbook web site.

9. The World Bank's criteria for middle-income classification is a GNP per capita of $766 to $9,385 in 1995. Namibia's per capita GNP in 1995 was $2,000.

10. *Annual Report* (Windhoek: Standard Bank Namibia, 1996).

11. While there is a degree of uncertainty with respect to the impact of the South African measure, it remains doubtful if a policy of exchange controls could effectively counter an outflow of capital in the case of a loss of confidence in the Namibian economy.

12. The Namibian Economy: Quarterly Economic Review, at NEPRU Viewpoint, web site, http://www.worldnet.co.za/achill/namibia/busbul/reports.html#nepruq3.

13. *Current Namibia Stock Exchange News: Weekly Report 29*, August 1997, at NEPRU Viewpoint web site, http://www.worldnet.co.za/achill/namibia/busbul/reports. html#nepruq3.

14. *Emerging Stock Markets Factbook 1997* (Washington, D.C.: International Finance Corporation, 1997).

15. Ibid.

16. Namibia Stock Exchange. See NEPRU Viewpoint web site, http://www.worldnet.co.za/achill/namibia/busbul/reports.html#nepruq3.

17. *Emerging Stock Markets Factbook 1997.*

18. Ibid.

19. Ibid.

NIGERIA

COUNTRY

The Federal Republic of Nigeria has an area of 356,669 square miles (923,768 square kilometers) in West Africa. For comparison, the country's landmass is slightly more than twice the size of California. On December 12, 1991 the capital was officially moved from Lagos to Abuja; many government offices remain in Lagos pending completion of facilities in Abuja. The official language is English, though Hausa is the most widely spoken language.

The geographical location of Nigeria has resulted in the nation being a focal point for migratory routes. There are more than 250 ethnic groups in the country, each with its own customs, traditions, and language. The earliest people in Nigeria were the Noks, who inhabited the region between 500 B.C. and about A.D. 200. After centuries of tribal warfare and the rise and fall of a number of states the Portuguese traders and explorers reached the coast in the fifteenth century. They initiated a slave trade and the British were acquiring slaves by the seventeenth century. The British abolished the slave trade in 1807, but other nations continued the trade.

The British annexed Lagos in 1861 to start their official control of the region, and by 1886 Nigeria had become a separate British colony. In 1914 the region became the Colony and Protectorate of Nigeria. Nigeria was granted its independence in 1960. The subsequent period saw warfare between tribes. In 1967 civil war broke out as the eastern area, Biafra, declared its independence. By 1969 the region had been subdued and the Biafrans surrendered in 1970. Consequently, the government has been a military dictatorship with brief periods of civilian rule.

Official Religion	None[1]
Religions	Muslim, 50%; Christian, 40%; indigenous beliefs, 10%
Population	103,912,489 (July 1996 est.)[2]
	Nigeria is the most populous nation in Africa.
	Urban 38%
	Rural 62%
	Population under the age of 15: 47%
Ethnic Divisions	Hausa and Fulani (north), Yoruba (southwest), and Ibos (southeast) together make up 65% of population. non-Africans 27,000
Languages	English (official), Hausa, Yoruba, Ibo, Fulani
Education	Population over age 15 who are literate: 57.1%

The Political System

Nigeria is a federal republic with thirty states. A military government that seized power on November 17, 1993, dissolved the constitution and concentrated authority in the Provisional Ruling Council. Political parties were suspended after the military takeover. The military regime has made successive promises to allow political parties to register at various times, however no registrations have been permitted. On October 1, 1995, the military government announced it would turn power over to democratically elected civilian authorities in October 1998. However, the military leaders keep a tight control on dissidents and executed political prisoner Ken Saro-Wiwa despite international protests. Since November 1993, the Chief of State, Chairman of the Provisional Ruling Council, Commander in Chief of Armed Forces, and Defense Minister is General Sani Abacha.

Political Web Site   http://www.geocities.com/~derksen/election.htm

Legal System

Nigeria's legal system is based on English common law, Islamic law, and tribal law.

Suffrage is at twenty-one years of age and is universal.

The Economy

The economy is a mixed economy based on petroleum production and agriculture. Nigeria's military regime abandoned its structural adjustment program in 1985. Significant oil revenues have enabled the government to remain in power. Nigeria's petroleum and natural gas reserves are estimated at nearly one-third of Africa's total reserves. The Nigerian National Petroleum Corp. released a recent report announcing that it will invest $2.8 billion in its oil sector before 1998 to increase its crude oil reserves by 25 percent.[3] Foreign companies control most of Nigeria's petroleum production. To attract foreign investment, Nigeria altered many of its investment policies in 1995.[4] These changes included allowing foreign investors to source foreign exchange from wherever they want and eliminating prior limitations on the extent of foreign ownership.

Becaue of its dependence on oil revenues, the economy is particularly susceptible to oil price fluctuations. Oil prices in the world markets dropped in the early 1980s and then collapsed in 1986. Nigeria's export earnings fell from $26 billion in 1980 to $12 billion in 1985 and $6.4 billion in 1986.

The oil-rich Nigerian economy continues to experience political instability, corruption, and poor macroeconomic management. Nigeria's unpopular military rulers failed to make significant progress in diversifying the economy away from overdependence on the capital-intensive oil sector which provides almost all foreign exchange earnings and about 80 percent of budgetary revenues. The government's domestic and international arrears continue to limit economic growth and prevent an agreement with the IMF and bilateral creditors on debt relief. The largely subsistence agricultural sector has failed to keep up with rapid population growth.

Gross Domestic Product[5]

Nigeria is classified as a low-income country under the World Bank's classification of economies.[6] For comparability, GDP is expressed in purchase power parity terms.

GDP purchasing power parity	$135.9 billion (1995 est.)
GDP real growth rate	2.6% (1995 est.)
GDP per capita	$1,300 (1995 est.)

Inflation for the 1990 to 1995 period averaged 47.1 percent, Africa's second highest among stock exchange counties (following Zambia). The unemployment rate is estimated at 28 percent for 1992.

Central Bank: Central Bank of Nigeria

The Central Bank of Nigeria is the chief regulatory authority for the country's financial system. It was established by the Central Bank Act of 1958 and began operations on July 1, 1959. The Act of 1958 has been repealed and replaced with the CBN Decree 24 of 1991. Among its functions, the bank promotes monetary stability and a sound financial system and acts as banker of last resort to the banks. The promulgation of the CBN Decree 24 and Banks and other Financial Institutions Decree 25 gave the bank responsibility for licensing banks.[7]

Postal Address

Central Bank of Nigeria
Private Mail Bag 12194
Tinubu Square
Lagos
Nigeria
Tel.: +234 1 266–0100

The Nigerian central bank heavily regulates and controls banks. Sixty-percent Nigerian ownership is required in foreign ventures. The central bank fixes the discount rate and mandates lending to the agricultural and manufacturing sectors.[8]

Credit Rating

Nigeria has not been rated by international rating agencies for either domestic or foreign currency debt. By the 1980s, external debt had become a serious issue, though, in per capita terms, the debt was not unusually high. In 1986, when oil revenues collapsed, agreement for debt rescheduling was reached with the London and Paris Clubs (which assist developing countries with debt problems). The situation had again deteriorated by 1991 when further rescheduling took place. The 1996 budget allocated $2 billion for external debt servicing, though $5.27 billion was due.[9] Additional debt rescheduling is difficult with the present domestic political environment, so debt arrears continue to rise.

Currency

Monetary unit   Nigerian naira (N) = 100 kobo

The government's major objectives in exchange rate policy are to preserve the value of the domestic currency, maintain a favorable external reserve position, and ensure price stability. The government repealed the Exchange Control Act of 1962 and replaced it with the Foreign Exchange (Monitoring and Miscellaneous Provisions) Decree of 1995. The decree creates an Autonomous Foreign Exchange Market (AFEM) in order to achieve exchange rate stability. Policies from 1995 have been aimed at guiding the deregulation of the currency as it moves from fixed to flexible exchange regimes. The AFEM operates as follows:[10]

1. The central bank has been vested with the power to appoint authorized dealers and buyers of foreign currency.

2. The importation and exportation of foreign currency in excess of $5,000 or its equivalent shall be declared on the prescribed form for reasons of statistics only.

3. The issuance of Capital Importation Certificates is to be done by the banks without prior approval.

4. Banks are allowed to treat applications on the remittance of proceeds (net of withholding taxes) and other obligations in event of sale without prior approval.

There are no currency hedging opportunities available. Exchange rates are as follows: naira per US$1–21.886 (January 1996), 21.895 (1995), 21.996 (1994), 22.065 (1993), 17.298 (1992), 9.909 (1991).

There are a number of web sites providing updated currency exchange values. The following is an example:

http://www.bloomberg.com/markets/currency/currcalc.cgi

Attempts to tighten controls on the purchase and sale of foreign exchange in 1994 kept the official exchange rate artificially stable at N22 to the dollar. However, this "stability" came at a high price to Nigerian exporters. Their competitive advantage largely disappeared. The 1995 reopening of the foreign exchange markets was an important step toward stimulating Nigerian exports.

In the parallel market, the naira foreign exchange rate increased from about N10 to the dollar in 1990, peaked briefly at over N100 in late 1994, and fluctuated in the N75 to 85 range in early 1995. In January 1994 the government banned the formerly legal parallel market for the naira (N44 to the dollar at the time) which the IFC had used and limited foreign exchange transactions to the official rate only (N22 to the dollar). The forced switch to the official rate boosted the IFCG Nigeria Index for a one-time U.S.-dollar gain of nearly 100 percent.[11]

Privatization

The Nigerian National Petroleum Corporation has a stake in all large oil firms. A number of state-owned enterprises were privatized in the early 1990s. By the end of 1996, the government had sold eighty-six state-owned enterprises to private owners; however, the labor unions have been opposed to the privatization program.

"Capital is not in short supply. When Standard Chartered sold its remaining 10 percent stake in Nigeria's First Bank late last year (1996), the offer was three times oversubscribed. 'For the right kind of offer, the money is there,' says Mr. Wale Edun, chief executive officer of Denham Management, a Lagos-based investment house. 'Domestic savings from the banking system and return of capital from abroad are factors behind the increasing availability of funds. With the corporate sector performing well and the exchange rate stable, the market is a good investment.'"[12]

Despite the political uncertainty, foreign portfolio investment in the country via the capital markets increased to $32.98 million in 1996 from $1.137 million in 1995, according to Hayford Alile, Director General of the Nigerian Stock Exchange.[13]

THE STOCK EXCHANGE: NIGERIAN STOCK EXCHANGE

The International Finance Corporation ranks Nigeria's 1996 U.S.-dollar price index return performance at tenth of seventy-six nations ranked. The 1996 performance was 55.6 percent. Nigeria's exchange index was up 8.2 percent in local terms through August 1997; however, this was a 14-percent drop from the market peak in April 1997.

Nigerian Stock Exchange
P.O. Box 2457

Lagos
Nigeria
Tel.: (234–1) 266 0287/0305   Fax: (234–1) 266 8724/8281

Web Sites	http://mbendi.co.za/exng.htm
	http://www.afrocaribbean.com/nigeria/nigstex.html
Established	September 15, 1960
	Commenced operations June 5, 1961
Other Markets	Second tier securities markets launched in April 1985
Trading Days	Monday to Friday
Trading Hours	11:00–14:00
	The international time zone is GMT +1.

Different Exchanges

There are six trading floors in Nigeria, located in Lagos, Kaaduna, Port Harcourt, Kano, Onitsha, and Ibadan. The regional exchanges are not active.

Market Index

All listings are included in the exchange's only index, the Nigerian Stock Exchange All Share Index. The Nigerian Stock Exchange All Share Index 100 (1984) was 6992.10 at the end of 1996 and 8561.39 at end of March 1997.

The IFC maintains a Global Index and an Investable Index for the Nigerian stock market as part of its Emerging Market DataBase using NSE market information obtained directly from Reuters Electronic Contributor Systems.

Exchange Memberships

The exchange is an affiliate member of the Federation of International Stock Exchanges (FIBV). The exchange is an observer at meetings of the International Organization of Securities Commissions (IOSCO). The Nigerian Stock Exchange is also a founding member of the African Stock Exchanges Association (ASEA), of which the Director General/Chief Executive Officer of the exchange, Mr. Hayford Alile, is the current chairman.

STOCK MARKET ACTIVITY

Trading Structure

The trading structure is by open outcry auction, call over mechanism, and floor system.

Performance

The Nigerian market has experienced a great deal of volatility in its performance. In 1990 the market was one of the top ten performers in the world (+23.8%); in 1992 it was in the bottom five (–38.8%); it continued its low performance in 1993 (–18.2%); rebounded to second place in 1994 (+168.8%); dropped again in 1995 (–26.9%); and in 1996 (+55.6%) once again among the world's top-ten performers. The International Finance Corporation ranks the Nigerian market's 1996 price index in U.S.-dollar performance as tenth (of seventy-six) in the world. This performance places Nigeria in second place in Africa for the year.[14]

Indicator[15]	(End) 1995	(End) 1996	% Change
All-share index	5092.2	6992.1	37.3
Market Capitalization (N billion)	171.1	285.6	66.9
Turnover Volume (N million)	397.0	882.0	122.2
Turnover Value (N billion)	1.8	7.1	284.0
Number	31.0	36.0	16.1
Value (N billion)	7.1	21.5	202.8
Foreign Investment Portfolio Transactions (U.S. Millions)	1.1	33.0	
Average P/E Ratio	9.2	12.2	

Number of Listed Firms

Market capitalization increased 75 percent in 1996. Capitalization has grown at an annual compound rate of 17.2 percent since the end of 1990. During the first six months of 1997, the only initial public offering was a closed-end fund which raised $16 million for investment in Nigerian government debt obligations being traded on international markets. In the first half of 1997, the exchange approved eight new issues with a total market value of N1.2 billion (about $14 million).

Number of Listed Firms and Market Capitalization[16]

Year	Number of Firms	Market Capitalization (U.S. Dollars)
1990	131	1,372
1991	142	1,882
1992	153	1,221
1993	174	1,029
1994	177	2,711
1995	181	2,033
1996	183	3,560

A drawback of the exchange is the absence of Nigeria's largest companies. Government-owned companies such as the Nigerian National Petroleum Corporation (NNPC), the country's largest company, and Nigerian Telecommunications Ltd. (Nitel), which could triple the market's capitalization, are not listed on the exchange. Quoted companies may seek multiple and crossborder listing, subject to the Nigerian Stock Exchange Memorandum of Understanding with such international stock exchanges.

Liquidity

Liquidity in 1996 was 2.3 percent and turnover was $83.35 million. Comparing the first six months of 1997 with the first half of 1996 shows that average daily trading volume increased 139 percent to 5.5 million shares, while the daily turnover surged 165 percent to N5.8 billion. The exchange estimates that foreign currency transactions on the exchange were $33 million in 1996 and in the first six months of 1997 totaled $8.6 million.

Market Turnover Ratio

Year	1990	1991	1992	1993	1994	1995	1996
Turnover Ratio[17]	0.9	0.6	1.0	0.8	0.8	0.8	2.6

Market turnover increased significantly in 1996 from year-earlier levels. The International Finance Corporation ranks the Nigerian market seventy-first (of eighty-four) in terms of market turnover. This places the exchange tenth in Africa. In the first six months of 1997 the exchange processed a total of 31,710 deals for 672.5 million shares worth N5.8 billion (about $69 million) on the six trading floors.

In January 1997, Mr. Hayford Alile, director-general of the Nigerian Stock Exchange (NSE), released figures showing that last year the volume of shares traded increased 122 percent over 1995, with turnover value more than trebling from N1.83bn to N7.058bn ($23m to $85.5m). Mr. Alile lists four factors, including a review in the allocation system on trading floors, a new, more flexible price movement limit and a reduced settlement period from a fortnight to a week. Interest from abroad has, however, been limited. Foreign investment portfolio transactions in 1996 stood at just $32.98m, substantially more than the $1.137m of 1995, but less than that attracted to much smaller markets such as Ghana.[18]

Ownership

Only the local branch of Citibank meets the adequate capital requirements for service as a custodian bank.

Instruments Traded

Equities, preference shares, corporate debentures, and government bonds are traded. There are currently no derivative products traded and the exchange has no plans to institute them.

Brokerage Rates

Brokerage rates are fixed. Transactions are subject to a minimum commission of N10.

Government stocks, under 5 years maturity	4.5% of nominal value
Transactions involving Central Bank of Nigeria	1/16 of 1% of nominal value
Other securities	3% of consideration

Insider Trading

Insider trading is illegal in Nigeria. As soon as the holding of an individual or corporate body in a quoted company gets to 5 percent of the equity capital, the beneficiary must notify the exchange. Also, directors' interests must be disclosed.

Regulatory Controls

The Nigerian Stock Exchange is a Self-Regulatory Organization (SRO) strictly owned and managed by the Nigerian private sector. The exchange's oversight is carried out under the direction of the Securities and Exchange Commission (SEC).

Web Site   http://www.afrocaribbean.com/nigeria/nigsec.html

The Securities and Exchange Commission[19]

The Securities and Exchange Commission was established under the Securities and Exchange Commission Decree 1979 as the regulatory body for the Nigerian capital market. The SEC's main objectives are to protect investors' interests and to ensure orderly and equitable dealings in securities business as well as the promotion of capital market growth and development. The SEC's functions, among others, include the following:

1. Registration of securities to be traded on the trading floor of the Nigerian Stock Exchange.
2. Registration of the Nigerian Stock Exchange and its branches along with the monitoring of activities on the trading floors.

3. Registrations of capital market operators (i.e., stockbrokers, registrars, security dealers, issuing houses, fund managers, etc.).

4. Approving schemes for mergers, acquisitions, and all other forms of business combinations.

5. Creating the necessary atmosphere for orderly growth and development of the capital market.

Foreign Investment Restrictions

With the repeal of the Exchange Control Act of 1962 and the Nigerian Enterprises Promotion Decree of 1989, foreigners are now free to invest in Nigeria. In 1995, legislation was lifted that limited nonresident shareholders in local companies. In September 1997, the military rulers allowed foreign enterprises or any foreign entrepreneur to buy shares of any existing Nigerian company or enterprise which can be completed through direct ownership or through the Nigerian Stock Exchange without reference to the federal Ministry of Finance.[20]

Central Depository

There is no central depository.

Settlement

The clearing and settlement organization is the Central Securities Clearinghouse. The settlement cycle is T+5. Prior to April 1997, the market was still a cash market and therefore settlement for transactions on the exchange was on an account settlements basis. This was done fortnightly in accordance with the settlement roster issued at the beginning of each year to all dealing members. In April 1997, the Central Securities Clearinghouse, promoted by the exchange, inaugurated a computerized clearing and settlement system. The system permits T+5 share delivery and payment. This system sped settlements that previously took as long as six months. For investors' protection, the NSE Protection Fund was formally inaugurated in 1995.

Registration

The Nigerian Stock Exchange, through its Central Securities Clearinghouse, provides custodial services to all investors on request. To avoid concentration of share ownership in too few hands, nominal transfers are still limited to among and between family members and associated corporate entities.

Dividends and Capital Gains Taxation

The withholding tax on dividends is 10 percent. Capital gains taxes were cut 50 percent in 1996 to 10 percent. The Securities and Exchange Commission charges a transaction tax of 1 percent. The corporate income tax rate is 35 percent.

Future Development

The Automated Trading System is expected to be completed before the end of 1997. Data on listed companies performance is published daily, weekly, monthly, quarterly, and annually. Market and corporate information are also available on Reuters Electronic Information Network. The on-line code for the Nigerian stock market is NSXA. The NSE publications constitute important tools of information dissemination, as the exchange is the primary source of most statistical information on the capital market. Regular publications by the exchange include the Daily Official List, Weekly Stock Market Report, Monthly Statistics, Quarterly Report, Annual Report, and the annual NSE Factbook, which contains information on quoted companies, stockbroking firms, and issuing houses in Nigeria.

The Nigerian Stock Exchange is to open a new branch in the administrative capital, Abuja. The aim of this move is to break down the monopoly of the Nigerian Stock Exchange.[21]

Procedure for Foreign Investment on the Nigerian Stock Exchange

The following procedures are to be adopted by the foreign investors who intend to bring in investable funds under the new legislation:

1. The prospective investor appoints a local stockbroker of his or her own choice.
2. The broker and the investor agree on a bank in Nigeria for the investor.
3. The potential investor then informs the bank on how much he or she is investing.
4. Thereafter, the money is routed by electronic transfer to the designated Nigerian bank; cash movement for dealing in securities is not allowed.
5. On receipt of the funds, the bank issues the investor with a Certificate of Capital Importation. With this certificate, the investor, through his or her stockbroker, enters the market, invests in any company of his or her choice, and if at any point in time the investor wants to put out, he or she must go back to the bank with the Certificate of Capital Importation and transfer all proceeds abroad including profit, net of all taxes.

Secondary Securities Market

Dealing members may now buy and sell quoted securities on behalf of Nigerians and non-Nigerians within the rules and regulations of the stock exchange. Accordingly, current transfer forms that contain attestation of Nigerian citizenship should now be amended to allow transfers to Nigerians and non-Nigerians. All the securities listed on the Nigerian Stock Exchange Official List are still registered securities, in which case bearer note transactions remain inadmissible on the exchange.

As the total market capitalization of each quoted company is listed on the exchange, all divestments or sale of shares must be effected on the trading floors through stockbrokers licensed by the stock exchange. Investors should note that share certificates of companies quoted on the exchange are negotiable instruments, hence registrars should not seek the approval of the vendors before effecting transfers. In effect, owners should protect their certificates as they would their currencies.

Regional Affiliations

Nigeria has been a member of the Organization of Petroleum Exporting Countries (OPEC) since 1971. In addition, Nigeria is a member of the Economic Community of West African States.

NOTES

1. CIA Factbook web site at http://www.odci.gov/cia/publications/nsolo/factbook/ni.htm.

2. Ibid.

3. "Nigeria Pours New Investment into Oil Sector," *Comtex Scientific Corp., NewsEdge/LAN*, 7 May 1996.

4. U.S. Department of Commerce, ITA, *1996 Country Commercial Guide for South Africa* (Washington, D.C.: U.S. Government Printing Office, National Trade Data Bank, 1995).

5. CIA Factbook web site.

6. The World Bank's criteria for low-income classification is a GNP per capita of less than $765 in 1995. Nigeria's per capita GNP in 1995 was $260.

7. Statement, Federal Ministry of Finance, Nigeria, 2 October 1997.

8. Kim R. Holmes, Bryan T. Johnson, and Melanie Kirkpatrick, *1997 Index of Economic Freedom* (Heritage Foundation and Dow Jones & Company, Inc., 1997), 341–343.

9. Information concerning the Nigerian debt market was obtained from web site at http://www.tcol.co.uk/nigeria/nige2.htm.

10. Statement, Federal Ministry of Finance.

11. *Emerging Stock Markets Factbook 1994* (Washington, D.C.: International Finance Corporation, 1994), 252.

12. Antony Goldman, "Nigeria Sees Near-70% Rise in Market Value of Shares," *Financial Times*, 5 February 1997, 4.

13. "Press Digest—Nigeria," *Reuters, Ltd.*, 4 January 1997.

14. *Emerging Stock Markets Factbook 1997* (Washington, D.C.: International Finance Corporation, 1997).

15. Nigerian Stock Exchange, *Exchange Reports* (Lagos, 1997).

16. *Emerging Stock Markets Factbook 1997.*

17. Ibid.

18. "Nigeria Sees Near-70% Rise in Market Value of Shares," 4.

19. See SEC Data and Information from web site at http://www.afrocaribbean. com/nigeria/nigsec.html.

20. "Nigeria Dangles Investment Protection Law before Foreign Investors," *Deutsche Presse-Agentur,* 23 September 1997.

21. Goddy Ikeh, "Business and Finance; Nigeria Proposes Reform of Its Capital Market," *Africa News Service, Inc.,* 29 July 1997.

SOUTH AFRICA

COUNTRY

The Republic of South Africa has an area of 488,000 square miles (1,219,912 square kilometers) in South Africa. For comparative purposes, it is slightly less than twice the size of Texas. Botswana, Lesotho, Mozambique, Namibia, Swaziland, and Zimbabwe border it. The administrative capital is Pretoria, the legislative capital is Cape Town, and Bloemfontein is the judicial capital.

Primarily pastoral tribes had settled in the region by the fifteenth century. The first European settlement was a Dutch East India Company settlement at the Cape of Good Hope in 1652. As the settlement expanded the colonists came into increasingly violent confrontations with Bantu tribes. In the first Bantu War, the Xhosa temporarily halted the eastward expansion of the Boers (Dutch–Afrikaner farmers) in 1779. The British annexed the Cape in 1806. Diamonds and gold were discovered in the mid-1800s. Eventual conflicts led to the 1899 to 1902 Anglo–Boer War, which ended with the defeat of the independent republics of Orange Free State and Transvaal and the imposition of British rule. The Union of South Africa was created in 1910, giving political control to whites, and in 1948 the Afrikaner National Party won the elections and the new government specifically excluded non-whites from the political and economic systems. Black political activists formed the African National Congress (ANC) and actively opposed the system of apartheid. The international community began to oppose apartheid and the United Nations and the British Commonwealth imposed economic and political sanctions. After the 1989 elections, the new president, F. W. de Klerk, instituted reforms aimed at dismantling apartheid and introducing democracy. In 1991 the South African government eliminated some of apartheid's most vital legal supports: the Land Acts of 1913 and 1936, the Group Areas Act of 1966, and the Population Registration Act of 1950. In April 1994 Nelson Mandela was elected president. The reintegration of South Africa into the global community provides forward momentum for what some hope will be the renaissance of Africa.

To meet the higher demand for capital, South Africa's position reflects a balance of payments deficit. The deficit must be financed by way of sales of government assets; that is, privatizations, reduction in government spending, and the country's ability to borrow in international capital markets. With regard to the latter, in December 1994 the government successfully raised $750 million through a five-year Eurobond issue. The issue was priced at 193 basis points above U.S. treasuries. The strong demand for the Eurobond offering resulted in an increase in the initial size of the issue from $500 million.

Official Religion	None[1]
Religions	Christian (most whites and Coloreds and about 60% of blacks), Hindu (60% of Indians), Muslim 2%
Population	41,743,459 (July 1996 est.)
	Population under the age of 15: 36%
Ethnic Divisions	black, 75.2%; white, 13.6%; Colored, 8.6%; Indian, 2.6%
Languages	Eleven official languages, including Afrikaans, English, Ndebele, Pedi, Sotho, Swazi, Tsonga, Tswana, Venda, Xhosa, Zulu
Education	Population over age 15 that is literate: 82%

The Political System

The new era of a free and democratic South African republic began on April 27, 1994. An interim constitution replaced the constitution of September 3, 1984, and on May 8, 1996, the Constitutional Assembly voted 421 to 2 to pass a new constitution. After certification by the Constitutional Court, the constitution will gradually go into effect over a three-year period and come into full force with the next national elections in April 1999.[2] Nelson Mandela was inaugurated as president on May 10, 1994. As part of the transition, any political party that wins 20 percent or more of the National Assembly votes in a general election is entitled to name a deputy executive president; moreover, any party that wins twenty or more seats in the National Assembly is entitled to become a member of the governing coalition.

Legal System

South Africa's common law is based on Roman–Dutch law and English common law. South Africa accepts compulsory ICJ jurisdiction, with reservations.

Suffrage is at eighteen years of age and is universal.

The Economy

The South African economy is moving forward in the post-apartheid era. As the isolation of the economy ends, the distortions to efficient economic systems are also ending. South Africa's trade with its neighbors has already increased from a level of 3 percent before 1994 and 16 percent post-1994. Despite the optimism, the realities are that the unemployment rate for the black population is estimated at 32.6 percent (1996 est.), with an additional 11 percent underemployment. The economy must generate more than 300,000 jobs a year to maintain stability. The recent experience is that less than 5 percent of the entrants are absorbed. Economic development will be driven by the need to improve the living conditions of the nation's black population.

Gross Domestic Product[3]

The International Finance Corporation classifies South Africa as an upper middle-income country.[4] For comparability, GDP is expressed in purchase power parity terms. South Africa is the richest country on the continent, however it represents a significant gap between the per capita income of the whites and the blacks.

GDP purchasing power parity $215 billion (1995 est.)
GDP real growth rate   3.3% (1995 est.)
GDP per capita $4,800.00 (1995 est.)

Central Bank: The South African Reserve Bank

The South African Reserve Bank presents detailed financial information concerning the South African economy on its web site. The site is updated daily with the most recent market conditions and information.

Web Site   http://www.resbank.co.za/

Postal Address
South African Reserve Bank
P.O. Box 427
370 Church Street
Pretoria
0001
South Africa
Tel.: +27–12–313–3911   Fax: +27–12–313–3197

Credit Rating

South Africa has received a credit rating from both Moody's and Standard & Poor's. Standard & Poor's rating of the long-term foreign currency bonds is BB+ (speculative).

Standard & Poor's rating of the long-term local currency bonds is BBB+ (investment grade). The rating was assigned November 1995 and carries a positive outlook. Moody's rates South African debt as Baa3 (investment grade).

Currency

Monetary unit   rand (R) = 100 cents

The central bank eliminated the dual system of the commercial and financial rand on March 12, 1997.[5] The exchange controls are being gradually phases out, permitting South Africans to invest abroad. Exchange rates are as follows: rand per US$1–3.6417 (January 1996), 3.6266 (1995), 3.5490 (1994), 3.2636 (1993), 2.8497 (1992), 2.7563 (1991).

The forward market is free of any reserve bank controls, and is liquid up to twelve months. A currency option market in the South African rand is developing. There are a number of web sites providing updated currency exchange values. The following is an example:

http://www.bloomberg.com/markets/currency/currcalc.cgi

Privatization

The government is evaluating opportunities to sell off state-owned enterprises to the private sector. However, with the largest securities market on the continent, much has already been accomplished. The potential $3 billion sales of South Africa Telecom is contemplated. A potential consistent post-apartheid theme is black empowerment and the government is pursuing opportunities to foster black ownership of securities.

THE STOCK EXCHANGE: JOHANNESBURG STOCK EXCHANGE

As the continent's oldest and most developed exchange, the Johannesburg Stock Exchange (JSE) plays an important role in the development of Africa's stock exchanges. Yet 1996 was a difficult year for the South African securities markets. The Morgan Stanley Capital International South Africa Index declined by 20.1 percent, while the J. P. Morgan ELMI South African Bond Index declined by 9.1 percent in 1996, primarily as a result of a 28.3-percent depreciation in the South African rand.

The market continues to evolve. In a May 21, 1997 interview with exchange Executive President Russell Loubser, the market's continual evolution and development was stressed. The markets in South Africa have undergone significant change as the economy emerges from the strictures of the apartheid era. Mr. Loubser indicated that updating the operational functions of the exchange to create electronic clearing and settlement systems is a high priority.

Johannesburg Stock Exchange
P.O. Box 1174
Johannesburg
2000, South Africa
Tel.: (27 11) 377 2200   Fax: (27 11) 836 6454

E-Mail:	pr@jse.co.za
Established	November 1887
Trading Days	Monday to Friday
Trading Hours	9:30–16:00
	The market has transitioned from two sessions daily to a continuous session.
	The international time zone is GMT +2.
Web Site	http://www.jse.co.za/

The Johannesburg Stock Exchange is the most advanced and active exchange on the African continent. The extensive review of the South African markets provided by the Johannesburg Stock Exchange and the Reserve Bank of South Africa provides investors with current information concerning South African market conditions. The latter part of this section provides a review of the exchange provided by the JSE and precludes the need for the extensive market review provided for Africa's other developing exchanges. Appropriate addresses have been provided to connect the reader with extensive accurate financial information. The following notes are meant to provide only a brief overview of the market and current activities.

STOCK MARKET ACTIVITY

Trading Structure

In March 1996 the JSE began automated trading, converting the first group of stocks from floor trading. Using the Johannesburg Equities Trading (JET) System, the structure changed to a continuous order-driven system with central market principles. The system has dual trading capacity complemented by member firms voluntarily acting as market makers and fully negotiable brokerage with clients. The system provides improved transparency, security, and audit trails, and manages a central order book that is accessed via trading workstations which are linked to the JET System.[6]

Instruments Traded

Equities, preference shares, corporate debentures, government bonds, derivatives, and financial futures are traded. Traditional options are traded on an OTC basis.

Number of Listed Firms and Market Capitalization[7]

The Johannesburg Stock Exchange dominates the African markets with its $241.5 billion in market capitalization. The exchange capitalization has grown at an average annual compound rate of 7.5 percent from 1991. The value of average daily trading in 1996 was approximately $12.36 million, the highest in Africa.

Year	Number of Firms	Market Capitalization (U.S. Millions)
1991	688	168,497
1992	683	103,537
1993	647	171,942
1994	640	225,718
1995	640	280,526
1996	626	241,571

Liquidity

The South African market is one of the most liquid exchanges in Africa, placing fifty-fifth (of eighty-four) in the International Finance Corporation's review of world stock market turnover and third among African exchanges.[8]

Market Turnover Ratio

Year	1991	1992	1993	1994	1995	1996
Turnover Ratio[9]	7.2	4.6	7.1	8.5	6.5	10.9

Settlement

Settlement is physical.

Central Depository

South Africa has no central depository.

Brokerage Rate

As of March 1, 1996, commission rates are negotiable.

Dividends and Capital Gains Taxation

There are no capital gains taxes or taxes on dividends.

Foreign Investment Restrictions

South Africa, because of its market size and access to other countries in sub-Saharan Africa, allowed repatriation of profits and more market-oriented polices, and is generally considered to have the best foreign investment climate in sub-Saharan Africa.[10] Foreign investors are allowed 100-percent ownership in South Africa, and foreign investment is not normally screened. There are no restrictions on foreign investment.

On July 23, 1997, the Johannesburg Stock Exchange and Namibian Stock Exchange signed an agreement on information sharing. The agreement, which promotes regional cooperation, provides for the exchange of information between exchanges to improve surveillance and protection to their investors.

The value of inward investment announced in 1996 was R4.1 billion, marginally higher than the R3.9 billion reported in 1995. Though this might appear to be a disappointingly small increase, inward investment leapt dramatically in 1995 when compared with the previous years of economic isolation. While the sharp depreciation of the rand in 1996 reduced the net cost of South African assets to foreign buyers, international experience suggests that periods of currency volatility—which are symptomatic of a more general economic malaise—tend to curb investor appetites. Given the rand's weakness in 1996, it is perhaps surprising that foreign investment remained as strong as it did.

Buyers paid an average price–earnings ratio of 19 in 1996, against the JSE Overall Actuaries index average of 18. This compares with an average transaction PE of 20 and a JSE Overall Actuaries index PE of 16 in 1995. Buyers paid an average 112-percent premium to net asset value, compared to 123 percent reported in 1995. The premiums paid reflect the high values currently being placed on intangible assets such as brands, trademarks, and specialist know-how.

EXCHANGE INFORMATION[11]

History and Organization

The Johannesburg Stock Exchange was founded little more than a year after President Paul Kruger proclaimed as public diggings the nine farms that made up the Witwatersrand goldfields, the richest of their kind in the world at the time. Nine months later the JSE grew out of the Johannesburg Exchange & Chambers Company, housed on stands at the corner of Commissioner Street and Simmonds Street, and established by an enterprising thirty-six-year-old London businessman, Benjamin Minors Woollan. At a meeting of the Exchange & Chambers Company board and members on November 8, 1887, it was proposed "that the Johannesburg Stock Exchange be and hereby is established." This simple resolution was carried unanimously.

The second JSE building was built in 1890 on the same site as the original building, whose trading hall had proved too small to accommodate the growing number of members. Because of continuing space constraints, however, even the second Simmonds Street building was shortly outgrown and trading activities spilled over into the street. By means of chains, the Mining Commissioner closed off that section of Simmonds Street between Market Square and Commissioner Street to vehicular traffic. Trading in shares, land, and property went on throughout the day and into the night "between the chains," in Simmonds Street, which was now free of traffic. For many years thereafter the heading to the stock exchange price list in the *Star* was "Between the Chains."

In 1903, the JSE moved to new building located on Hollard Street. This well-proportioned three-story building covered the whole city block bounded by Fox and Main, Hollard and Sauer Streets. In a pre-skyscraper era, its graceful dome above the porticoed entrance was one of Johannesburg's landmarks. With this third home of the JSE, Hollard Street became the financial center of Johannesburg and was to remain so for more than half a century.

Because of brisk market activity toward the end of World War II, and fueled especially by the strong acceleration in industrial activity, it was daily becoming more apparent that the Hollard Street premises were again inadequate. From the date of the members' resolution in 1947 to rebuild, eleven years were to pass before the demolishers moved in. During the construction period a temporary home was found for the JSE in Protection House situated in Fox Street. The second exchange in Hollard Street was built on the site of the old one and officially opened in February 1961.

The fifth and last move to date took place in 1978 when the JSE took up residence at 17 Diagonal Street, the heart of South Africa's financial market. For the first time in its history, the JSE's stockbrokers, staff, and offices were to be housed in one building. At the appointed time on December 12, 1978, the historic old handbell was rung to signify the start of trading in the current premises. However, at 4 P.M. on Friday, June 7, 1996, the final bell was rung for the close of trade on the trading floor, thus ending a 108-year era of open outcry trading and giving way to a new era of high-tech computer trading. Monday, June 10, 1996, saw all trade being conducted on the JET System, a system which had been gradually phased in over the previous three-month period, commencing March 1996.

The Role of the JSE in South Africa

The JSE was founded to enable the new mines and their financiers to raise funds for the development of the fledgling mining industry. However, the majority of the companies listed today are non-mining organizations. The exchange successfully fulfils its main function—the raising of primary capital—by rechanneling cash resources into productive economic activity, thus building the economy while enhancing job opportunities and wealth creation.

It is an essential cog in the functioning of a capitalist economy and provides an orderly market for dealing in securities, thereby creating new investment opportunities in the country. Liquidity is perhaps the most important objective of any stock exchange—the success with which the primary market fulfils its function of raising new investment capital is dependent upon it. As a national institution the JSE must make the services it provides—primary and secondary markets in equities—available to the nation as a whole. The best method of achieving this is to ensure that the nation is suitably educated in the advantages and risks of share ownership.

Structure and Administration of the JSE

The exchange is directed by an honorary committee of sixteen people, all with full voting rights. The elected stockbroking members (who may not number less than eight and not more than ten) may appoint an executive president and five nonmembers to the committee. Policy decisions are made by the committee and carried out by a full-time executive headed by the executive president. The JSE is governed by its members but, through their use of JSE services and facilities, these members are also customers of the exchange.

Though there is only one stock exchange in South Africa, the Stock Exchanges Control Act (1985) does allow for the existence and operation of more than one exchange. Each year the JSE must apply to the Minister of Finance for an operating licence which vests external control of the exchange in the South African Financial Services Board.

Purpose and Benefits of a Stock Exchange

The exchange is structured without bias toward any particular business or social community; its overall benefit to the economy is twofold. A listing on the JSE enables large sums of capital to be raised for expansion, the financing of new businesses, and the creation of new employment opportunities. For the person in the street it represents, in the medium to long term, one of the best means of investment. The capital appreciation from holding shares over a period of time comfortably exceeds the rate of inflation. For those who are knowledgeable about the performance of selected shares, speculative buying and selling may be appealing, but the risk is high.

Amendments to the Stock Exchanges Control Act 1985

A research subcommittee, under the chairmanship of Professor Michael Katz, was formed by the JSE Committee in 1992 in anticipation of the subsequent significant changes in the South African political and economic environment. The JSE Committee adopted the majority view recommendations contained in the 500-page report of the subcommittee.

It is important to note that the restructuring of the stock exchange was largely dependent on Parliament agreeing to appropriate amendments to the 1985 Act. Following the agreement on the amendments, the Stock Exchanges Control Amendment Act was subsequently approved by Parliament in September 1995.

The restructuring plan was approved by the JSE Committee, thus ensuring the stock exchange's efficient and successful deregulation, and also its meaningful contribution toward the needs of the new political and economic era. This plan will further enhance the JSE's attractiveness to local and foreign investors. The restructuring has impacted on membership, trading principles and systems, clearing and settlement, transfer and registration, capital requirements of member firms, and the financial structure of the JSE.

Operations of the JSE

The JSE operates an equities market with many of its members also trading bonds and financial futures. Traditional options are traded on an OTC basis.

Membership.   Corporate limited liability membership with ownership by nonstockbrokers was introduced on November 8, 1995, supplementing the present membership of sole traders, partnerships, or unlimited liability corporate members. However, the member firm will be the trading entity and not the individual. Foreigners may also operate as member firms. In addition, every member firm must appoint an officer who has passed the compliance officer examination. It will be that officer's prime responsibility to ensure the member firms' compliance with the provisions of the Stock Exchanges Control Act (SECA), the rules, and the JSE Committee directives and decisions.

The South African Institute of Stockbrokers.   The institute was founded in November 1995 to represent, train, qualify, and discipline stockbrokers independently from the JSE. Aspiring stockbrokers must pass the examination of the Institute and have been employed by a member firm for a period of at least six months. There are two categories of membership: practicing and nonpracticing stockbrokers.

Trading

Trading Structure.   In March 1996 the JSE commenced automated trading, converting the first group of stocks from floor trading. Using the JET System, the structure then changed to continuous order-driven with central market principles; dual trading capacity, complemented by member firms voluntarily acting as market makers; and fully negotiable brokerage with clients.

Significant improvements arise for investors, listed companies, and the JSE itself from the JET System, through improved transparency, security, and audit trails which greatly enhance investor protection. The JSE recognizes the need to assist the Reconstruction and Development Programme by encouraging the participation of new investors and entrepreneurs in the equities market. Equally important is to attract a greater number of international players and to improve the service to existing market participants. The anticipated ease of trading and increased liquidity makes the cost of raising capital cheaper. The JET System does just that.

The central order book ("the book") is the cornerstone of, and is managed by, the JET System. The book is accessed via trading workstations, which are linked to the JET System. Dealers enter buy and sell orders on the workstations, which are immediately included anonymously in the summary display of the aggregate of orders in the order book for all dealers to view. The order book is divided into a bid and offer side and organized on the principle of priority where orders, when registered in the book, are ranked first in priority of price and then time within price. The bid with the highest price is placed on the top left of the order book and the offer with the lowest price at the top right. The system continuously seeks to match the bids and offers, comparing new orders and those in the book to each other and executing trades whenever the terms of the orders match. Dealers are advised immediately of matched trades, and a code number is recorded for client identification purposes.

The JET principles and trading rules have been developed following principles aimed at optimizing investor protection. The system allows for maximum efficiency and equal participation by all players, both large and small. The JSE's rules also allow member firms the choice of dealing in either single or dual capacity. Dual trading capacity is where a member firm acts as either an agent, on behalf of, or as a principal with a client. The member firm may therefore sell a client shares from its own holding of shares. However, the member firm must inform the client in which capacity it is acting prior to the transaction being effected. If no information is provided, it will be assumed that the member firm is dealing as an agent. The introduction of dual trading capacity and fully negotiable commissions was made simultaneously with the automation of trading in March 1996.

How to Invest through the JSE

Purchasing Shares.   Investors do not buy shares in or through the JSE itself, but through member firms. When a potential investor approaches a member firm, discussion takes place with one of its stockbrokers about the proposed investment and it is likely he will also give you advice. Decisions need to be made about which shares to purchase and how much to invest, preferably with a view to medium- to long-term investment of three to five years.

On instruction from the stockbroker, a dealer executes your order at the price agreed upon. Alternatively, you might have imposed certain price limits within which the dealer must buy or sell your shares, but these limits should be reasonable with regard to time and price. From the date of purchase there are seven business days within which to pay for your shares and a share certificate could follow a few weeks later. Share certificates are issued by the relevant transfer secretary who records share ownership and who should also be informed in the event of losing the share certificate (a fee is levied for the replacement of lost or stolen certificates).

Selling Shares. Selling shares is almost a reversal of purchasing. In the course of the administration of your securities you might ask your stockbroker to sell all or part of them at the best price possible or within certain limits. Buying or selling limits are usually set when you want to obtain a certain price for your shares and you are prepared to wait until this price is met. Sellers give their share certificates to the member firm and sign a transfer deed, which allows the shares to be transferred to the buyer. Once the sale is executed, sellers receive the proceeds from the sale within seven working days.

Step-by-Step Guide to Buying or Selling Shares

How to Buy Shares. You will need to have approximately R2,000 available in cash. Contact the JSE public relations department (tel.: 011 377 2200) and ask to be referred to a member firm. The member firm will open an account for you in your name. While the member firm's stockbroker will give advice on your investment, remember the final decision lies with you.

The stockbroker will then instruct a dealer to purchase X number of shares in a particular company for you. With the implementation of the dual trading capacity and JET System, and after receiving your instructions, the dealer will enter your order, via his trading workstation, onto the central order book managed by the JET System. The system continuously seeks to match the bids and offers, comparing new orders and those in the book to each other and executing trades whenever the terms of the orders match.

When the order is executed, you will receive a broker's note containing relevant details and will then be asked to pay for those shares. A share certificate will be sent to you within four to seven weeks. This document is proof of ownership of the shares. Brokerage is now fully negotiable between the client and the member firm.

Dependence on paper in the form of share certificates and transfer documents will eventually be eliminated. The JSE, in consultation with other interested parties, is supporting the implementation of an electronic scrip registry which, as an interim measure, would be facilitated through a central depository.

How to Sell Shares. Contact your stockbroker and advise him which shares you wish to sell. Again, if you do not have a stockbroker, contact the JSE public relations department and ask to be referred to a member firm. The stockbroker will ask you to sign a transfer deed enabling the shares to be registered in the buyer's name and to forward the share certificates, together with the transfer deed, by registered mail to him. When your shares have been sold, you will receive a broker's note with relevant details. The charges will be fully negotiable between you and the member firm.

Rights of a Shareholder

A shareholder has the right to vote at shareholder meetings and general meetings of the company. The company may also be forced by the shareholders to hold a meeting under certain circumstances where they can influence the agenda or voice their opinions. Although not explicitly expressed in the Companies Act, shareholders must be kept informed at all times. A prospectus must be distributed when a company wants to raise capital. Shareholders have the right to receive dividends, but this is a legitimate expectation and not a legal right. Shareholders are entitled to expect a high degree of diligence, competence, and integrity from the directors of the company. Shareholders have the right to be informed by the company regarding any information or developments which might influence its share price.

JSE Guarantee Fund

The JSE has established a Guarantee Fund with assets in excess of R80 million. The fund offers protection to clients who suffer a loss arising out of transactions in listed shares consequent upon the default or bankruptcy of a member firm. Payment of claims to qualifying clients is made immediately following the default of a member firm. The fund then claims against the member firm's estate.

Rise and Fall of Share Prices

Initially, the prelisting statement or prospectus, financial statements, and any projected profits are the investor's guide in determining the value of the share. The share price, from the day of listing, is influenced by supply and demand based on the value which investors place on that equity. Where demand for a share exceeds supply, the price tends to rise. On the other hand, where supply exceeds demand, the price tends to fall. The same is true of gold and oil, commodities of international importance. The general tendency, particularly where gold is concerned, is for share prices to rise or fall in line with changes in the rand price of gold.

Investment Knowledge

In forming an opinion about the performance of various equities, one should study the most recent interim and annual reports published by the relevant companies. The member firm one deals with will be able to supply information about the forecast for a company, its share performance in the past, and its dividend yield.

A further valuable source of information is the JSE Monthly Bulletin, which contains current and historical information on companies' shares. Also, obtainable from newsagents, is a selection of stock market handbooks, updated and published twice a year. These handbooks cover the nature of business, the names of the directors, share capital information, forecasts and dividend dates, financial statistics, and shareholding percentages for each listed company. In addition to these sources, anyone studying the performance of various companies would also benefit by reading financial newspapers and magazines for background material. Mining and investment companies deserve special mention. When assessing whether to invest in a company listed under these sectors, one must bear the following in mind.

With regard to mining companies an obvious question would be, "For how long will the company be able to mine profitably?" The supply will end one day and the mine might reach the stage when it becomes unprofitable to continue mining the remaining deposits. When this happens the mine will close and be liquidated, returning as much capital as possible to shareholders. By taking the life of the mine into consideration, one is able to determine whether it is possible to recover the cost of one's shares over this period and what the dividend yield is likely to be. Known as amortisation, this process is usually quite complex, as one needs to take one's personal financial situation into account, especially from a tax point of view. However advice may be sought from a member firm. Mining shares are, by their very nature, more volatile than other shares, hence the timing of the purchase or sale decision is of utmost importance. If one's interest lies in gold shares, one must be aware that these shares are affected by the international gold price, quoted in U.S. dollars.

When selecting shares in industrial companies, the nature of the particular business and the outlook for that sector must be taken into account. By conducting a comparative analysis with the company's competitors one can gauge the success and, consequently, the marketability of those shares. Be critical of the prospects for that type of company in light of the country's circumstances and against a global backdrop. Is this sector of the industry susceptible to world market influences? Again, annual and interim reports should be studied and analyzed.

Services Provided by a Member Firm

Member firms supply the following services: administration of securities, equity and bond trading, general investment planning, futures and options trading, money market deposits, research and investment advice, corporate finance advice, and assisting companies with listing requirements.

Fidelity Insurance Cover

The insurance policy, which has cover up to R350 million, serves as an initial protection for member firms against, among other things, criminal acts by a stockbroker or the employees of a member firm using the money or shares of its clients. In addition, the policy provides protection to member firms that have dealt in good faith and received tainted scrip—in other words, scrip that has been forged, stolen, lost, or the like.

Listing Categories

When applying for a listing, a company will qualify for one of three possible listings: the Main Board, the Development Capital Market (DCM), or the Venture Capital Market (VCM). The listing requirements for the three categories are detailed in the following sections.

Main Board Requirements

- A subscribed capital, excluding revaluations of assets, of at least R2 million in the form of not less than one million shares in issue.
- A satisfactory profit history for the preceding three years, the last of which reported an audited profit before taxation of at least R1 million.
- A minimum of 10 percent of each class of equity shares to be held by the public.
- A minimum of 3,000 public shareholders for equity shares.
- The minimum initial issue price of shares to be not less than 100 cents per share.

The JSE may list companies that do not strictly comply with these requirements, but this will only occur in exceptional circumstances. It should be noted that pyramid companies, investment entities, and mineral companies that are listed on the Main Board have certain modified criteria for listing.

To promote the socioeconomic development of South Africa, the JSE has introduced the Financial-Redevelopment sector to the Main Board and, to promote industrial development in South Africa, has also introduced the Industrial-Development Stage sector to the Main Board.

Financial-Redevelopment Sector

In evaluating a listing of a redevelopment entity, the JSE will have regard, inter alia, to the fundamental principle that the principal objective of the redevelopment entity must be the provision of assistance, whether through investment, loan, or other means acceptable to the JSE, to persons, communities, or undertakings which, in the opinion of the JSE, are of a socioeconomic development nature. The JSE may admit the securities of a redevelopment entity to listing subject to whatever conditions it deems necessary (which may include requirements that are different from those contained in the listings requirements), notwithstanding that the normal requirements regarding details of assets and liabilities and profit records are not given, and/or the applicant's assets consist wholly or substantially of cash or short-dated securities.

Industrial-Development Stage Sector

The JSE may list the securities of substantial industrial companies that are in the developmental stage and which, accordingly, do not have the profit history required for a Main Board listing. The applicant should have a subscribed permanent capital prior to the offering of securities to the public of at least R20 million, and will have to provide a forecast of future profits and losses during and at least one year after the development stage.

Development Capital Market Requirements

Recognizing the need to encourage the growth of small to medium-size businesses and companies which are not able to list on the Main Board, the JSE created the DCM in 1984. While still demanding quality and stability of a DCM company, the criteria to be met are less onerous than those of the Main Board. It is expected that DCM companies will use the capital raised to expand to a level where they meet the requirements for a Main Board listing.

The principal requirements of a DCM listing include the following:

- A subscribed capital, excluding revaluations of assets, of at least R1 million, in the form of not less than 1 million shares in issue.
- A satisfactory profit history for the preceding two years (or in exceptional circumstances, a lesser period), the last of which reported an audited profit level of at least R500,000 before taxation (mineral companies are exempt from this requirement).
- A minimum of 10 percent of each class of equity shares in issue to be held by the public.
- A minimum of 75 public shareholders for equity shares.
- The minimum initial issue price to be not less than 50 cents per share.

Venture Capital Market Requirements

To assist companies specializing in venture capital projects (venture capital conglomerates) or single venture companies, the JSE formed the VCM in 1989. Prior to the submission of an application for listing, the JSE requires a memorandum giving a summary of the nature of business of the applicant, its modus operandi, and its business plans and prospects. If the memorandum is approved, the company may make a formal application for listing.

A single venture company must draw up an analysis of its prospects, based on its market segment growth, competitive analysis, and market share. From this, it should present a three-year business plan with forecast balance sheets, profit and loss accounts, and cash flows. A venture capital conglomerate must have as its dominant business the professional operation of a company which holds and will in future hold a portfolio of investments in ventures, each of which is characterized by the fact that the venture capital conglomerate has an investment in each underlying venture, which is substantially an equity one; is able to add value to each of its underlying venture projects through providing support services and proper financial disciplines; has conducted adequate research into the management strength and commercial viability of each of its underlying ventures; and has drawn up a business plan for the next three years in respect of each underlying venture and of the combined portfolio, with forecast balance sheets, profit and loss accounts, and cash flow statements.

The principal requirements of a VCM listing include the following:

- A subscribed capital, excluding revaluations of assets, of at least R500,000, in the form of not less than 1 million shares in issue.

- The JSE would like the entrepreneurs to remain financially committed to the VCM company and, accordingly, it will not list securities held by the entrepreneurs of the VCM company amounting to 75 percent of their shareholdings (as held immediately prior to any marketing of securities in conjunction with the application for listing) for a period of at least two years subsequent to listing being granted.

- No profit history is required, but it should, in its analyses of future earnings, indicate credible returns on capital which, on a timeweighted basis, are above average.

- A minimum of 5 percent of each class of equity shares to be held by the public.

- A minimum of seventy-five public shareholders for equity shares.

- The minimum initial price of shares to be not less than 50 cents per share.

- The majority of directors and managers must have had successful records of achievement in their respective trades.

- At the beginning of its prospectus or prelisting statement, there must be a warning of the speculative nature of investment in such a company.

A company may be delisted as a result of a takeover or merger, or, in the case of a "cash shell," if it has not acquired new business within eight months of becoming a cash shell in terms of JSE criteria.

Types of Companies Listed

The nature of business of listed companies varies greatly, ranging from mining and industrial concerns through to textiles, fishing, and entertainment.

They are all public limited liability companies, with a shareholder's liability limited to the purchase price of his shares. However, by their restrictive and exclusive nature, closed corporations, partnerships, sole proprietorships, and proprietary limited companies are unable to list.

Global and Local Market Trends

Since South Africa has reentered the global village, the JSE, in particular, has been plunged into the world of a twenty-four-hour global stock market. The market is influenced by the trends of the world's major stock markets and by the sometimes shock occurrences on the markets of other emerging countries. The domestic influence of our own growth cycles will still be of major consequence in dictating the market trends. Thus, before buying or selling shares, one first should ascertain any global factors which may be influencing the market and then establish which phase of our own cycle is occurring. Markets are traditionally expensive at or near the top of a cycle and inexpensive at the bottom.

Interest rates play a major role in determining stock market trends. The norm is to associate bull markets (those in an upward trend) with low interest rates, and bear markets (those in a downward trend) with high interest rates. Interest rates are determined by the demand for capital; this pushes them up and normally indicates that the economy is at, or near, the top of a cycle and that shares are probably expensive. Low interest rates indicate low demand for capital, thus liquidity builds up on the economy, driving share prices down.

Specific Sectors and Companies

Once an investor has determined the trend of the market, and thus the economy, his next task is to determine which sectors of the economy will perform best. He may, for example, decide that the tourism or building sectors will grow the fastest over the next three to five years. Having selected a sector, he will then have to select a company in whose shares he will invest. To do this properly he will consider a host of things, namely the products manufactured or services offered, the financial stability of the company, the quality of management, the competition which the company faces, and its overall track record.

Having established a value for the company, and assuming he is happy with the timing, the investor will then purchase the shares. Having made the investment he will then begin a monitoring process in which he will assess the company's progress by studying the results which are published every six months in the form of interim and final financial statements. He will also be entitled to attend the annual general meeting of the company and vote on any major decisions which are made.

Risk and Investments

The wise and successful investor always considers his risk, and never puts all his eggs in one basket. He does not expose himself, either, to investments which are considered to be speculative. A young investor with a full working life ahead will be able to adopt an aggressive investment policy, placing most of his funds in high-growth equities. A more mature investor who has, for example, only a few years to retirement will be more conservative and would keep only a portion in equities and diversify his investments into property, bonds, and cash. An elderly widow would, for example, require income rather than capital growth. She would have few equities (if any) and would seek secure high-yielding investments, bearing in mind the old adage that the higher the yield the higher the risk. A conservative investor would consider investing in unit trusts rather than individual shares, as the spread of companies within the trust would afford him far less risk.

The JSE and the Big Bang

The history of the JSE has been one of traditional stockbroking in which stockbrokers acted as agents, buying and selling shares on behalf of their clients. Only individuals could be stockbrokers and the commissions they charged were fixed. They competed with each other on service only, while advertising was prohibited. The JSE has now moved away from this environment into one with negotiable commission, corporate ownership (mainly the local and foreign banks), and principal dealing (member firms dealing directly with their clients). The "Big Bang" took place in the United States in 1976 and in London in 1986. We are, therefore, following a global trend, which should lead to higher turnovers on the JSE as well as to more competitive rates and services for the investors. Most of South Africa's major banks have become member firms of the JSE and can now offer stockbroking services through all of their branches.

Krugerrands

The Krugerrand was listed on the JSE on April 9, 1979. It is a 22-carat gold bullion coin weighing one troy ounce. It is obtainable in denominations of one ounce, half-ounce, quarter-ounce, and a tenth of an ounce and is considered legal tender. It is generally purchased as a hedge or protection against currency fluctuations, hence many investors include Krugerrands or gold shares in their portfolio. Because Krugerrands are listed on the JSE, trading is controlled by the rules and directives of the exchange. The establishment of an official market for Krugerrands has led to improved efficiency on the formation of prices where the margin between buyers' and sellers' prices has been significantly narrowed. Bid and offer prices, plus volumes traded, are published in the media daily. Krugerrands can be bought and sold through a member firm, being subject to negotiable commission, and also from either a bank or a coin exchange.

Literature Available from the JSE

The literature listed is available at no charge, unless more than two copies are required:

Facts at Your Fingertips (statistical information of particular interest to local and foreign investors)

How to Read the Share Price Page in the Newspaper

Understanding the JSE–Actuaries Indices

The JSE Main Indices (35 years in perspective)

List of members (equities)

The JET System

An Investor's Guide to the Restructured JSE

For further information, contact the following address:

JSE Public Relations Department
P.O. Box 1174 Johannesburg 2000
Tel.: 377–2200   Fax: 834–7402

NOTES

1. CIA Factbook web site at http://www.odci.gov/cia/publications/nsolo/factbook/sf.htm.

2. Ibid.

3. Ibid.

4. The International Finance Corporation classifies a market as middle income when the GNP per capita is between $766 and $9,385 for 1995. (*Emerging Stock Markets Factbook 1997* [Washington, D.C.: International Finance Corporation, 1997], 3).

5. Roger Mathews, "S. Africa Relaxes Forex Curbs," *Financial Times*, 13 March 1997, 9.

6. An extensive discussion of the JET system is available on the exchange's web site at http://www.jse.co.za/.

7. *Emerging Stock Markets Factbook 1997* (Washington, D.C.: International Finance Corporation, 1997).

8. Ibid.

9. Ibid.

10. U.S. Department of Commerce, ITA, *1996 Country Commercial Guide for South Africa* (Washington, D.C.: U.S. Government Printing Office, National Trade Data Bank, 1995).

11. Adapted from the Johannesburg Stock Exchange web site at http://www.jse.
co.za/thejse/aguideto.htm, and is accurate as of November 6, 1997. Used by permission.

SWAZILAND

COUNTRY

The Kingdom of Swaziland (in SiSwazi, Umbuso WeSwatini) has an area of 6,704 square miles (17,364 square kilometers). It is the second smallest country in Africa. (Gambia being the first.) For comparative purposes, it is slightly smaller than the state of New Jersey in the United States. It is a land-locked country surrounded by South Africa and Mozambique. The administrative capital is Mbabane and the legislative and royal capital is Lobamba.

During the eighteenth century the Bantu-speaking Swazi people established the center of the Swazi nation. King Sobhuza I consolidated his power in the 1820s and 1830s. In 1846 his successor Mswazi sought British assistance against the Zulus. In 1890 the Swazi people agreed to a provisional government of British, South African, and Swazi representatives. The Swazis did not consent to the institution of South African administration in 1893, but in 1894 they signed an agreement permitting South African administration without annexation.

With British control of Transvaal in 1903, the British Consul administered Swaziland by proclamation. The British transferred this control to the high commissioner for Basutoland (now Lesotho), Bechuanaland (now Botswana), and Swaziland. The British denied a 1949 request by the Union of South Africa for control. The 1963 constitution provided for limited self-government, in 1967 the Kingdom of Swaziland was proclaimed under British protection, and full independence as a constitutional monarchy was granted in 1968.

Official Religion	None[1]
Religions	Christian 60%, indigenous beliefs 40%
Population	998,700 (1997)
	Urban 34%
	Rural 66%
	Population under the age of 15: 43%
Ethnic Divisions	African 97%, Non-African 3%
	The population is mostly homogenous with 84% Swazis.
Languages	English (official, government business conducted in English), SiSwati (official)
Education	Population over age 15 who are literate: 77%

The Political System

The Kingdom of Swaziland is a constitutional monarchy. In 1973 and 1977 King Sobhuza II dismissed Parliament and abolished the constitution. Two years later in each case a new constitution was enacted. King Sobhuza II died in 1982. His son, Prince Makhosetive, was crowned King Mswati II in 1986.

The 1978 constitution provides for a bicameral parliament, but its powers are purely advisory. The Parliament consists of a sixty-five-member House of Assembly and a thirty-member Senate. The King, who has absolute power, appoints ten members to the House of Assembly and twenty members to the Senate. The other House members are elected from candidates nominated within the framework of traditional local councils. The House of Assembly elects the remaining senators. The head of government is the Prime Minister, Dr. Sibusiso Bamabas (since 1996).

Political Web Site   http://www.geocities.com/~derksen/election.htm

Legal System

The Swazi legal system is based on South African Roman–Dutch law in statutory courts and Swazi traditional law and custom in traditional courts.[2]

Suffrage is at eighteen years of age and is universal. Fifty-five of the sixty-five seats in the House of Assembly were filled by popular vote in the elections of September and October 1993. None of the thirty seats in the Senate were filled by popular vote.

The Economy

Swaziland is a small country with limited domestic markets, therefore export-oriented industries are vital to its economic performance. Swaziland is targeting and developing new markets, and South Africa, with its revised constitution, has been identified as one of the areas where export promotion efforts should be concentrated. Swaziland is closely linked with South Africa and participates in the South African Customs Union.

Due to the 1980s sanctions on South Africa, the Swazi economy recorded high growth rates as corporations relocated to Swaziland. The political transition in South Africa in 1994 resulted in Swaziland losing its previous advantage as an investment location, thus limiting the long-term capital inflows. The Swaziland economy is based on diverse agricultural and manufacturing activities. High population growth continues to thwart development efforts, resulting in unemployment, poverty, and other adverse factors.

Gross Domestic Product[3]

Swaziland is classified as a middle-income country under the World Bank's classification of economies.[4] The diversity of Swaziland's economy is reflected in the contribution of manufacturing to the economy, contributing approximately 30 percent of GDP, which is extremely high for Africa. For comparability, GDP is expressed in purchase power parity terms.

GDP purchasing power parity	$3.6 billion (1995 est.)
GDP real growth rate	3.9% (1996 est.)
GDP per capita	$3,700 (1995 est.)
Unemployment rate	30% (1992 est.)

GDP in 1996 was estimated at SZL5.072 billion in current prices and SZL1.549 billion in 1985 prices.

Central Bank: Central Bank of Swaziland[5]

The central bank's mission is to contribute to Swaziland's national economic development through promotion of monetary stability and by fostering an environment which ensures a stable and a sound financial system. The bank seeks to achieve this mission by, among other things, doing the following:

- promoting sound monetary policies within the framework of economic objectives.
- managing the exchange rate policy and the official reserves in the best interests of the country.
- safeguarding the integrity and efficiency of the financial sector so as to enhance service quality.
- conducting research in economic matters, particularly in national and international monetary issues.
- developing and motivating competent staff to handle the tasks required to fulfil its mission.
- monitoring good working relationships with domestic, regional and the international financial community.

Postal Address
Central Bank of Swaziland
P.O. Box 546
Warner Street
Mbabane
Swaziland
Tel.: 268–42161, 268–43222   Fax: 268–45417

The Central Bank's 1997 Annual Report is at web site http://www.realnet. co.sz/cbs/report97/cbsrep97_1.html.

Credit Rating

Swaziland has not been rated by international rating agencies for either domestic or foreign currency debt.

Interest Rates[6]

Swaziland's interest rate policy continues to be influenced by developments in the South African market. This is reflected in increases in the nominal rates of interest, during the year, which is partly explained by the maintenance of a minimum differential between Swazi rates and those in South Africa. It is the central bank's aim to narrow the spread between the lending and borrowing rates.

The level of interest rates in Swaziland moved in the same direction as those in South Africa during the year 1996–1997. The inflation rate based on a new basket of goods was 6.1 percent for the year ending March 1996, 6.5 percent for the year ending March 1997, and 7 percent for the year ending November 1997. (Note that a computational error resulted in the year ended March 1997 inflation rate originally being reported as 18.9 percent.) The discount rate has been maintained at 16.8 percent from May 1996 to date, up 1.8 percentage points from the level of 15 percent in March 1996. The prime lending rate followed closely the rate in South Africa, with a margin of only 0.5 percent, and closed the year at 19.8 percent. The spread is wider on deposit rates; for example, the thirty-one-days term deposits rate was 5 percentage points below the South African rates for the year in March 1997.

Currency

Monetary unit   lilangeni (SZL) (plural, emalangeni) = 100 cents

The Rand Common Monetary Area links the South African rand, Namibian dollar, Swaziland emalangeni, and Lesotho maloti. The emalangeni is currently pegged to the South African rand on a one-to-one basis. The Common Monetary Area Agreement, which links Swaziland's lilangeni to the South African rand, is unlikely to change in the immediate future. The depreciation of the rand and the emalangeni against the major reserve currencies continued during 1996. Though the trend in exchange indicates minor recovery in some cases, toward the end of 1996, the lilangeni deteriorated against the U.S. dollar and pound sterling.[7] The forward market in the South African rand is free of any South African Reserve Bank controls, and is liquid up to twelve months. A currency option market in the South African rand is developing in the Johannesburg market. Exchange rates are as follows: Emalangeni per US$1–4.89 (February 17, 1998), 4.59 (July 30, 1997), 3.6417 (January 1996), 3.6266 (1995), 3.5490 (1994), 3.2636 (1993), 2.8497 (1992), 2.7563 (1991), 2.5863 (1990); note that the Swazi emalangeni is at par with the South African rand.

There are a number of web sites providing updated currency exchange values. The following is an example:

http://www.bloomberg.com/markets/currency/currcalc.cgi

Payments are made freely within the Common Monetary Area (Swaziland, Lesotho, Namibia, and South Africa). Exchange control regulations only apply outside this area. The Central Bank of Swaziland administers exchange control, and authorized dealers (commercial banks) are empowered to approve certain foreign exchange transactions. Residents who wish to buy and sell foreign currency (i.e., currencies other than emalangeni, maloti, Namibian dollar, or the rand) or gold must use an authorized dealer.

Web Site   http://mbendi.co.za/stanbic/stsw01.htm

THE STOCK EXCHANGE: SWAZILAND STOCK EXCHANGE

The Swaziland Stock Exchange (SSE) is a small exchange. The share market was established in 1990 and at the end of 1996 the market had a total capitalization of $471 million. The exchange has evolved from its early days, when daily volume totaled $822, to today when trading value average much more than that.

Mr. Andy McGuire
Chief Executive Officer
Swaziland Stockbrokers Ltd.
2nd Floor, Dhlanudeka House
Walker Street
P.O. Box 2818
Mbabane
Swaziland
Tel.: (268) 46163   Fax: (268) 44132

Web Sites	http://mbendi.co.za/exsw.htm
	http://www.worldnet.co.za/achill/swazilan/busbul/stock.html
Established	July 9, 1990
Trading Days	Monday to Friday
Trading Hours	10:00–12:00
	The international time zone is GMT + 2.

Market Index

All listings are included in the only index, the SSM Index, which is unweighted. There are five listed public companies.

STOCK MARKET ACTIVITY

Trading Structure

The stock market operates on a matched bargain basis.[8] Brokers act as agents and do not trade as principals. The SSE operates on a specialist matching system. Dealers in Swaziland are permitted to purchase or sell securities as agents on behalf of customers, provided that they are licensed to do so. Trades can be carried out by netting without initiating two separate transactions. Over-the-counter transactions are permitted by private treaty.

Performance

The Swaziland Stock Exchange local market index increased 41 percent in 1996, and the market price index increased 9.9 percent in U.S.-dollar terms. Swaziland's performance ranked it forty-seventh (of seventy-six) in the International Finance Corporation's 1996 World Stock Market Performance ranking.[9] The 1996 price–earnings ratio was 9.7, with a dividend yield of 5.2 percent.

Market Valuation[10]

Year	Price–Earnings Ratio	Dividend Yield
1993	11.5	5.0
1994	10.6	5.6
1995	7.4	5.7
1996	9.7	5.2
1997	6.8	9.1

Number of Listed Firms

The number of listed firms, which had been constant at four since 1993, increased to five firms in 1996. There are two unit trusts which also trade on the exchange. One firm, Fridge Master, is jointly listed on the Johannesburg Stock Exchange. In addition, one firm, GROPROP, has been suspended from trading by the exchange. The market capitalization in U.S. dollars increased 39 percent from 1995 to 1996. U.S.-dollar valued capitalization has grown at an annual compound rate of 16.6 percent since the end of 1993.

Number of Listed Firms and Market Capitalization[11]

Year	Number of Firms	Market Capitalization (U.S. Millions)
1993	4	297
1994	4	338
1995	4	339
1996	5	471
1997	4	137

The increase in market capitalization was the result of an increase in the number of listed firms, but a 22-percent depreciation in the exchange rate from 1995 to 1996 restrained the growth in dollar terms. The market's year-to-year increase in emalangeni terms was 78.5 percent. The market's local currency annual compound growth rate from 1993 to 1996 was 29.7 percent.

Liquidity

The 1996 Swaziland market liquidity is very low as reflected by the market's turnover ratio. The 1996 average daily trading was approximately $37,275. This contrasts with an average of $822 when the market opened. The International Finance Corporation ranks the Swaziland market turnover as eighty-first (of eighty-four) in the world. The exchange ranks last in Africa in terms of overall turnover.[12]

Market Turnover Ratio

Year	1993	1994	1995	1996	1997
Turnover Ratio[13]	0.0	0.7	0.1	0.6	0.1

Quarterly Swaziland Stock Exchange Equity Trading Summary[14]

Year	Transactions	Shares	Value (SZL)
1996	52	3,310,497	10,083,427
1997	32	134,144,036	1,738,888,447

Instruments Traded

Equities, corporate debentures, and government bonds are traded. The exchange lists three government bonds and three corporate debentures for trading. There are currently no derivative products traded and the exchange has no plans to institute them.

Brokerage Rates

The brokerage commissions are not fixed by statute or government regulation, or by the rules of the stock exchange or association of brokers or dealers. However, there is only one dealer and commissions are fixed.

Orders up to SZL49,999	2.0%
Orders from SZL50,000 to SZL99,999	1.5%
SZL100,000 or greater	1.0%

There is a basic stock exchange handling fee of SZL15 charge per transaction. Government bonds are sold on a different commission schedule. This will change in the last half of 1998 when the new Securities Act and revised Companies Act are promulgated into law.

Margin/Securities Lending

There is no legal restriction on a broker lending securities to a customer for a short sale; however, this is not practiced by the market dealer. A broker purchasing securities as an agent may not lend the purchaser part of the purchase price against the security as collateral. However, a registered commercial bank in Swaziland may make a loan against securities collateral and this is a common practice. There are no price limits or daily trading ranges for exchange transactions.

Insider Trading

There are no laws restricting the ability of directors, officers, or substantial shareholders of domestic corporations in the purchase or sale of shares of their corporations unless the Articles of Association of the relevant corporation specifically prohibit such actions. The laws relating to insider trading as they apply in the Republic of South African relating to publicly listed companies would be applicable in Swaziland on the basis of common law and the decided cases in that regard in the Republic of South Africa. Courts in Swaziland follow South African case law. A new set of listings requirements fashioned by customizing the requirements of the Johannesburg Stock Exchange is expected to be operative by the beginning of 1999. In these requirements there are specific provisions which deal explicitly with insider trading.

Dividends and Capital Gains Taxation

A withholding tax of 10 percent is applied to interest earnings. Nonresident taxes on dividends are at the rate of 15 percent. If the investor is a South African company, the rate is reduced to 12.5 percent. There is no capital gains tax or tax on dividends from companies and distributions paid to residents. Swaziland has double tax agreements with various countries in Africa, including South Africa. Swaziland welcomes foreign investment and most business activities are open to foreign investors.

Regulatory Controls

The Stock Exchange Committee, chaired by the Governor of the Central Bank of Swaziland, is responsible for approving listings, approving membership applications, and amendment and enforcement of stock market rules and regulations.

As the supervisor of the exchange, the committee is responsible for the maintenance of an orderly and efficient market. The Listings Committee chaired by the Deputy Governor of the Central Bank of Swaziland is responsible for the evaluation of applications for new listings and recommendations for new listings and sustained listings. Together, the Stock Exchange and Listings Committees provide the regulatory framework for the market with the Central Bank of Swaziland acting as the final authority.

The Swaziland Stockbrokers Limited (SSL) provides the trading arena for the stock market. SSL is a licensed financial institution that operates under the supervision of the Central Bank of Swaziland pursuant to the provisions of the Financial Institutions Order of 1975. Swaziland Stockbrokers Limited is currently the only broker in Swaziland. The firm acts as an agent between buyers and sellers and does not take positions in listed securities. There is an application at the central bank for at least one more stockbroking license.

Domestic securities may be listed and traded on a foreign stock exchange with the consent of the central bank if the stock exchange is outside the rand monetary area, South Africa, Swaziland, Lesotho, and Namibia. These shares may not be traded on foreign over-the-counter markets.

Foreign Investment Restrictions

There are no limitations on foreigners purchasing and owning or selling securities of domestic corporations. It is necessary for a foreigner to obtain the consent of the central bank relating to the purchase or sale of securities for exchange control purposes. Swaziland has accepted IMF Article VIII rules, which hold that all current transactions and most capital transactions are free of controls. Repatriation of capital is allowed, provided the appropriate authority has approved the investment. In addition, income may be repatriated under the same conditions.

Central Depository

There is no central depository.

Settlement

Settlement requires physical possession of the share certificates and that they be presented at the office of the brokers.

Registration

Physical possession of a certificate is necessary to exercise ownership rights. The possession by an agent or custodian is sufficient as long as the agent is duly authorized to hold the certificates. Physical delivery of the certificate is necessary to transfer ownership.

Buy-Ins

The consequences of a fail or a breach, as it is known under Swazi law, would be the cancellation of the contract by the innocent party subject to its rights to claim damages in terms of either the agreement, if specified, or the common law, if not specified. In this event, no transfer takes place.

Voting

Foreign security holders are entitled to enjoy the same benefits of ownership as afforded to domestic securities holders. The exchange regulations provide for foreign shareholders to be notified of any meetings or required actions by publication at least two months before the date of the meeting in a leading daily newspaper published in London.

Legal Issues

Domestic courts would enforce a custody agreement clause providing for the application of New York law, if they have jurisdiction. However, a judgment of a U.S. court is not automatically enforceable in the domestic courts.

INTERNET RESOURCES

General Information

http://www.realnet.co.sz

Business Sites

Swaziland Business Yearbook 1997 at http://www.realnet.co.sz/real/sbyb/sbyb.html
Economic and Social Reform Agenda at http://www.realnet.co.sz/real/esra/esra.html
1997 Budget Speech at http://www.realnet.co.sz/real/budget97/budget97.html

News

Swaziland Observer (latest daily edition of the newspaper) at http://www.realnet.co.sz/
real/observer/today/observer.html

Swaziland Today (Swazi government newsletter) at http://www.realnet.co.sz/real/
govt/sgt-nl.html

NOTES

1. CIA Factbook web site at http://www.odci.gov/cia/publications/nsolo/
factbook/wz.htm.

2. Ibid.

3. Ibid.

4. The World Bank's criteria for middle-income classification is a GNP per
capita of $766 to $9,385 in 1995. Swaziland's per capita GNP in 1995 was $1,170.

5. Mission Statement and Policy Statement are from the central bank's 1996–
1997 Annual Report at web site: http://www.realnet.co.sz/cbs/report97/cbsrep97
_mission.html.

6. Ibid.

7. Stanbic Bank's Swaziland in Figures 1995/6.

8. Exchange information was obtained from the exchange and from MBendi,
a private company that maintains African data and web sites. See web site http://
mbendi.co.za/exbo.htm. Used with permission.

9. *Emerging Stock Markets Factbook 1997* (Washington, D.C.: International Finance
Corporation, 1997).

10. Swaziland Stockbrokers Limited, Michael S. Matsebula, Chairman, Mbabane,
Swaziland, 25 February 1998. Data provided by the Central Statistical Office,
Mbabane, Swaziland. 1996 market capitalization was recalculated from that reported
by the International Finance Corporation as the reported U.S.-dollar market capitalization was incorrect due to an error in the exchange rate.

11. Ibid.

12. *Emerging Stock Markets Factbook 1997.*

13. Swaziland Stockbrokers, 25 February 1998.

14. Ibid.

TUNISIA

COUNTRY

The Republic of Tunisia (in Arabic, al-Jumhuriyah at-Tunisiyah) has an area of 59,664 square miles (154,530 square kilometers), making it the smallest country in North Africa. For comparison, the landmass is the size of Georgia. The capital is Tunis. The official language is Arabic, though French is widely spoken.

The Phoenicians founded a group of trading outposts and ports on the North African coast. Carthage was founded in the eighth century B.C. near present-day Tunis.[1] In 146 B.C., after the Punic Wars, Rome gained control of Carthage. In the mid-seventh century the Muslim Arab invasion displaced the Romans. After a number of subsequent conquests, Tunisia was conquered by the Ottoman Turks in 1574 and controlled until the late nineteenth century.

European rivalries for influence between the French, British, and Italians helped maintain the region's independence until an 1881 deal in which Britain occupied Cyprus and France took Tunisia as a protectorate. Following World War I, Tunisians demanded more home rule. Full independence was granted in 1956, and Habib Bourguiba, a leader in the independence movement, headed the government and a republic was founded. The ruling party proceeded with social reforms and the enfranchisement of women. Bourguiba was declared mentally unfit to rule in 1987 and was removed from office. General Zine al-Abidine Ben Ali succeeded Bourguiba and saw a rise in Islamic fundamentalism. The population is relatively homogeneous, with the Arabs having conquered the indigenous Berbers.

Official Religion	Muslim[2]
Religions	Muslim, 98%; Christian, 1%; Jewish, 1%
Population	9,019,687 (July 1996 est.)[3]
	Urban 53%
	Rural 47%
	Population under the age of 15: 37%
Ethnic Divisions	Arab-Berber, 98%; European, 1%; Jewish, less than 1%
Languages	Arabic (official and one of the languages of commerce), French (commerce)
Education	Population over age 15 that are literate: 67%

The Political System

The country is governed as a multiparty republic with one legislative house—the Chamber of Deputies. The Chief of State is President Zine El Abidine Ben Ali (since November 7, 1987). He was reelected without opposition for a five-year term in the last election, held on March 20, 1994, and the next elections are scheduled for 1999. The legislature is unicameral. The Chamber of Deputies (Majlis al-Nuwaab) elections were last held March 20, 1994, and the next elections are scheduled for 1999.

Political Web Site   http://www.geocities.com/~derksen/election.htm

Legal System

The legal system is based on the French civil law system and Islamic law; there is some judicial review of legislative acts in the Supreme Court in joint session. Suffrage is at twenty years of age and is universal.

The Economy

Tunisia boasts a mixed economy with both public and private sectors. During its Eighth Development Plan (1992–1996), Tunisia achieved economic growth of 4.5 percent on average.[4] The economic restructuring was designed to liberalize the economy and began in 1993.[5] The industrial sector of the economy is increasing; however, agriculture continues to dominate the economy. The government initiated an irrigation and water development project in the 1980s to make agriculture less dependent on rainfall.

Tunisia has moved forward to implement structural reforms and progressive macroeconomic policies. The policies of fiscal responsibility have resulted in a decline in inflation to less than 5 percent per year, and external debt has declined from 55 to 52 percent of GDP from 1991 to 1996.[6] Despite this progress, unemployment remains high at 15 percent. In 1996, economic growth reached 6.9 percent. Tunisia has some of the largest reserves in Africa of phosphate rock. The phosphate is used in the chemical industry and for fertilizers for export. In addition, the country has substantial oil reserves and some of Africa's largest natural gas fields.

Economic Indicators[7]

Indicator	1993	1994	1995	1996 (IMF Staff Estimate)
Real GDP	2.2	3.3	2.4	6.9
Consumer Price Index	4.0	4.7	6.3	3.7
Interest Rate (money market)	10.5	8.8	8.8	7.8

The economic indicators demonstrate the progress that the Tunisian government has made in stimulating the economy. Over the 1991 to 1996 period, savings have been maintained at an average rate of 22 percent of

GDP. Real GDP growth increased from 2.2 percent in 1993 to 6.9 percent in 1996, while the CPI declined from 4 percent to 3.7 percent over the same period. Interest rates declined 270 basis points over the four-year period. Growth for 1997 was expected to reach 5.7 percent.[8] However, agricultural losses kept the growth well below target at approximately 3.5 percent.

Gross Domestic Product[9]

Tunisia is classified as a middle-income country under the World Bank's classification of economies.[10] For comparability, GDP is expressed in purchase power parity terms.

GDP purchasing power parity	$37.1 billion (1994 est.)
GDP real growth rate	6.9% (1996)
GDP per capita	$4,250 (1994 est.)
Unemployment rate	16.3% (1997 est.)

Central Bank: Bank al-Markazi al-Tunisi//Banque centrale de Tunisie[11]

Postal Address

Banque Centrale de Tunisie
Rue Hédi Nouira
1001 Tunis
Tunisie
Tel.: +216–1–254–000 216–1–354–000   Fax: +216–1–340–615 216–1–354–214
Web Site   http://www.idsonline.com/business/srouai/bct/

Currency

Monetary unit   Tunisian dinar (TD) = 1,000 millimes

Tunisian currency is convertible for current transactions. However, Tunisian law prohibits the export or import of Tunisian bank notes or coins. Exchange rates are as follows: Tunisian dinars per US$1–0.9635 (January 1996), 0.9458 (1995), 1.0116 (1994), 1.0037 (1993), 0.8844 (1992), 0.9246 (1991).

There are a number of web sites providing updated currency exchange values. The following is an example:

http://www.bloomberg.com/markets/currency/currcalc.cgi

Privatization

As a cornerstone of Tunisia's structural adjustment program, the nation has moved forward with the privatization of state-owned enterprises. Twenty-seven firms were scheduled for privatization in 1996, versus twenty in 1995. Since its inception in 1991, ninety-two companies employing more than 28,000 Tunisians had been privatized through the end of 1997. During 1998 to 2000, the country plans to privatize sixty companies.[12]

| Web Site (French) | http://www.tunisie.com/BusinessInfo/privatisation/ndex.html |
| Web Site (English) | http://www.investintunisia.tn/html/opportunities.html |

THE STOCK EXCHANGE: TUNIS STOCK EXCHANGE/ BOURSE DES VALEURS MOBILIERES DE TUNIS

The Tunisia Stock Exchange (TSE) has a new electronic trading system, Super CAC, donated by France at an estimated cost of 13.5 million francs. Tunis is the first emerging market to adopt the computerized trading platform, which is derived from those operating in larger exchanges such as Paris, Brussels, and Toronto. The system was launched in parallel with a new paperless clearing and settlement platform, also based on French technology.[13]

Bourse des Valeurs Mobilieres de Tunis
19 bis, Rue Kamal Ataturk
1001 Tunis
Tel.: (216) 1 259 411   Fax: (216) 1 347 256

Web Site	http://mbendi.co.za/extu.htm
Established	1969
Trading Days	Monday to Friday
Trading Hours	10:00–11:30 The international time zone is GMT + 1.

Market Index

The Tunis Stock Exchange Index includes all listed companies except for new listings, which are included after a one-year period.

STOCK MARKET ACTIVITY

Trading Structure

Three companies traded on the Super CAC electronic system are traded continuously, subject to a price fluctuation limit of 3 to 4 percent a day, while the remaining companies trade on the fixed system, subject to a price fluctuation limit of 3 percent a day. Previously, trading was done on the exchange's floor using the open-outcry method.

The Tunis Stock Exchange has recently launched its new automated trading system in cooperation with the SBF–Paris Bourse and the French depository Sicovam.[14] The new system has been designed on the model of the Paris Stock Exchange's own trading system, the Super CAC. The system started operations at the end of 1996, but it reached its full capacity in the first quarter of 1997. The introduction of the automated system is part of a comprehensive move intended to upgrade the Tunisian market to international standards.

The new system should bring more liquidity and transparency to the market and attract domestic and foreign investors. The privatization program in course, especially among large public businesses, is expected to induce new listings to the stock exchange in the near future.

Performance

The International Finance Corporation ranked the Tunisian market price index in U.S.-dollar performance as sixty-second (of seventy-six) in the world in 1996. The market price index declined 6.5 percent during the year.[15]

African Stockbrokers—Tunisia

A list of African stockbrokers licensed to conduct trading on the Tunis Stock Exchange can be found at web site http://www.africa.co.uk/brokers/tunis-sb.htm. There are ten brokers listed at the web site. The site includes address and telephone contact information.

Instruments Traded

Equities, corporate debentures, and government bonds are traded. Most shares traded on the exchange are common, though some preferred shares, both with and without voting rights, are outstanding. The Banque Nationale de Developpement Touristique issued Tunisia's first Eurobond in June 1997.[16] There are currently no derivative products traded and the exchange has no plans to institute them.

Market Valuation[17]

Year	Price–Earnings Ratio	Dividend Yield
1991	10	3.74%
1992	12	3.40%
1993	12	3.85%
1994	25	2.49%
1995	21	2.51%
1996	18	3.00%

The price–earnings ratio fell 17 percent in 1996 from the end of 1995; however, market valuation has increased 80 percent from the levels afforded the market in 1991. The number of firms listed on the exchange increased 20 percent from the end of 1995. The number of listed firms has doubled since 1991.

Number of Listed Firms and Market Capitalization[18]

Year	Number of Firms	Market Capitalization (TD Millions)
1991	15	611
1992	17	793
1993	19	1,000
1994	21	2,525
1995	25	3,655
1996	30	3,951

This information reflects those firms that meet the full listing requirements of the exchange. A second or parallel market is open to smaller firms unable to meet the requirements for a listing on the main market. The number of firms listed increased 20 percent in 1996 and market capitalization increased 8.1 percent from 1995. At the end of September 1997, there were thirty-three listed companies. By the end of June, thirty-one listed stocks had been fully converted into the electronic trading system. There are no foreign firms listed on the Tunis Stock Exchange.

Liquidity

The International Finance Corporation ranks the Tunisian market turnover as sixty-fourth (of eighty-four) in 1996. This places the market turnover at sixth place among African exchanges.

Market Turnover Ratio

Year	1991	1992	1993	1994	1995	1996
Turnover Ratio[19]	5.3	4.2	5.2	17.0	19.8	6.8

Market turnover declined significantly in 1996. The daily trading volume was valued at $1,275,455. In the first eight months of 1997, the global volume of transactions on the Tunis Stock Exchange reached TD196 million against TD164 million during the same period of 1996, increasing by 20 percent. Electronic trading was introduced in October 1996 and prices declined due to increased transparency, activity, and liquidity. Turnover increased significantly.[20]

Brokerage Rates

Commission rates are between 0.6 percent and 0.8 percent, depending on the broker. Commission rates are negotiated by the Association des Intermediares en Bourse.

Insider Trading

Insider trading is illegal on the Tunis Stock Exchange.

Dividends and Capital Gains Taxation

Foreigners are exempt from dividend and capital gains taxes. The following have signed double taxation agreements with Tunisia: Germany, Austria, Belgium, Canada, South Korea, Denmark, Egypt, France, Indonesia, Italy, Jordan, Norway, the United Kingdom, Sweden, the United States, and the North African countries.

Regulatory Controls

The Conseil de Marché Financier (Tunisian Securities and Exchange Commission) was set up in 1995 and is responsible for supervising the TSE. As a public supervisory body, it monitors the market's activity.

Foreign Investment Restrictions

Tunisia operates within the IMF Article IV rules—current transactions and most capital movements are exempt from currency control and can be bought and sold freely. Present exchange controls guarantee the free transfer of profits to nonresidents under the following conditions: when the company's shares are registered on the listed securities market, or when at least 50 percent of the company's total gross income is derived from exports.

Until 1995, foreigners could not buy local shares without a special authorization from the central bank. A December 1996 law increased the foreign investment thresholds, and foreign investors are allowed to own up to 49 percent of the share capital of listed companies.[21] Foreigners may also invest in open-ended mutual funds. In 1996, foreign investment represented nearly 20 percent of private investment in Tunisia.[22] Foreign investor activity on the Tunis Stock Exchange rose from virtually zero in 1996 to $20 million during the first six months of 1997 as a result of the lifting of investment limits for foreigners in Tunisian stocks from 10 percent to 49 percent in January 1997. Tunisia is a good example of increased foreign investment as a result of improved trading facilities.

Banque Internationale Arabe de Tunisie (BIAT) became Tunisia's first global depositary receipt (GDR) on February 10, 1998. The issue raised $40 million and was listed on the London Stock Exchange on February 17, 1998.

Central Depository

Tunis has a central depository.

Settlements

Settlement and transfer are carried out by STICODEVAM, a centralized clearinghouse, and are T+7.

Listing Requirements

Companies listed on the TSE must do the following:

1. Publish net operating results and submit them to the public no later than one month before the AGM.
2. Publish board meeting reports, general meeting reports, and the auditor's report.
3. Submit, after general meetings, a copy of the financial statement, a copy of the resolutions approved by the general meeting, a copy of the report of the board meeting, and a copy of the certified public accounts.
4. Submit unaudited statements to the stock exchange no later than two months after the end of each half year.
5. Publish details of any major changes that could affect the value of their shares.

NOTES

1. Carthage was founded in 814 B.C. by Queen Elyssa.
2. CIA Factbook web site at http://www.odci.gov/cia/publications/nsolo/factbook/ts.htm.
3. Ibid.
4. International Monetary Fund, Press Information Notice No. 97/3, 5 June 1997.
5. In 1993 and 1994, the authorities proceeded with structural reforms designed to liberalize the economy. See web site at http://www.idsonline.com/srouai/bct/imfra95.htm.
6. International Monetary Fund.
7. Ibid.
8. See web site at http://www.investintunisia.tn/html/diversification.html.
9. CIA Factbook web site.
10. The World Bank's criteria for middle-income classification is a GNP per capita of $766 to $9,385 in 1995. Tunisia's per capita GNP in 1995 was $1,820.
11. The Central Bank of Tunisia was created by Law No. 58–90 on September 19, 1958.

12. "Tunisia," *Middle East Economic Digest*, News Section, 2 January 1998, 25.

13. Samer Iskandar, "Stock Market, A Catalyst for Development," *Financial Times*, 22 September 1997, Survey—Tunisia 97, 4.

14. Tunis Stock Exchange Inaugurates New Trading System," *FIBV Web Site*, 24 April 1997. See http://www.fibv.com/Focus0424.htm.

15. *Emerging Stock Markets Factbook 1997* (Washington, D.C.: International Finance Corporation, 1997).

16. "Tunis Stock Exchange Continued to Fall," Info-Prod Research (Middle East) Ltd., *Middle East News Items*, 3 August 1997.

17. IFC, *Factbook*.

18. Ibid.

19. Ibid.

20. "Arab Stock Exchanges Unite to Build Clearinghouse," Institutional Investor, Inc., *Global Money Management*, 23 June 1997, S1.

21. "New Economic Measures Announced by the President," Africa News Service, Inc., *Africa News*, 31 December 1996. Previous limits on foreign ownership restricted foreigners to 10 percent of a company listed on the exchange and 30 percent of an unlisted company without central bank approval.

22. Tunisia Foreign Investment web site at http://www.investintunisia.tn/html/diversification.html.

ZAMBIA

COUNTRY

The Republic of Zambia has an area of 290,586 square miles (752,614 square kilometers). For comparative purposes, the country is slightly larger than the state of Texas. The capital is Lusaka.

Evidence from archaeological excavations indicates that early humans were in present-day Zambia between 1 and 2 million years ago. About 2,000 years ago, early Iron Age settlers were in the region. Modern peoples came in the seventeenth and eighteenth centuries from neighboring Zaire and Angola. The Portuguese established trading outposts in the early eighteenth century, and in 1851 David Livingstone reached the upper Zambezi River and discovered Victoria Falls (1855) and subsequently explored the region. During the 1890s, most of the Zambian chiefs concluded treaties with the British South Africa Company. Consequently, the company administered the region until 1924, when it became a British protectorate. From 1911 to 1964 the territory was known as Northern Rhodesia.

An independence movement was begun in the early 1950s by the United National Independence Party (UNIP) and the African National Congress. Independence was granted in 1964.

Official Religion	None[1]
Religion	Christian, 50% to 75%; Muslim and Hindu, 24% to 49%; indigenous beliefs, 1% (Many participants practice more than one religion making exact estimates difficult.)
Population	9,159,072 (July 1996 est.)[2]
	Urban 42%
	Rural 58%
	Population under the age of 15: 48%
Ethnic Divisions	African 98.7%, European 1.1%, other 0.2%
Languages	English (official), Bemba, Kaonda, Lozi, Lunda, Luvale, Nyanja, Tonga, and about seventy other indigenous languages
Education	Population over the age of 15 who are literate: 78%

The Political System

The nation is a multiparty republic with a unicameral legislature, the National Assembly. Upon independence in 1964, the United National Independence Party (UNIP) took power and Kenneth Kaunda became president. In 1973 a new constitution ensured the one-party system. Constitutional amendments permitting opposition parties were signed into law in 1990. In 1991, Kaunda and his party were defeated by the Movement for Multiparty Democracy (MMD). With a peaceful transition, Frederick Chiluba became the next President. Chiluba has served as Chief of State since October 31, 1991. The last election was held on November 18, 1996, and Chiluba received 70.2 percent of the vote, with the leading opposition candidate, Mungomba receiving 12.1 percent. The next election is scheduled for November 2001. The National Assembly has 159 members; 150 members are elected for a five-year term in single-seat constituencies, 8 members are appointed, and one is the Speaker. In the November 1996 elections, the MMD captured 127 seats, or 60.8 percent.

Political Web Site   http://www.geocities.com/~derksen/election.htm

Legal System

The Zambian legal system is based on English common law and customary law. The Zambian courts conduct a judicial review of legislative acts in an ad hoc constitutional council. Zambia has not accepted compulsory ICJ jurisdiction.

Suffrage is at eighteen years of age and is universal.

The Economy[3]

At independence, Zambia pursued a laissez-faire economic policy. In 1968 the founding President, Kenneth Kaunda, pursued the principles of African Socialism, which he called "Humanism." In 1969 the government began a policy of nationalization, beginning with the copper industry. By 1975, the state controlled almost 80 percent of the economy. In the 1960s and 1970s, to the detriment of its own economy, the country participated in sanctions against white-led Rhodesia.

The focus of the economy has been predominantly on mining, but the agriculture potential is significant.[4] Declining copper revenues resulted in growing discontent. With the election of a new government in 1991, privatization was pursued as a government policy. At that time, the state assets were earning an average return of less than 5 percent, with inflation over 200 percent. Economic indicators demonstrate the cyclical nature of Zambia's economics from negative to positive real GDP growth.

Economic Indicators[5]

Despite continuing progress in privatization and budgetary reform, Zambia's economy is showing little improvement. Inflation, while slowing somewhat, continues to be a major concern. Inflation for 1997 was 18.6 percent and by October 1997, the commercial bank base rate was 42 percent, while yields on ninety-one-day treasury bills were 21.4 percent. Four of Zambia's twenty banks collapsed in 1995, and the nation's debt stood at about $7 billion. The total external debt was 195 percent of GDP in 1996. Zambia's copper mining sector, which accounts for over 80 percent of the nation's foreign currency proceeds, is facing lower production rates and declining prices.

Indicator	1991	1992	1993	1994	1995	1996
Real GDP Growth Rate	0.0	−1.8	6.8	−8.6	−4.3	6.4
Inflation Rate	93.4	191.3	187.3	53.3	46.0	35.2
FDI as % of GDP	1.0	—	—	1.3	2.8	3.9
Total external debt as % of GDP	212.5	213.7	206.7	202.0	193.9	194.6
Central Bank Discount Rate	—	47.0	72.5	59.1	48.2	63.1
Prime Lending rate	—	54.6	113.3	70.6	45.5	54.2

Gross Domestic Product[6]

Zambia is classified as a low-income country under the World Bank's classification of economies.[7] For comparability, GDP is expressed in purchase power parity terms. Recognizing the population growth rate, per capita GDP has declined from 1991 levels.

GDP purchasing power parity	$8.9 billion (1995 est.)
GDP real growth rate	6.4%
GDP per capita	$900 (1995 est.)

Central Bank: Bank of Zambia

Postal Address

Bank of Zambia
P.O. Box 30080
Bank Square
Cairo Road
Lusaka
Zambia
Tel.: +260–1–228888/896 or + 260–1–229885
Fax: +260–1–221791 or +260–1–226844

Credit Rating

Zambia has not been rated by international rating agencies for either domestic or foreign currency debt.

Currency

Monetary unit   Zambian kwacha (K) = 100 ngwee

The Zambian kwacha is an independently floating currency. The Exchange Control Act was repealed in 1994. A forward market exists up to three months. As of September 24, 1997, the exchange rate for the Zambian kwacha was 1324 per dollar. Further exchange rates are as follows: Zambian kwacha per US$1–1,427.50 (December 1997), 1,297.00 (December 1996), 909.09 (December 1995), 833.33 (1995), 769.23 (1994), 434.78 (1993), 156.25 (1992), 61.7284 (1991).

There are a number of web sites providing updated currency exchange values. The following is an example:

http://www.bloomberg.com/markets/currency/currcalc.cgi

Privatization

The government is moving forward with efforts to transform the economy into a market-oriented economy. The Zambia Privatization Agency (ZPA), created in June 1992, is responsible for evaluating bidders for the state-owned enterprises that are to be privatized. As of June 30, 1997, forty companies were ready for privatization or under negotiation and thirty-one more are being prepared. There are renewed interests in foreign investment in Zambia on account of its structural adjustment programs, which include plans to privatize numerous state-owned enterprises.[8]

The government pursued privatization as a means to make resource allocation more optimal, to reduce the drain on national finances from the losses of the parastatals, to introduce market-based efficiencies into the economy, to secure better access to foreign technological transfers, and to develop capital markets. The first initial public offering of shares by a parastatal, Chilanga Cement, took place in 1995.

The government's plans were to privatize all 275 state-owned enterprises over a period of five years.[9] Within the first four years of the program, 157 companies have been privatized. A further nine companies have reached the stage of Heads of Agreement, thirty-one more are under negotiation as of December 1996, and fifty-nine more are due for privatization in 1997. The government has promulgated regulations and procedures to ensure the fairness and transparency of the privatization process. The ZPA, representing the government as seller, aims to secure the highest price on the open market. The ZPA also arranges for independent valuations of SOEs to provide additional support to the assessment of the market value of the SOE. The purpose is to eliminate the possibility of underpricing. In addition, the ZPA's aim of negotiating for the highest possible price is strengthened by conducting negotiations through independent negotiating teams as provided under Section 32 of the Privatization Act.

To select a buyer, the ZPA considers the consistency with privatization principles and objectives, the potential for new private-sector economic development, the operational considerations and constraints, and the financial value of the offer. The privatization process is designed to encourage individual and institutional share ownership.

A typical example of the privatization efforts was the listing on June 9, 1997 of Zambian Breweries PLC on the Lusaka Stock Exchange. The government floated the residual of 13 million shares held by the government to complete the company's privatization. The flotation was oversubscribed by 61 percent and attracted 1,825 new first-time investors and shareholders. On its first day of trading, the shares traded at K200 per share, an increase of 33 percent on the offer price of K150 per share. For the week ending September 25, 1997, the shares were up 67 percent over the listing price. The bid–ask spread for the shares was 4 percent.

The greatest privatization process ahead is the Zambia Consolidated Copper Mines (ZCCM). Zambia is the fourth largest copper producer in the world; however, due to the lack of investment in new equipment and technology, production has declined from 720 thousand tons in 1969 to less than 400 thousand tons in 1996. ZCCM is listed on the London Stock Exchange and has a current market capitalization of $400 million. The transition involves unbundling of the conglomerate into nine autonomous units for separate sale to major international mining houses. ZCCM will retain a minority shareholding in each privatized unit, but the government will later divest its 60.7 percent holding in ZCCM, leaving the copper mining industry totally private in 1998. In March 1997 the government received twenty-seven bids from fifteen international mining companies for the copper concern. Investment information can be obtained from the following sources:

Zambia Investment Centre
P.O. Box 34580
Lusaka
Tel.:   +260 1 2521 30
Fax: +260 1 252150
E-mail: invest@zamnet.zm
Zambia Investment Agency
P.O. Box 30819
Lusaka
Tel.: +260 1 223858   Fax: +260 1 227250

E-mail: zpa@zamnet.zm

Privatization Web Site   http://www.pangaeapartners.com/zampriv.htm

THE STOCK EXCHANGE: LUSAKA STOCK EXCHANGE

The government established the Lusaka Stock Exchange (LuSE) to enhance the private sector's financial and capital markets and to attract foreign investment. Thus, the exchange serves an important function in the government's privatization program. The number of firms listed on the Lusaka Stock Exchange remained constant from 1995 to 1996. However, trading volume increased from $300,000 in 1995 to $2.8 million in 1996.[10]

Lusaka Stock Exchange, Ltd.
Mr. Charles Mate, General Manager
Lusaka Stock Exchange Building
Private Bag E 731, Lusaka, Zambia
Cairo Road
P.O. Box 34523
Lusaka
Zambia

Tel.: (260–1) 228 391/537/594   Fax: (260–1) 225 969

E-Mail: luse@zamet.zm

Web Sites: http://www.zamnet.zm/zamnet/zambus/luse/luse1.htm
                       http://www.africa.cis.co.za/achill/zambia/busbul/stock.html

The weekly Lusaka Stock Exchange market report from Pangaea Securities can be found at http://www.pangaeapartners.com/zchart.htm.

Established	1993
	Trading began February 21, 1994
	Officially opened April 27, 1995
Trading Days	Monday to Friday
Trading Hours	10:00–12:00
	The international time zone is GMT + 2.

Market Index

The LuSE established two indexes, an all-share index and a free-float index, on January 2, 1997. Neither index includes ZCCM, which, though contributing 61 percent of the market capitalization, trades very intermittently because there are only 10,000 shares in the LuSE depository. The free-float index seeks to reflect those shares that are considered accessible to investors and not "locked up" through institutional or individual holdings.

Instruments Traded

Equities, corporate debentures, and government bonds are traded. There are currently no derivative products traded and the exchange has no plans to institute them.

Bond Market

The Zambian financial markets offer short-term debt instruments that have little to no default risk, low price risk, and fair marketability. The Bank of Zambia issues treasury bills on behalf of the Zambian government on a discount basis. The bills are available on both a competitive and a noncompetitive basis. Prices are established in a weekly treasury bill auction.

The LuSE opened its market to trading in bonds on August 9, 1995. The Bank of Zambia lists two types of bonds for trading: government auction bonds and statutory reserve bonds. Auction bonds are one-year issues on behalf of the government. Interest income and capital gains on the bonds are not subject to withholding tax. Statutory reserve bonds are held by commercial banks and are variable rate interest bonds. The first offering is to be redeemed in twelve tranches between February 1, 1996 and November 2, 1998. The creation of a secondary market to list and trade government bonds will assist in developing financial and capital markets and improve the liquidity in the financial system. In addition, the long-term securities assist in developing capital markets yield curves and longer-term sources of domestic capital. Bond trading settlement can be on a T+1 settlement. On request, settlement can be achieved on trade date as well. Commissions are fully negotiable and an indicative scale is 0.75 percent, with 0.15 percent going to the exchange.

The LuSE is a centralized exchange. Thus, securities of public companies that are not listed are also quoted and traded on a second tier market within the Lusaka Stock Exchange.

STOCK MARKET ACTIVITY

Trading Structure

There is a single price auction mechanism at the opening of the market, and continuous order matching thereafter.

Market Valuation[11]

Year	Price–Earnings Ratio	Dividend Yield
1995	6.6	2.5
1996	8.4	6.9

The 27-percent increase in the market's price–earnings ratio from 1995 to 1996 reflects the markets willingness to pay a higher multiple for a firm's cash flow. Average dividend yields increased significantly as well. By March 1998, the average dividend yield had declined to 5.51 percent with a PE ratio of 5.79.

Number of Listed Firms and Market Capitalization[12]

Year	Number of Firms	Market Capitalization (U.S. Millions)
1994	7	—
1995	8	436
1996	8	229

While the number of listed firms remained constant in 1996, the market capitalization declined 47.5 percent, reflecting the performance of the stock exchange. At the end of 1996 there were no foreign firms listed on the exchange.

Liquidity

The exchange's first trade took place on March 1, 1994, in Standard Chartered Bank shares. Trading took some time to establish itself, as five trades for a total volume of 15,185 shares in Standard Chartered Bank took place in March 1994, with prices moving from K100 to K84 per share. Additional firms were added to the exchange in May, June, and August. By September, trading activity had increased with the full introduction on the exchange of three collective schemes run by Meridien Financial Services. The number of trades increased from 116 in August to 208 in October. In its first year of operation, to the end of December 1994, a total of 3,934,020 shares were traded on total turnover of K255.658 million and 977 trades. Full-year results for 1995 were 898 trades on a volume of 7,917,400 shares and a turnover value of 216.7 million. The 1996 results show an increase to 1,376 trades, 241,001,900 shares, and a turnover value of K3,428,160,378. For the week of September 19, 1997, there was record trading volume on the Lusaka Stock Exchange, with more than 35,000,000 Standard Chartered Bank shares worth K402 million ($303,625) changing hands on Monday. Average daily trading volume for 1995 was approximately $1,360, increasing to $12,725 in 1996.

Brokerage Rates

For equities, 1.25 percent is the rate charged by the broker. Of this amount, 0.25 percent goes to the exchange. For bonds, the rate is 0.75 percent, with 0.15 percent going to the exchange.

Custody Services

Two local banks meet the U.S. Securities and Exchange Commission's 17f5 requirements concerning custodial stands. Barclays Bank of Zambia Limited (P.O. Box 31936, Lusaka, tel.: 228858) is the subcustodian of the Lusaka Stock Exchange. The bank provides custodial services to foreign funds investing in Zambia.

Trading Shares on the LuSE

Domestic investors must contact any broker who is a member of the stock exchange. Foreign investors have the choice of contacting a broker directly or transacting through a subcustodian. Barclays Global Securities Services coordinates the link into Barclays Bank Zambia, which provides subcustody services in the LuSE depository.

Insider Trading

Insider trading is illegal.

Dividends and Capital Gains Taxation

There are no capital gains taxes. Taxes are withheld on dividend inome at the 15 percent rate. There is a property transfer tax of 2.5 percent deductible on proceeds from disposal of unlisted securities.

Regulatory Controls

The Securities Act of 1993 established the Securities and Exchange Commission (SEC). The SEC has powers to regulate and supervise the securities industry in Zambia. The regulatory powers of the commission have four major requirements:

1. Any person dealing or advising on securities must be licensed by the SEC.
2. Any securities market must be licensed as a securities exchange by the SEC.
3. All securities of a public company which are publicly traded must be registered by the SEC.
4. Collective investment schemes must be authorized by the SEC.

Foreign Investment Restrictions

To facilitate investment on the exchange, there are no exchange controls, no restrictions on shareholding levels, and no restrictions on foreign ownership. However, in the privatization of a parastatal local investors will be given preference. Dividends can be remitted in full.

Central Depository

The exchange was established with the mandatory use of a central share depository system.

Settlement

The exchange conforms to G30 recommendations, with a manual order matching system with automated clearing and settlement. Settlement is T+3 by book entry. There is a trade-for-trade netting, clearing, and settlement process.

Voting

Voting by proxy is permitted. Foreign shareholders enjoy the same rights as domestic shareholders.

INTERNET RESOURCES

Government

Government of the Republic of Zambia at http://www.zamnet.zm/zamnet/grz/govstate.html, provides official statements and press summaries.

Business

Zambian Investment Centre at http://www.zamnet.zm/zamnet/zambus/zic/zichome.html, has investment information, investment guarantees, and social economic indicators.

Export Board of Zambia at http://www.zamnet.zm/zamnet/zambus/ebz/ebz.htm, includes trade regulations, monetary and banking system, and a list of export companies.

Lusaka Stock Exchange at http://www.zamnet.zm/zamnet/zambus/luse/luse1.htm, has highlights, stock news, background, bond market, and the design and structure of the Zambian securities market.

Ernst and Young Investment Profile at http://mbendi.co.za/ernsty/cyzaeyip.htm, provides general background information on Zambia, including procedures on how to establish a business, taxation, and incentives. Maintained by a private entity, Mbendi.

Information Services

Telecommunications Sector Profile for Zambia at http://rtr.worldweb.net/zambia.htm.

News

The *Post* at http://www.zamnet.zm/zamnet/post/ post.html, is Zambia's leading independent newspaper.

Times of Zambia at http://www.zamnet.zm/zamnet/times/times.html.

Zambia Daily Mail at http://www.zamnet/zadama/zadama.html.

Zambia Today at http://www.zamnet.zm/zamnet/zana/zamtoday.html, is a compilation of news stories published by the Zambian media.

INTRODUCTION TO THE LUSAKA STOCK EXCHANGE[13]

Background to LuSE

The Lusaka Stock Exchange was established with preparatory technical assistance from the International Finance Corporation and the World Bank in 1993. The exchange opened on February 21, 1994. In their first two years of operation, the UNDP and the government of Zambia funded the LuSE and Securities and Exchange Commission as a project on financial and capital market development in Zambia under the multicomponent private-sector development program. The LuSE is made up of stockbroking corporate members and is incorporated as a nonprofit limited liability company. Currently, there are six members of the exchange. Three firms handle most trades, but by value of the trades Pangaea Securities Zambia handles by far the bulk of the transactions.

Role

The formation of the exchange is part of the government's economic reform program aimed at developing the financial and capital market in order to support and enhance private-sector initiative. The Lusaka Stock Exchange is also expected to attract foreign portfolio investment through recognition of Zambia and the region as an emerging capital market with potentially high investment returns. Another important role of the exchange is to facilitate the divestiture of government ownership in parastatals and realization of the objectives of creating a broad and wide shareholding ownership by the citizenry via a fair and transparent process.

Modern Stock Exchange

With this in mind, the Lusaka Stock Exchange has been set up as a modern stock exchange based on the most current international standards and practices. These include, for example, the following: use of a central share depository system, a trade-for-trade netting clearing, and settlement process, a rolling settlement three days after the trade (T+3), and the exchange meets G30 recommendations for clearing and settlements system design and operation.

Strong Investor Protection Legislation and Centralized Market

Supporting legislation enacted as the Securities Act No. 38 of 1993 backs up the rules and listing requirements of the LuSE. The Securities Act regulates the entire Zambian securities market and is specifically designed to ensure adequate investor protection and support the operation of a free, orderly, fair, secure, and properly informed securities market. The act creates and defines a central market in which both unlisted and listed securities trade on the exchange, as opposed to the dual market system.

A compensation fund was established under the act and is designed to compensate persons who suffer a pecuniary loss occasioned by default of a licensed dealer or licensed investment advisor. The compensation fund is a mechanism aimed at creating investor confidence in case of default by the dealer or investment advisers, which otherwise would lead to investors losing confidence in the securities industry in Zambia.

Fiscal Investment Incentives

Several incentives have been put in place to promote rapid development of the capital market in Zambia. These include the following: no exchange controls, no restrictions on shareholding levels, no restrictions on foreign ownership, no capital gains tax, corporate income tax reduced to 30 percent for companies listed on the LuSE, and no property transfer tax on listed securities.

DESIGN AND STRUCTURE OF THE SECURITIES MARKET

Publicly Traded Securities

The Securities Act No. 38 of 1993 defines publicly traded securities as those of a public company that has more than fifty shareholders or those that the SEC has, by notice, declared to be publicly traded. Under the act, all such companies are required to register their securities with the SEC and are required to submit annual reports and accounts to the commission.

They are also obliged to report to the SEC any facts concerning the company that may affect the value of the shares.

Central Market System

The Zambian securities market has been designed as a "unified market," where virtually all trading is conducted through a stock exchange. This is in contrast to the "dual market" system, in which only selected stocks are listed and traded on the exchange (sometimes referred to as the organized exchange or exchange market), and the balance is traded off the exchange as unlisted stocks (usually referred to as traded over-the-counter and sometimes called a decentralized market). The central market design of the Zambia market means that securities of public companies that are not listed are also quoted and traded on a second tier market within the Lusaka Stock Exchange.

Advantages of a Central Market

There are several advantages to the unified market system. First, it channels all trading activity through one market. This enhances liquidity and market depth. Liquidity is the ability to buy or sell both quickly and without substantially moving prices. Market depth refers to the ability to transact at the current market price and is particularly important when large volumes are involved. Both liquidity and market depth ultimately dictate the success or failure of a market. Thus, centralizing the market is an effective method that attempts to compensate for the low volumes and thin trading activity so typical of infant and start-up stock markets. A central market creates the necessary critical mass to enhance market liquidity. Second, the unified market avoids duplication and makes more efficient use of natural resources. Third, it gives maximum transparency in securities dealing, reduces the opportunity for malpractice, and improves the reliability of pricing.

Price Discovery

The advantages of the centralized structure of the stock market in Zambia are borne out by the empirical evidence to date on the price formation of shares on the LuSE. The stock price movement charts show a general characteristic pattern of initially high market entry pricing followed by large significant drops in prices with increased trading activity and, over time, gradual leveling off to stable price movements. This pattern is particularly noticeable for example, in the price movement charts for Chilanga Cement, Rothmans, and Standard Bank.

The logical explanation for the initial downward trend in prices is that this represents the price discovery process of the market at work. Price discovery is being driven by the formalization of the market, namely a central market, regulation requirements, disclosure of company information, and the interplay of demand and supply. The net result is market transparency, which in turn improves market efficiency and price formation.

ZAMBIAN GOVERNMENT BOND MARKET

Zambian Treasury Bills

The Zambian financial markets offer short-term debt instruments that have (1) little to no default risk, (2) low price risk, and (3) fair marketability. The Bank of Zambia issues treasury bills on behalf of the Zambian government on a discount basis. The bills are available on both a competitive and a noncompetitive basis.

In the process of liberalizing the economy, the Bank of Zambia has now resorted to a competitive pricing policy, in which the price is established through a weekly tender process. Currently, treasury bills with a maturity period of 28, 91, and 182 days are available on an auction basis. Bidders must have their bids by Thursday at 10:00 for availability the following Monday.

There are two methods of purchasing treasury bills via Pangaea Securities: By competitive bids, the bank awards the highest prices (smallest discounts) first, in order to achieve the best possible interest rate. In this way, the bidders themselves determine interest rates on the treasury bills. By noncompetitive bids, non-auction bills are also available for "smaller" investors at each auction, with the rate determined on the basis of the average rate of the competitive bids. Noncompetitive bids may be made for amounts between Kw1 and 20 million.

Under the current legislation, the income earned on treasury bills is subject to a 15-percent withholding tax at the Bank of Zambia. The bills are rediscountable at the bank, at a penalty, but can also be traded in the market. They can also be used as collateral for obtaining loans. The current T-bill rates available are in the Pangaea Weekly Lusaka Stock Exchange Market Report.

Zambian Government Bonds

The Zambian financial markets also offer medium term debt instruments that have (1) little to no default risk, (2) low price risk, and (3) fair marketability. The Bank of Zambia, on behalf of the Zambian government, auctions government bonds with tenders of twelve and eighteen months. The tenders are normally held by 10:00 A.M. on a Tuesday, every four to six weeks, depending on the borrowing needs of the government. The size of each tender depends on the amount of money the government needs to raise. The results of the auction are communicated to the bidders on the Wednesday following the auction. The settlement is done three days after the auction on a Friday.

There are two methods of obtaining treasury bonds via Pangaea Securities: By competitive bids, the Bank of Zambia uses the Dutch Auction Tender System, in which successful competitive bidders receive the yield at which they bid. The minimum acceptable competitive bid is K20 million. There are no restrictions on the number of bids that a bidder may place. The bids are chosen starting with the lowest annual percentage yield. By noncompetitive bids, up to 10 percent of the tender on issue is reserved for noncompetitive bidders per auction. This is to facilitate the participation of small personal investors and range in amount from K1 million to K20 million. The noncompetitive bids are allocated at the weighted average yield struck in the competitive portion of the particular auction.

Semiannual coupon interest payments will be paid and the bonds will be redeemable upon maturity at the Bank of Zambia by physical presentation of the certificate. Interest income earned on the bonds is not subject to tax under the current legislation. The current bond rates available are in the Pangaea Weekly Lusaka Stock Exchange Market Report.

The bonds are transferable by endorsement at the Bank of Zambia and hence can be traded in the market. The bonds will be listed on the Lusaka Stock Exchange, and therefore there will be a central and market-based avenue for investors to liquidate the bonds before maturity if need arises. It will also provide other investors an opportunity to purchase bonds in an organized secondary market. However, buyers should be aware that the market is in its infancy and liquidity is currently limited.

Privatization and Its Objectives

The government has set privatization high on its policy agenda. The primary objective behind privatizing is to improve the efficiency of asset utilization, but other underlying objectives include reducing the drain on the government's fiscal resources; optimizing the use of the government's management resources; securing enhanced access to foreign market technologies and capital; widening the base of ownership (Zambian citizens are encouraged to buy shares in recently privatized blue chip companies at concessionary prices through the Lusaka Stock Exchange); increasing long-term job creation; reallocating assets tied up in parastatal enterprises to higher priority government expenditures such as social services and investment in human capital and national infrastructure; increasing the role of the private sector in the ownership and management of national economic resources; and stimulating capital market development.

Institutional Arrangements

The Zambia Privatization Agency was created by an Act of Parliament passed in June 1992. The members of the ZPA board are appointed by the president on recommendation by Parliament. Members of the private-sector-dominated board are drawn from a cross-section of society. The members of the ZPA board are responsible for approving recommendations made by the ZPA management. For each transaction, negotiating teams comprising an independent Chairman, a private lawyer, and at least two technical consultants from the ZPA staff assists management. A Zambian Chief Executive, recruited after an international executive search, is at the helm of ZPA and is assisted by a team of Zambian and expatriate (mainly American) technical consultants.

Total Divestiture

A Divestiture Sequence Plan, which has been revised four times, has been prepared so that the SOEs are divested in tranches. Small and medium-size companies were initially targeted for sale as the political and economic cost of mishandling their privatization was an acceptable risk. Moving up the learning curve, ZPA has subsequently graduated to the privatization of major industries and politically sensitive institutions. The ZPA has now begun the privatization of Zambia Consolidated Copper Mines, the largest company in the eighteen-country Common Market of Eastern and Southern Africa region.

Competition

One of the main objectives for the privatization program is fostering competition. Under the program the following principles are applied:

1. Private monopolies are discouraged; where they are unavoidable, the soon to be enacted Competition Act will provide regulations for fair trading.
2. Where possible, SOEs are broken up into their component parts to provide competition in the industry in which they operate (an example is Zambia Breweries).
3. Protectionist policies are not condoned.

Transparency

The following provisions in the act achieve the transparency of the program:

- Negotiations are carried out by a team of independent negotiators appointed by the agency for each sale. Such appointments give due consideration to professional qualification, experience, and business standing.
- The ZPA publishes the following information in the *Government Gazette*:

  1. The names of the approved SOEs to be privatized.
  2. The names of registered consultants, valuers, merchant bankers, advocates, and public accountants.
  3. The bidders and the bid prices.

4. The successful bidder(s) and the reason for selection of such bidder(s).

5. The price of shares and any special conditions of the sale of shares.

Valuation and Pricing

Section 22 (2) of the Privatization Act provides for each SOE to be sold at its market value, defined as that price agreed between a willing buyer and seller. The ZPA, which represents the state as seller, aims to secure the highest price on the open market. The ZPA also arranges for independent valuations of SOEs to provide additional support to the assessment of the market value of the SOE. The purpose is to eliminate the possibility of underpricing the SOE. In addition, the ZPA's aim of negotiating for the highest possible price is strengthened by conducting negotiations through independent negotiating teams as provided under Section 32 of the Privatization Act.

Considerations Used when Selecting a Buyer

The criteria for evaluating the tender offers received can differ from one case to another. Tenders from bidders are evaluated on the basis of specific criteria announced in advance and can include some or all of the following: consistency with privatization principles and objectives, protection of the public interest, the bidder's commitment to continue operating the business, competition or transfer of monopoly, extent to which the proposal offers job protection or retrenchment to employees, the bidder's intention to offer expanded or related services, the bidder's bringing in foreign exchange for the investment, potential for new private-sector economic development, proposed preliminary business plan for upgrading the performance of the company, and the potential for private-sector activity and job creation.

Freedoms of a Privatized Company

A sales agreement signed by the seller and purchaser marks the change from an SOE to a private company. Each party to the agreement has the responsibility to honor his or her obligations. The purchasers are accorded all rights and freedoms of normal private commercial operators, except to honor the commitments embedded in the sales agreement. Specifically, no requirements are imposed on new owners regarding future production and sales. New owners also have the authority to set the optimal size and composition of their labor force.

Post-Privatization Monitoring

The objective of privatization is to bring about a turnaround in the enterprise's performance, thereby leading to economic development. Areas of followup to determine the impact of privatization will include the impact on public-sector borrowing requirements, new employment creation, improvement in the quality of goods and services, impact on prices, impact on industrial relations and other welfare issues, and the overall impact on productivity, capital formation, and balance of payments.

Privatization Modes of Sale

The ZPA recommends various options for privatizing SOEs for Cabinet approval. In certain cases, it may be appropriate for the government to determine modes of sale without any recommendations. The modes of sale employed by the ZPA include public offering of shares, private sale of shares through negotiated or competitive bids, offer of additional shares in an SOE to minority shareholders, sale of assets or business of the SOE, reorganization of the SOE before sale of the whole or part of it, and lease or management contracts.

THE FUTURE

The Zambian privatization program has achieved an exemplary record of success in terms of political acceptance, attraction of foreign and domestic capital into the acquisition of SOEs, transparency and accountability, and the retention of employment in the newly privatized companies. It is now common knowledge that the companies awaiting privatization are shedding more jobs than those which have been privatized.

The economy will begin to recover when there is a fresh injection of capital into the productive sectors. The $20-million sale of the Zambia Sugar Company to Tate & Lyle PLC, $7-million sale of a commercial farm to the Commonwealth Development Corporation, and the impending privatizations of Zamtel, a portion of the Electricity Supply Company, and the copper mines will compel the infusion of hundreds of millions of dollars in purchase consideration and new investment that will help reinvigorate an economy in slumber. The future for Zambia looks bright and the privatization process will remain the beacon.

NOTES

1. CIA Factbook web site at http://www.odci.gov/cia/publications/nsolo/factbook/za.htm.

2. Ibid.

3. Pangaea Partners, Ltd., Economic Overview, July 1997, at http://www.pangaeapartners.com/zampriv.htm. Used by permission.

4. Only 15 percent of the arable land is under cultivation at present. The land has abundant water resources, holding 45 percent of the Southern African region's water resources.

5. Bank of Zambia. See web site at http://www.zamnet.zm/zamnet/zambus/luse/statis.htm.

6. CIA Factbook web site.

7. The World Bank's criterion for low-income classification is a GNP per capita of less than $765 in 1995. Zambia's per capita GNP in 1995 was $400.

8. U.S. Department of Commerce, ITA, *1996 Country Commercial Guide for Zambia* (Washington, D.C.: U.S. Government Printing Office, National Trade Data Bank, 1995).

9. Pangaea Partners, Ltd., Economic Overview.

10. Neither the information nor any opinion expressed constitutes an offer to buy or sell any securities or options or futures. Pangaea Partners (Zambia) Limited, Pangaea Securities Limited, their affiliates, directors, officers, and employees may have long or short positions in Zambian securities including T-bills and T-bonds.

11. LuSE Weekly Stock News. See web site at http://www.zamnet.zm/zamnet/zambus/luse/luse6.htm. Used by permission.

12. Ibid.

13. The material from the stock exchange web site is used by permission of the LuSE and is illustrative of the development of emerging markets in an age of technological access. The discussion on Zambia's privatization program is adapted from the Pangaea Partners web site (used by permission). Pangaea Partners provides expert investment banking and financial consulting services in emerging markets. Founded in 1989, the firm has offices in six countries and specializes in projects involving fundraising or financial advice, privatization and merger and acquisition (M&A) transactions for buyers and sellers, capital markets development, and consulting services and training for commercial and export banks in emerging markets, such as those in the former Soviet Union, Africa, the Middle East, and the Caribbean.

ZIMBABWE

COUNTRY

The Republic of Zimbabwe has an area of 150,873 square miles (390,759 square kilometers). For comparison, the country's landmass is slightly larger than that of Montana. The official language is English, though Shona is more widely spoken. The population is rural, with only one-fourth living in an urban setting. The capital is Harare (once known as Salisbury).

The British South Africa Company was formed in 1889 by Cecil Rhodes to colonize and promote regional trade. In 1922, the Europeans chose to become a British colony rather than join the Union of South Africa. The British crown annexed Southern Rhodesia in 1923. In 1965, the white Rhodesian Front government unilaterally declared its independence from Britain, resulting in economic sanctions during the 1960s and 1970s. After a decade of struggle, the white minority government consented to hold multiracial elections in 1980. Robert Mugabe of the Zanu-PF party won the elections. From 1911 to 1964, Zimbabwe was known as Southern Rhodesia, from 1964 to 1979 as Rhodesia, and from 1979 to 1980, Zimbabwe Rhodesia. From independence in 1980 it has been formally known as the Republic of Zimbabwe.

Official Religion	None[1]
Religions	Syncretic (part Christian, part indigenous beliefs) 50%, Christian 25%, indigenous beliefs 24%, other 1%
Population	11,271,000 (1996 est.)
	Urban 26%
	Rural 74%
	Population under the age of 15: 44%
Ethnic Divisions	African 98% (Shona 71%, Ndebele 16%, other 11%), white 1%, mixed and Asian 1%
Languages	English (official), Shona, Sindebele (the language of the Ndebele, sometimes called Ndebele), numerous minor tribal dialects
Education	Population over age 15 who are literate: 85%

The Political System

The nation is an independent republic, with the president as head of state and a unicameral legislature. The Legislature of Zimbabwe consists of an Executive President and Parliament, which comprises a House of Assembly.

Parliament has a maximum life of five years after which it is automatically dissolved. Elections were held in May 1995 and gave President Robert Mugabe's ruling Zanu–PF party a five-year mandate. The Zanu–PF party has ruled the country since independence in 1980. In the 1995 elections, the party ran unopposed in 55 of 120 elected seats. The president nominates thirty MPs, including ten "traditional leaders" and eight provincial governors.

The president is elected by the legislature to a six-year term. Mugabe has ruled since December 31, 1987. Mugabe stood for reelection as executive president in 1996. The president, in consultation with the Judicial Service Commission, appoints the judiciary.

Legal System

The Zimbabwean legal system is a mixture of Roman–Dutch and English common law.

Suffrage is at eighteen years of age and is universal.

The Economy

Zimbabwe began its significant structural adjustment program in 1991. However, real progress was only apparent in 1993 when exchange control and foreign payments were liberalized. Other structural adjustments were made in price deregulation, labor laws, investment regulation, and the commercialization of some state enterprises. As part of the adjustment program, interest rates were allowed to respond to the market and foreign exchange in the Zimbabwean dollar was partially floated. The partial flotation lead to a 17-percent devaluation of the currency in January 1994. In addition, quantitative import controls were lifted. Portfolio investment was liberalized in 1993 when foreign investors were permitted to trade on the stock exchange. After the liberalization, foreign direct investment increased threefold, from $20 million to more than $60 million a year.

The economy's performance is dependent upon weather conditions. The 1991–1992 and 1994–1995 droughts adversely impacted the country's agricultural production. In 1997, the market experienced significant drought fears from El Niño, the phenomenon of water warming in the southeastern Pacific Ocean that disrupts weather patterns. Zimbabwe also has rich mineral deposits. Gold, nickel, asbestos, coal, copper, chrome, iron ore, silver, and tin are mined.

From independence in 1980, real GDP growth has been at an annual 2.8-percent rate, below the annual population growth rate of 3.1 percent. Consequently, real income is lower now than at independence. The country experiences a significant debt problem, with the national debt estimated at 95 percent of GDP in 1995. More than 23 percent of the budget is devoted to paying the interest on the national debt. In September 1997, Barclays

Bank, in its bulletin, indicated a slowdown in economic growth with GDP between 4 and 5 percent.[2]

Gross Domestic Product[3]

GDP purchasing power parity	$18.1 billion (1995 est.)
GDP real growth rate	2.4% (1995)
GDP per capita	$1,620 (1995 est.)
Unemployment Rate	At least 30% (1997 est.)

Inflation Rate

The consumer price inflation rate in 1995 was 25.8 percent.[4] Inflation dropped in August 1997 to 17.99 percent for the month, down from 19.1 percent in July 1997. The inflationary decline was the result of a drop in the food component of the basket used to measure consumer price changes. Inflation has been on a downward trend despite the inflationary pressures inherent in the economy.

Central Bank: Reserve Bank of Zimbabwe

Negative real interest rates were experience by the market for most of the 1980s and the early 1990s, until the reserve bank introduced real positive rates of interest in mid-1993.

Postal Address

Reserve Bank of Zimbabwe
P.O. Box 1283
76 Samora Machel Avenue
Harare
Zimbabwe
Tel.: 263–4–790731, 263–4–729071, 263–4–739701 or 263–4–796251
Fax: 263–4–739787, 263–4–708976, or 263–4–707800

Currency

Monetary unit   Zimbabwe dollar (Z$) = 100 cents

The Zimbabwe dollar is a freely floating currency. Though some accounts are blocked, these are sums that were invested before independence in 1979, when sanctions were in place. A forward market exists up to six months. Zimbabwe has experienced a stable real exchange rate, however the currency was devalued in 1991 and 1994. Exchange rates are as follows:

Zimbabwe dollars per US$1–9.3633 (January 1996), 8.6580 (1995), 8.1500 (1994), 6.4725 (1993), 5.0942 (1992), 3.4282 (1991). In 1997, the stability of the Zimbabwe dollar was threatened by the uncertainty of the government's plan to pay Z$4 billion ($270 million) in pensions to veterans of the independence struggle. By November 1997, the local currency collapsed, trading at Z$25 to the U.S. dollar, depreciating 23 percent for the year. By year end 1997, the rate was Z$17 to the U.S. dollar.

There are a number of web sites providing updated currency exchange values. The following is an example:

http://www.bloomberg.com/markets/currency/currcalc.cgi

Privatization

Significant privatization has been delayed in Zimbabwe, as many parastatals need recapitalization and restructuring before they can be effectively sold. In 1996 the government disposed of $564 million worth of its holdings. The typical listed firm has a capital structure of 70 percent equity and 30 percent debt. The government has articulated a goal of attracting as many shareholders as possible to privatizations. Reflecting the nature of the challenge the state faces in transitioning its economy, it was reported that during 1996 parastatals had operating losses of $1.3 billion.

In August 1997, Zimbabwe conducted the privatization initial public offer (IPO) of the Commercial Bank of Zimbabwe. This was the country's second IPO, following the ten-times oversubscribed offer of 15 percent of Dairibord Zimbabwe Limited in July 1997.[5] In the offering, domestic investors received an allocation of 27 percent of the shares, 26 percent was reserved for private investors and the National Investment Trust, and a 25-percent block was designated for a strategic partner. Employees can receive up to 2 percent. The firm's shares will be traded on the over-the-counter market initially. The offer was one-and-a-half times oversubscribed.

The privatization of the Cotton Company of Zimbabwe (COTTCO) in September 1997 illustrates the distribution of shares in an initial public offering. The government retained a 25-percent position in the company, listing 75 percent of its stake on the exchange. Small cotton growers were offered 20 percent of the company's total shareholding, while commercial farmers were offered 10 percent. In addition, employees received 5 percent, the National Investment Trust received 10 percent, institutional investors received 15 percent, and the general public (domestic investors) received 15 percent.[6] The shares will be listed on the stock exchange in December 1997. It is estimated the government would realize in excess of $1.9 billion in privatizing its major holdings.

Markets received a boost on September 8, 1997, when the government directed pension funds with more than $25 billion worth of assets to invest at least 10 percent of their portfolio with Africa Resources Investments, which was formed by the government as a vehicle for black economic empowerment. This development, which has surprised the entire pension industry, comes after a 15 percent profits tax introduced in the July budget. It comes just four months after the government reduced from 55 percent to 45 percent the amount of money insurance companies and pension funds are required by law to invest in prescribed assets.[7]

THE STOCK EXCHANGE: ZIMBABWE STOCK EXCHANGE

The first stock exchange in Zimbabwe opened its doors very soon after the arrival of the pioneer column in Bulawayo. It was, however, only operative for about six years, from 1896 to the end of the South African War. Other exchanges were established in Gwelo and Umtall, the former now only remembered by the name of the building which housed it. The latter, also founded in 1896, thrived on the success of local mining, but with the realization that deposits in the area were not extensive, activity declined and it closed in 1924. After World War II, a new exchange was founded in Bulawayo and dealing started on January 2, 1946. A second floor was opened in Salisbury in December 1951, and these two centers, trading by telephone, continued operating until it was decided that legislation should be enacted to govern the rights and obligations of both members of the exchange and the general investing public. The Zimbabwe Stock Exchange Act took some five years from the first draft until it reached the statutes book in January 1974. The members of the exchange continued to trade as before, but it became necessary for legal reasons to bring into being a new exchange coincidental with the passing of the legislation. The present exchange, the Zimbabwe Stock Exchange (ZSE) dates from the passing of the act in 1974.

Mr. Mark Tunmer
Chairman
Zimbabwe Stock Exchange
8th Floor Southhampton House, First Street
P.O. Box UA 234
Union Avenue
Harare
Zimbabwe
Tel.: (263–4) 736 861/791 045   Fax: (263–4) 791 045, (263–4) 70–8368

Web Sites   http://www.africa.co.uk/exchange/ex-zim.htm
                              http://mbendi.co.za/exzi.htm

Broker Information   http://www.zimbabwe.net/business/sagit/index.htm

Handbook   First handbook published on September 9, 1997

Established	January 1946
Trading Days	Monday to Friday
Trading Hours	9:00–12:00
	The international time zone is GMT + 2.

Market Indexes

There are two local indexes in Zimbabwe, the Zimbabwe Industrial Index and the Zimbabwe Mining Index. The indexes include all the companies in their sector and track daily movement in relation to the base year.

Trading Structure

There is a call-over system on a matched bargain basis. There is no method of obtaining the best execution and no price limits or daily trading ranges for exchange transactions. Shares trade in lots of 100.

Market Valuation[8]

Year	Price–Earnings Ratio	Dividend Yield
1991	7.0	5.8
1992	2.0	6.1
1993	8.8	3.6
1994	8.3	5.0
1995	7.4	5.2
1996	14.6	2.9

In January 1998 the price–earnings ratio was 11.63 times and the dividend yield was 5.03 percent.

Ownership

The exchange estimates the following breakdown between private and institutional investors:

| Private | 15% |
| Institutional | 85% |

The number of listed firms declined 2 percent from 1995. However, local currency market capitalization increased 163 percent. The local currency capitalization has grown at an annual compound growth rate of 49.1 percent since 1991.

Number of Listed Firms and Market Capitalization[9]

Year	Number of Firms	Market Capitalization
1991	na	7,101
1992	62	3,433
1993	64	9,937
1994	65	14,087
1995	66	19,849
1996	65	52,257

There are two foreign firms listed on the exchange. For U.S. investors who wish to invest in Zimbabwe without leaving the U.S. market, Mhangura Copper Mines Ltd. trades on the U.S. over-the-counter market.

Instruments Traded

Equities, preference shares, corporate debentures, municipal stocks, and government bonds are traded. There are no derivative products traded and at this time the exchange has no plans to offer such products.

Liquidity

Zimbabwe's turnover ratio places it fifty-seventh (of eighty-four) in the world in terms of market activity. This places it fourth among African exchanges. The value of average daily trades has increased to $1,159,000 in 1996 from $681,800 in 1995, a 70-percent increase.

Market Turnover Ratio

Year	1992	1993	1994	1995	1996
Turnover Ratio[10]	2.0	5.2	11.5	7.6	8.8

During the first week of September 1997, a foreign investor invested $180 million in industrial conglomerate and bourse market leader Delta Corporation Ltd., after acquiring a parcel of 10 million shares from the counter in the biggest ever single deal on the local market.[11]

Settlement

Settlement of all trades takes place on T+7, with physical delivery. All scrip remains in the control of the transfer agent, which may be either a listed company or a professional/institutional body that keeps the registers on their behalf. Clearing is by transaction. If settlement is not made within a reasonable period, the broker repurchases the securities at the expense of the defaulting client.

Central Depository

There is no central depository. There are three principal transfer secretaries in Zimbabwe that handle share registers. In addition, some companies act as their own transfer secretaries.

Brokerage Rates[12]

On the first Z$50,000	2.0%
On the next Z$50,000	1.5%
Over Z$100,000	1.0%

Margin/Securities Lending

A broker is entitled to lend the purchaser the purchase price or part thereof and to take the securities that he has purchased as security by way of a pledge, but he must not take more shares than is necessary. Banks may also lend in this capacity. However, a company may not assist in the purchase of its own shares.

Regulation

Brokers are subject to audit and inspection by the Stock Exchange Committee, which is not a government agency, but the organization established by the stock exchange itself. However, certain government representatives sit on the Stock Exchange Committee. There is a government official known as the Registrar of the Stock Exchange, who has powers of supervision and other regulatory duties.

Legal Issues

The common law in Zimbabwe is Roman–Dutch law, which is the same common law of South Africa. It is doubtful that the courts would recognize ultimate beneficial ownership of a security that is reflected only on the books of a foreign entity. The law requires each company to maintain a share register and to register all transfers in the register. Thus, the register is prima facie evidence of ownership and the courts would not recognize foreign ownership not so recorded in the register.

In 1984, a number of securities listed on foreign stock exchanges were dealt with on the stock exchange in Zimbabwe. These securities were denominated in foreign currency and carried a premium. The government expropriated all of these foreign securities on the grounds that the country was extremely short of foreign currency and needed to use securities to obtain foreign currency. Compensation paid was equal to the market value of the security on the stock exchange where it was listed.

Courts would enforce a clause which made the subcustody agreement as governed by New York law or any foreign law. This issue would be enforced as long as the foreign jurisdiction provided the same protection as would apply in Zimbabwe. A judgment of a U.S. court would not be enforceable in Zimbabwean courts simply on the basis that such a judgment had been obtained. The matter might be reopened and relitigated under certain circumstances.

Insider Trading

There is no specific legislative bar to insider trading. However, under the common law directors owe a fiduciary duty to the shareholders and must not act dishonestly for their own benefit. In certain circumstances, a director using confidential information for his own benefit could be guilty of fraud.

Regulatory Controls

The ZSE is a proprietary body licensed under the Zimbabwe Stock Exchange Act of 1974 and the Zimbabwe Stock Exchange Amendment Act, 1984. The ZSE is set up in terms of the act and regulated by its provisions. The act provides for the following:

- the Committee of the Exchange
- the appointment of a Registrar and a Register of Stockbrokers
- discipline of stockbrokers
- the method of transfer for certain securities and certification of instruments of transfer
- various miscellaneous provisions relating to the control of registered stockbrokers and the exchange by the Minister of Finance

A committee, the members of which are elected by the whole body of members, rules the exchange. The committee consists currently of seven members; five from the stockbroking companies and two government-nominated representatives (one from the Ministry of Finance, one from a merchant bank). The function of the committee is to examine all applications for quotations, to maintain a watch on the operations of existing companies, and to settle disputes between members. Externally, it is controlled by the act; internally, by its own comprehensive rules and regulations which follow closely those of the London Stock Exchange. The exchange provides two comprehensive documents that cover the membership rules of the exchange and the procedures necessary for gaining a listing on the exchange.

Foreign Investment Restrictions

On June 22, 1993, it was announced that non-Zimbabwe residents could invest in ZSE listed companies, though the following regulations governing the participation of foreign investors have been set:

- Foreign investors may now participate on the ZSE provided they finance the purchase of shares by inward transfer of foreign currency through normal banking channels.

- The purchase of shares will be limited to 40 percent of the total equity of the company, with a single investor acquiring a maximum of 10 percent of the shares on offer. This is over and above any foreign holdings in existence on May 1, 1993.

- The investments will qualify for 100-percent dividend remissibility rights subject to deduction of the relevant withholding tax (15 percent at the time). Disinvestment proceeds will be freely remissible.

Any amounts arising from capital gains made on disposal of such investments will be freely remissible subject to the deduction of a capital gains tax, reduced to 10 percent on April 1, 1993. Foreign investors may also bring in hard currency to invest up to a maximum of 15 percent of their assets in primary issues of bonds and stocks. The United States is the third largest investor in Zimbabwe, with about forty-five U.S. companies operating in the country in 1995.[13] Zimbabwe has one of the most highly skilled labor forces in Africa, but high inflation and interest rates in the country tend to discourage foreign investment.[14] Total trade on the ZSE since the liberalization of the financial sector four years ago has risen to Z$6.14 billion ($533.9 million) as of the end of August 1997.[15] Foreign investors account for 23 percent of quoted securities.

Operating Procedures

No prior exchange approval is necessary for a foreign investor to participate on the Zimbabwe Stock Exchange. Authorized dealers on behalf of nonresident investors will receive forex which they will convert in Zimbabwe dollars at the official exchange rate for onward transmission to a stockbroker to purchase of shares. Shares purchased on behalf of the foreign investors will be registered into either their own names or the names of nominee companies.

The share certificates, once registered accordingly, should be endorsed "Non-Resident," and for dual quoted shares a further endorsement "For Sale Within Zimbabwe Only" will be required. Authorized dealers will be responsible for such endorsement. The certificates may be delivered to the foreign investor or his bankers according to instructions.

For the purpose of dividend payments, current exchange control policy requires that the companies submit specific applications for authority to remit dividends. The investors will enjoy 100-percent dividend remittance rights, provided the purchase of the shares was negotiated on the Zimbabwe Stock Exchange and not privately.

The transfer secretary of each listed company will be responsible for ensuring that the 10 percent per foreign investor and 40 percent overall limits are adhered to. If shares are to be registered in the name of local nominee company, it will be the responsibility of that company to inform the transfer secretary on whose behalf the shares are held subject to compliance with the 40-percent and 10-percent limits. This regulation does not apply to old investors.

Should the new collective foreign ownership exceed the 40-percent limit, the transfer secretary will be obliged to report to the stock exchange, who should give a directive to the foreign investor responsible for exceeding the limit to sell sufficient shares to bring the collective ownership below the 40-percent ceiling. Any losses incurred will be dealt with on a last in, first out basis. On disinvestment, the stockbroker, on instruction, will sell the shares, and authorized dealers, after satisfying themselves with the transactions, will arrange a draft to be sent to the foreign investor. No exchange control approval will be required. Authorized dealers should submit monthly returns of all transactions effected over the period (i.e., amounts received, shares purchased, and any disinvestments) on behalf of all their clients.

Trading

The quotations (bids and offers) on the official stock market price list refer to parcels of 100 shares or more. Any transaction of a lesser number is known as an odd-lot transaction. The average price at which a sale or purchase of an odd lot takes place is slightly different, to the disadvantage of the client, owing to marketing difficulties. Investors should, where possible, endeavor to maintain share holdings in numbers of 100. Trades are manually processed.

Registration

Shares must be registered, whether in a foreign shareholder's name or a local (Zimbabwe) nominee name. The principal transfer secretaries in Zimbabwe are the following:

First Transfer Secretaries (Private) Limited
First Merchant Bank
P.O. Box IIA
Harare

KPMG Peat Marwick
P.O. Box 1122
Bulawayo

Zimbabwe Banking Corporation
Central Scrip Administration
P.O. Box 3198
Harare

In addition, some companies act as their own transfer secretaries and occasionally offer their services to other companies. The purchase contract note is the legal document that acts as proof of ownership of shares until the share certificate arrives. On delivery by the seller of the shares purchased, the stockbroker will complete the transfer deed in the name of the new owner. The duly executed transfer deed together with the relative share certificates is lodged with the registrar of the company whose shares were purchased.

The registrar records the name and address of the transferee in the register of shareholders in the place of the previous owner whose name is deleted, and sends back a new share certificate via the stockbroker. This certificate is a legal document that confirms title to the shares owned. It is of no value to anyone else and can be replaced if lost.

The procedure for selling securities is similar to buying, but the total amount on the sale contract note shows the net sale proceeds payable by the stockbroker to the seller. The sale contract note shows the administrative charges deducted from the consideration, and these include commission, contract stamps, and basic charge. Once the stockbroker sells shares, a blank transfer deed is sent to the seller for signing. The duly executed transfer deed should be returned by registered mail to the stockbroker, together with the share certificate. Occasionally it takes up to two months for these formalities of the transfer of ownership to be completed.

All stockbrokers and individuals that act for stockbrokers and deal on the stock exchange have to be licensed. When a principal buys or sells on the stock exchange, he must use a registered stockbroker. A stockbroker may purchase shares for his own account and benefit. Banks may be licensed to act as stockbrokers, but under the Banking Act they would be required to obtain the approval of the Registrar of Banks and it is unlikely under current circumstances that approval would be granted. Banks that own shares, either because they were pledged to them or because of an underwriting contact, are only allowed to keep the shares for as long as is necessary to realize their security. A foreign entity could not obtain a stockbroker's license, as only residents of Zimbabwe or Zimbabwean companies are legally entitled to obtain a license.

A domestic corporation would be entitled, provided exchange control approval was obtained, to appoint a registrar and transfer agent in a foreign country. It would be very unlikely that such permission would be granted, but there are eight companies listed on the stock exchange which have registers outside Zimbabwe as well as a register within Zimbabwe. In these cases, the share certificates are endorsed to show which can be traded on the foreign register and which can only be transferred on the local register.

Buy-Ins

If settlement is not made within a reasonable period, then the broker will repurchase the securities at the expense of the defaulting client.

Corporate Actions

Quoted companies are required by the Zimbabwe Stock Exchange to circulate to shareholders and publish interim results and dividends, annual reports and accounts, and the date of the annual general meeting. Notices must appear in two of the following:

* *The Herald* (principal daily newspaper)
* *Chronicle* (Bulawayo)
* *The Financial Gazette* (weekly financial newspaper)
* *Independent*
* Wire Services

When making a dividend declaration, certain general requirements are stipulated and there are a number of regulations governing the payment of dividends, newspaper advertisements, director's meetings, and the submission of figures to the exchange. The ZSE follows the London Stock Exchange City for mergers and takeover actions, except that a takeover bid is triggered when a shareholding reaches 50 percent.

Dividends and Capital Gains Taxation

Companies declare dividends once or twice each year with no particular schedule.

Dividends may be remitted at 100 percent to foreign investors. Dividend income due is taxable at the rate of 15 percent, which is deducted by the company declaring the dividend. This dividend income received is not subject to further taxation. Capital gains accruing from the sale of securities are subject to a 10 percent capital gains tax. An annual inflation allowance of 15 percent per annum is allowed as a deduction and capital gains amounting to less than $5,000 in any tax year are not assessed.

Securities Lending

Short trading is permitted after certain formalities are completed, but they are not common, as there is no stock borrowing or lending mechanism.

Voting

Annual general meetings are usually announced in the local newspapers. Proxy voting forms are required to be circulated by companies with any documents which require action by shareholders. Foreign holders of shares are entitled to vote their securities in the same way as local holders. In addition, foreign shareholders are not restricted to fewer votes for each share held.

INTERNET RESOURCES

Government

The Official Home Page of Zimbabwe at http://www.zimweb.com/Embassy/ Zimbabwe, includes information about the embassy, travel requirements, and news updates.

Business

http://www.zimweb.com/Business/html, from the government's official web site, includes information about exchange control, importing, and investing in Zimbabwe.

Zimbabwe Investment Climate at http://www.zimtrade.co.zw/zic/zic.htm, provides information on investment opportunities, tax exemptions, export processing zones, and investment incentives.

The Zimbabwe Business Directory at http://www.zimbabwe.net/business, is a listing of all business-related sites advertising through the Zimbabwe network.

Zimbabwe Stock Exchange at http://mbendi.co.za/exzi.htm, provides an overview of the exchange, regulations, market listing, and contact information. It is maintained by a private entity, Mbendi Information Services.

Ernst and Young Investment Profile at http://mbendi.co.za/emsty/ cyzieyip.htm, gives general background information on Zimbabwe, including procedures on how to establish a business, taxation, and incentives. It is maintained by a private entity, Mbendi Information Services.

U.S. Department of Commerce's International Trade Administration 1997 Country Commercial Guide at http://www.ita.doc.gov/uscs/ccgozimb.html, is an overview of Zimbabwe's commercial environment (economic, political, and market analysis) from an American perspective.

Telecommunications Sector Profile for Zimbabwe at http://rtr.worldweb.net/ Textonly/zimprl.htm

News

Zimbabwe *Independent* at http://wwwl.samara.co.zw/zimin

NOTES

1. CIA Factbook web site at http://www.odci.gov/cia/publications/nsolo/factbook/zi.htm.

2. "Bank Expects Economic 'Slowdown'," ZBC Radio, Harare, 1800 gmt, 11 September 1997.

3. CIA Factbook web site.

4. Ibid.

5. "Zimbabwe Launches Second IPO," *Privatization International Ltd.*, 1 September 1997.

6. "Zimbabwe Cotton Firm Launches Share Offer," African News Service, Inc., *Africa News*, 30 September 1997.

7. *Financial Gazette*, 8 September 1997.

8. International Financial Corporation.

9. Ibid.

10. Ibid.

11. "Zimbabwe: Foreign Investor Buys Delta Shares," Africa News Service, Inc., *Africa News*, 12 September 1997.

12. Zimbabwe Stock Exchange, *Exchange Report* (Harare, 1997).

13. U.S. Department of Commerce, ITA, *1996 Country Commercial Guide for Zimbabwe* (Washington, D.C.: U.S. Government Printing Office, National Trade Data Bank, 1995).

14. "U.S. Urges for Improving Investment Climate in Zimbabwe," Comtex Scientific Corp., *NewsEdge/LAN*, 25 April 1996.

15. "Business and Finance; ZSE in Multibillion Dollar Trade," Panafrican News Agency, Harare, Zimbabwe, 10 November 1997.

EMERGING MARKETS

As the macroeconomic environments open to a market-driven orientation, more African nations recognize the contribution that a securities market makes to capital mobilization. A number of nations have indicated a desire to move forward with the establishment of an exchange to include Algeria, Ethiopia, Malawi, Mozambique, Tanzania, and Uganda, among others. The following provides basic information on the markets in Malawi, Tanzania, and Uganda. These markets can be classified as preemerging securities exchanges, and the pace of their development is dependent upon the political and economic environment into which they are introduced.[1]

MALAWI

The Malawi Stock Exchange

In September 1997, the Sugar Corporation of Malawi Limited (Sucoma) was the third company to list shares on the exchange. The government's offering of a 4.32-percent stake was valued at $3.7 million and was targeted at local investors and will be followed by a second offering aimed at international institutional investors in early 1998. Sucoma, majority-owned by South Africa's Illovo, increased the exchange's market capitalization from $12.5 million to $110 million. The National Insurance Corporation and Blantyre Hotels are the other companies with shares listed on the Malawi exchange at the end of August 1997.

Malawi Stock Exchange
Stockbrokers Malawi Limited
P.O. Box 2598
Hanover Street
Blantyre
Tel.: (265) 621 817   Fax: (265) 624 351

| Web Site | http://mbendi.co.za/exma.htm |
| Established | March 1995 |

The Malawi Stock Exchange opened for business for the first time on November 11, 1996, with 2,300 Malawi citizens buying shares in the first company to be listed, Malawi's largest insurance firm, the National Insurance Company. The International Finance Corporation and a Dutch development bank provided 40 percent of the $500,000 required to establish the exchange.

Trading Days	Monday to Friday
Trading Hours	9:00–12:00
Trading Structure	Call-over mechanism with floor system

Instruments Traded	Government bonds and treasury bills, equities are to be introduced in the near future
Membership	Corporate and individual
Clearing	By transaction
Settlement	Physical delivery
Depository	None

Brokerage Rate

0 to 50,000 kwacha	2%
50,000 to 100,000 kwacha	1+%
Over 100,000 kwacha	1%

Web Site   http://www.sadc-usa.net/members/malawi/default.html

Dividends and Capital Gains Taxation

Capital gains tax is applicable if shares are sold within twelve months of purchase. However, actual taxation implementation has not been resolved.

Foreign Investment Restrictions

There are no foreign exchange controls. A shareholding of up to 30 percent of a registered company is allowed. Nonresident participation is allowed through brokers. After the minimum six-month holding period, there is no restriction on repatriation of capital. Income is remittable after tax deduction.

Credit Rating

Malawi has not been rated by international rating agencies for either domestic or foreign currency debt.

Central Bank: Reserve Bank of Malawi

Reserve Bank of Malawi
P.O. Box 30063
Lilongwe 3
Capital City
Malawi
Tel.: +265–78–0600   Fax: +265–73–1145

TANZANIA

Dar-es-Salaam Stock Exchange

The Dar-es-Salaam Stock Exchange is in a development stage. The exchange's first company, Tanzania Oxygen, listed at the start of 1998. The exchange is a result of the Banking and Financial Institutions Act of 1991, followed by the Capital Markets and Securities Authority Act in 1994.

c/o Capital Markets & Security Authority
4th Floor Twigga Building
Samora Avenue
Dar-es-Salaam
Tanzania
Tel.: +255 51 11 3903   Fax: +255 51 11 3846
Web Site   http://mbendi.co.za/exta.htm

Central Bank: Bank of Tanzania

Postal Address

Bank of Tanzania
P.O. Box 2939
10 Mirambo Street
Dar es Salaam
Tanzania
Tel.: +255–51–21291   Fax: +256–41–258442

UGANDA

The Uganda Securities Exchange was launched June 6, 1997. Uganda's market license to operate the exchange is held by the Uganda Securities Exchange (USE) Limited, unofficially known as the Kampala Stock Exchange. It is a company formed by eight licensed brokerage dealers and investment advisers.[2] For Uganda, 85 percent of the 107 parastatal firms will have been disposed of, mostly through bids, by the end of 1997. Thirty-seven firms are pending disposition as of the end of the first half of 1997. Privatization began five years ago.

East African Development Bank bonds began trading on the Uganda Securities Exchange on January 5, 1998. Central bank treasury bills were added in February 1998. The ninety-one-day maturities are auctioned weekly and are transferable as they are in bearer treasury bills certificates.

Mr. S. Rutega
Kampala Stock Exchange
c/o Capital Markets Authority
P.O. Box 7120, Kampala, Uganda
Tel.: (256) 41 244–737   Fax: (256) 41 230–878

The board overseeing the privatization of government-owned entities slated twelve entities for sale by the end of 1997; however, structural details prevented this from happening. The Ugandan Securities Exchange was incorporated in

May 1997, and the Capital Market Authority appointed brokers in June 1997. Regulations are based on the London and New York exchanges' codes.

Web Site   http://mbendi.co.za/exug.htm

Ugandan Investment Code 1991

A critical component of African development is the ability of governments to transition from closed and protected economies to open economic systems. An example of laws designed to promote the investment opportunities in Africa is the Ugandan Investment Code, enacted January 25, 1991.

The code was enacted to make provision in the law relating to local and foreign investments in Uganda by providing more favorable conditions for investment; to establish the Uganda Investment Authority; to repeal the Foreign Investment (Protection) Act and the Foreign Investment Decree 1977; and to provide for other related matters.

Central Bank: Bank of Uganda

Postal Address

Bank of Uganda
P.O. Box 7120
Kampala Road
Kampala
Uganda

A goal of the three East African stock exchanges—Kenya, Uganda, and Tanzania—is to form a single East African exchange with three trading floors. In early 1998, the three exchanges reached an agreement to cross list companies.

NOTES

1.Exchange data are provided by MBendi Information Services (Pty) Ltd., and used with permission. Mbendi is an African company founded in 1995 by a group of professionals with extensive worldwide experience of strategic management, information systems, and the corporate world.

Tel.: +27 (0) 21 616–316   Fax: +27 (0) 21 616–316
E-mail: MBendi@MBendi.co.za
Web Site: http://www.mbendi.co.za

2. "Ugandan Stock Market," *International Market Insight Reports*, 3 July 1997.

CHAPTER FOUR

AFRICAN INVESTMENTS

As markets develop, the role of foreign investors becomes increasingly important. Research has demonstrated that investors benefit from international diversification. Because an international portfolio is vulnerable to economic conditions in various countries, the variability in returns will most likely be less than that of an entirely domestic portfolio.

The correlation between African market returns and more developed exchange returns is important to investors as long as securities market returns in different national markets are less than perfectly correlated. The low correlation between African markets and developed exchanges, including those in the United States, the United Kingdom, and Japan, make it worthwhile for investors to diversify in African markets. The correlation between African markets and the U.S. S&P 500 index is 0.149; the IFC Asian index, 0.055; and the IFC Latin America Index, −0.011. These estimates are consistent with individual market correlations reported by the IFC for Nigeria and Zimbabwe and developed markets.[1] The correlation between South Africa and the other African exchanges is 0.086, indicating that there is a significant African diversification benefit to investors beyond the South African market.

Africa's financial infrastructure development is proceeding as nations reorient to market-directed economies. Most securities markets have eased restrictions on foreign direct investment and offered incentives to encourage market participation. However, Africa's annual share of new foreign direct investments to developing countries has slipped to 5 percent annually from about 11 percent in the 1980s, even though the investment flow has been a steady $3 billion over recent years.

Yet the United Nations report, *Foreign Direct Investment in Africa, 1995*, reports that Africa topped the rest of the world in rates of return on investments by

American multinational companies in natural resources, manufacturing, and services for most of the past fourteen years.[2] The report showed that in 1993, U.S. companies rang up a 25.5-percent return on book value of their African investments, while similar ventures in all developing and developed countries scored 16.6 percent and 8.6 percent, respectively. The oil industry, especially in Egypt and Nigeria, accounts for about two-thirds of the foreign direct investment total in fifty-four African countries.[3] The U.N. report noted that multinational corporations are frightened off from Africa by factors such as poor infrastructure, small domestic markets, unskilled labor forces, and high external indebtedness.

As equity markets develop and present investors with opportunities to participate in Africa's renaissance, the current debt burdens of Africa stand out in need of relief. Debt reduction and forgiveness must be extended to those African countries that pursue policies of economic and political liberalization. Africa's debt burden of $340 billion is almost as large as its total GDP. Africa is moving toward free competitive markets and overcoming the difficulties in the transition from centrally planned economies to open markets.

African markets present unique risks to a portfolio investor. Table 4.1 presents a summary of risk measurements for the markets of Africa. Evaluating the African markets' shortfalls in the ratings highlights the importance of financial institutions, access to bank financing, short-term finance, and capital markets. The absence of these factors has a significant negative impact on the country's rating. Access to international capital and financial market infrastructure are both critical elements in evaluating risk ratings in all three surveys. As Africa's capital markets evolve, the risk ratings should demonstrate improvements. The African nations without stock exchanges rate lower in the risk assessments.

Political instability is also a factor in risk analysis. This is a particularly critical element in the analysis of the *Euromoney* rating of Nigeria. The *Euromoney* rating of Zambia shows the greatest decline from September 1996 to March 1997. Mauritius shows the greatest increase over the same period.

Mutual Funds

After considering the risks of investing in African markets and reviewing the details of Africa's securities markets, the following provides practical investment alternatives for pursuing African markets. The presentation of information should not be considered a recommendation to purchase or sell particular securities or countries. Recognizing the risks peculiar to emerging proceed securities markets, investors should act with care and only after a review of their financial objectives and risk tolerance. Due to the liquidity constraints imposed by most African exchanges, short-term investments should be avoided. In an October 13, 1993, report on the region, Morgan Stanley noted that the region was entering a period of change. The report notes

Table 4.1
Country Risk Profiles

Country	ICRG Risk Rating 12/96	Institutional Investors 9/96	9/97	Euromoney 9/96	3/97
Botswana	79.0	49.8	51.2	51.1	61.8
Côte d'Ivoire	64.0	18.5	20.1	39.8	38.8
Egypt	67.5	35.1	39.7	45.7	54.7
Ghana	62.0	29.6	31.5	49.6	47.9
Kenya	67.5	27.9	28.6	42.3	41.2
Mauritius	---	50.8	51.9	51.3	67.8
Morocco	71.5	39.3	40.9	---	53.7
Namibia	79.0	---	---	30.8	33.5
Nigeria	50.5	15.2	15.3	31.1	26.8
South Africa	72.5	46.3	46.4	62.3	69.9
Swaziland	---	---	33.3	---	53.4
Tunisia	73.0	45.5	47.9	61.6	62.9
Zambia	56.0	16.5	16.0	32.8	21.8
Zimbabwe	56.0	32.5	33.8	46.1	42.0

Source: ICRG, *International Country Risk Guide*, Political Risk Services, December 1996; Purcell, Kit, "It's Like Growth Stocks," *Institutional Investor*, September 1997, p. 177; and Dobson, Rebecca, "Switzerland Takes a Tumble," *Euromoney*, March 1997, p. 164.

After decades of struggling with socialism and misguided economic policies, Africa is entering a period of secular change. The continent is poised for growth. Of its 50 countries, 28 have economic reform programs in place. Fourteen stock markets are up and running, with four more planned within the next two years. Under increasing pressure from the international community, African governments are showing greater commitment to monetary reform, privatization, and free trade policies. Although most stock markets are still in their infancy, we believe that emerging market Investors can find extraordinary opportunities and undervalued assets.[4]

It is expected that the development of mutual funds will revolutionize the local securities markets. The funds will enable smaller investors to participate in the exchanges, while receiving the diversification benefits of a portfolio that eliminates company-specific risk factors. Examples include the 1994 introduction of the $230-million Morgan Stanley Africa Fund, and Alliance Capital Management's $92-million Southern Africa Fund.[5] In 1997, the firm raised an additional $130 million for the Nile Growth Company, a Luxembourg listed closed-end mutual fund, to invest in Egypt. Over $1 billion has been directed toward African markets by equity fund managers.

African Funds

To ensure that investors were advised concerning the risks of investing in African markets, the Morgan Stanley Africa Fund Prospectus notes

Investing in securities of African issuers involves certain risks and considerations not typically associated with investing in securities of U.S. issuers, including generally (a) controls on foreign investment and limitations on repatriation of invested capital and on the Fund's ability to exchange local currencies for U.S. dollars, (b) greater price volatility, substantially less liquidity and significantly smaller market capitalization of Securities markets, (c) currency devaluation and other currency exchange rate fluctuations, (d) more substantial government involvement in the economy, (e) higher rates of inflation, (f) greater social, economic and political uncertainty and (g) the risk of nationalization or expropriation of assets and the risk of war.[6]

As emerging markets opportunities expand, the following African funds present multiple-year track records that may be evaluated. Given the high transaction costs and custodial requirements in emerging markets, individual investors may elect to pursue the markets through a mutual fund alternative. The following is a partial list of "long" established African funds.

Africa Emerging Markets Fund—Equities   *Launched November 12, 1993*
State Street Cayman Trust Co, Ltd., P.O. Box 1984, Elizabeth Square, Grand Cayman, Cayman Islands, British West Indies, Tel.: (1 809) 949 6644

First African Asset Fund Ltd.—Income   *Launched November 13, 1992*
Carlson Investment Management Inc., 36 Silver Birch Drive, New Rochelle, NY 10804, USA, Tel.: (1 914) 633 5735

Mauritius Fund, Ltd., Manager—Equity   *Launched January 15, 1993*
Mauritius Fund Management Company Ltd., P.O. Box 52, Sir William Newton Street, Port Louis, Mauritius

Morgan Stanley Africa Investment Fund, Inc.—Equity   *Launched February 4, 1994*
Morgan Stanley Asset Management Inc., 1221 Avenue of the Americas, 21st Floor, New York, NY 10020, USA, Tel.: (1 212) 296 7000

New South Africa Fund Inc.—Equity   *Launched March 11, 1994*

Robert Fleming Inc., c/o Custodial Trust Company, 101 Carnegie Center, Princeton, NJ 08540, USA, Tel.: (1 609) 951 2300

Nigeria Emerging Market Fund—Income   *Launched October 1, 1992*

International Asset Transactions LP, 730 Fifth Avenue, Suite 2101, New York, NY 10019, USA, Tel.: (1 212) 262 2845

Old Mutual South Africa Trust plc.—Equity   *Launched July 1, 1994*

Mutual Intl. Asset Managers (Guernsey) Ltd., Fairbairn House, P.O. Box 121, Rohais, St. Peter Port, Guernsey, Channel Islands

Southern Africa Fund Inc.—Equity   *Launched February 25, 1994*

Alliance Capital Management LP, 1345 Avenue of the Americas, New York, NY 10105, USA, Tel.: (1 212) 969 1000

Fund Allocations

Mutual funds provide an opportunity to diversify into African securities markets; however, the performance of the fund is dependent upon the allocations of the portfolio manager. Managers are constrained by market developments and custodial support. Despite the promise offered by African markets, investment was constrained by regional institutional details. Under the provisions of the prospectus, the Morgan Stanley Africa Fund was permitted to invest only in securities traded in African markets with custody arrangements meeting the requirements of the Investment Company Act of 1940. At the fund's inception, custody arrangements meeting the requirements were only available in Mauritius, Morocco, and South Africa. As markets evolved, custodial arrangements have been expanded to permit investments in other markets. To provide insights into the allocation of portfolio assets, Table 4.2 examines the weightings of the fund at year end. Table 4.2 presents an overview of the fund's multiyear implementation of the investment strategy. As market opportunities arose, the fund decreased its holdings in South Africa and deployed assets to new markets, such as Egypt and Zimbabwe.

COMPARATIVE HIGHLIGHTS

Competition for foreign direct investment is intense as the world's markets increase their integration. Africa is rich in raw commodities and agricultural products. African markets are at roughly the same stage in development as other emerging markets were a few years ago. Inevitable comparisons are drawn between the emerging regions of Asia, Latin America, and Africa. Tables 4.3 and 4.4 provide a comparison between the regions. The comparison illustrates the opportunities and challenges confronting the region.

Table 4.2
Morgan Stanley Africa Investment Fund, Inc.

	1994	1995	1996
Algeria	1.5	2.0	0.0
Australia	0.4	0.0	0.0
Botswana	0.0	0.0	1.3
Egypt	0.0	0.7	15.0
Ireland	0.0	0.0	0.5
Ghana	0.0	1.6	1.3
Kenya	0.0	0.0	0.8
Côte d'Ivoire	2.5	2.4	2.8
Mauritius	0.0	2.3	7.2
Morocco	13.1	15.1	3.7
Nigeria	6.6	3.6	0.0
Switzerland	0.0	0.0	0.8
South Africa	72.1	66.4	46.4
United Kingdom	2.0	2.6	2.5
United States	4.9	7.6	0.4
Zimbabwe	1.1	4.2	16.9
Other			1.7
Total Allocations	**104.2%**	**108.5%**	**101.3%**
NAV	$14.43	$17.05	$16.86
Market Value	$11.38	$12.88	$13.63
Total Investment Return:			
Market Value	(15.37%)	20.84%	16.26%
Net Asset Value	7.34%	26.14%	8.64%
Net Assets (Thousands US$)	$222,929.00	$263,428.00	$260,522.00

Source: "Morgan Stanley African Fund Annual Report," Morgan Stanley Asset Management, Inc.,
1221 Avenue of the Americas, 21st Floor, New York, NY 10020, 1994, 1995, and 1996.

As noted in Table 4.3, Africa's economic growth exceeded Latin America's growth in 1995 and 1996 after lagging in the overall 1990 to 1995 period by 0.9 percent. Both regions have high absolute levels of external debt, while Africa's burden relative to GDP is significantly higher.

Zaire's 1996 inflation was over 23,000 percent and Angola's was 950 percent. Latin America's dramatic improvement in inflation is clearly evident in the change from 1992 to 1996. In contrast, African inflation has been stable over this period, declining 300 basis points overall after spiking to 29 percent in 1993. However, 1996 inflation remains 500 basis points higher

Table 4.3
Percentage Economic Growth Rates of Emerging Regions

	1990-95	1993	1994	1995	1996
Asia	6.6	6.7	7.1	8.0	7.1
Latin America	3.4	3.5	5.6	1.1	3.3
Sub-Saharan Africa	**2.5**	1.8	2.9	3.1	5.0

Source: "Sub-Saharan Africa: Turmoil and Progress," *Rand Focus: The Treasury Financial Newsletter of First National Bank of Southern Africa Limited*, May/June 1997.

Table 4.4
Inflation Rates of Emerging Regions

	1992	1993	1994	1995	1996
Asia	2.8	3.7	3.9	2.4	2.6
Latin America	376.0	826.0	352.0	24.0	16.0
Sub-Saharan Africa*	**24.0**	**29.0**	**28.0**	**29.0**	**21.0**

Source: "Sub-Saharan Africa: Turmoil and Progress," *Rand Focus: The Treasury Financial Newsletter of First National Bank of Southern Africa Limited*, May/June 1997.
Note: *Excluding Zaire and Angola.

in Africa than in Latin America, and 18.4-percent higher than Asia. This comparative illustration highlights the relative stability of Asia's macroeconomic development policies. As Africa's economies open and are disciplined by a market orientation, the potential for development is enormous given the size of its markets and the wealth of its resources.

In a historical context, many view the African continent as the cradle of civilization. The richness of its archaeological record presents the oldest evidence of civilization. From the splendor of Egyptian civilization to the diversity of its cultures today, Africa commands a central place in the evolution of world civilization. However, the twentieth century's record of unfilled promises and missed opportunities presents us with challenges to the perceptions of historical greatness. The current progress in structural adjustment programs and the development of financial infrastructure offers a positive opportunity for the future. Recognizing the richness of its natural endowments and the values inherent in free economic systems, the African continent presents investors with risks and opportunities. Balancing the two presents the key to Africa's future financial infrastructure development.

NOTES

1. See *Emerging Stock Markets Factbook 1994* (Washington, D.C.: International Finance Corporation, 1994), 48.

2. *Foreign Direct Investment in Africa, 1995* (New York: United Nations, 1995).

3. "Foreign Investment in Africa Is Lagging, Despite Good Returns, UN Report Says,"

Fred R. Bleakley, *Wall Street Journal*, 14 July 1995, A8.

4. "Emerging Markets Investment Research," Morgan Stanley Report, 13 October 1993.

5. These mutual funds are listed on the New York Stock Exchange as closed-end mutual funds.

6. Morgan Stanley African Fund Prospectus, October 1993, Morgan Stanley Asset Management, Inc.

SELECTED BIBLIOGRAPHY

Aryeetey, Ernest, Hemamala Hettige, Machiko Nissanke, and William Steel. "Financial Market Fragmentation and Reforms in Sub-Saharan Africa." World Bank Technical Paper No. 356, Washington, D.C., 1997.

Bachmann, Heinz, and Ken Kwaku. *MIGA Roundtable on Foreign Direct Investment Policies in Africa: Proceedings and Lessons*. PAS Research Paper Series. Washington, D.C.: World Bank, 1994.

The Botswana Share Market: Procedure for Listing and General Requirements for Listed Companies. Gaborone: Exchange Publication, n.d.

Botswana: Tax Information Summary 1995. Gaborone: Coopers & Lybrand, n.d.

Bourse des Valeurs D'Abidjan Organisation du Marche Financier en Côte D'Ivoire, 1994. Abidjan: Stock Exchange Publication.

Claessens, Stijn, and Sudarshan Gooptu. *Portfolio Investment in Developing Countries*. Washington, D.C.: World Bank, 1993.

Clark, Robert A. "African Securities Markets: A Study in the Development of Africa's Emerging Securities Markets." *Journal of International Financial Markets, Institutions & Money* 6 (1996): 39–54.

Culagovski, Jorge, Victor Gabor, Maria Cristina Germany, and Charles Humphreys. "African Financing Needs in the 1990s." In *African External Finance in the 1990s*, edited by Ishrat Husain and John Underwood. Washington, D.C.: World Bank, 1991.

Emerging Stock Markets Factbook 1997. Washington, D.C.: International Finance Corporation, 1997.

Foreign Direct Investment in Africa, 1995. New York: United Nations, 1995.

Gassman, Amy. "Ashanti Goldfields Co. Limited (ASL)." In *U.S. Research*. New York: Goldman Sachs, 1997.

Government of Botswana, Ministry of Finance and Development Planning. *Financial Assistance Policy (FAP)*, 1 October 1995. Gaborone: Botswanan Government Publication, 1995.

Hartland-Peel, Christopher. *African Equities: A Guide to Markets and Companies.* London: Euromoney, 1996.

Husain, Ishrat, and John Underwood, editors. *African External Finance in the 1990s.* Washington, D.C.: World Bank, 1991.

IMF Policy Development and Review Department. "Experience under the IMF's Enhanced Structural Adjustment Facility." *Finance & Development,* September 1997, pp. 32–35.

Jiyad, Ahmed M. "Privatisation in the Arab Countries, Programmes, Achievements, and Lessons." Bergen, Norway: Centre for Development Studies, Norwegian School of Economics and Business Administration, 1996.

Kibazo, Joel. "Enticement Comes Out of Africa." *Financial Times,* 23 December 1996, p. 21.

Kwaku, Ken. *MIGA Roundtable on Foreign Direct Investment Policies in Africa: Proceedings and Lessons.* Washington, D.C.: World Bank, 1994.

The LGT Guide to World Equity Markets 1996. London: Euromoney, 1996.

The LGT Guide to World Equity Markets 1997. London: Euromoney, 1997.

Marsden, Keith, and Thérèse Bélot. *Private Enterprise in Africa: Creating a Better Environment.* Washington D.C.: World Bank, 1987.

Oliver, Roland. *The African Experience.* New York: HarperCollins, 1992.

Senbet, Lemma. "Perspectives on African Finance and Economic Development." *Journal of African Finance and Economic Development* 2 (1996): 1–22.

Shelby, David. "The Cairo Stock Exchange? It Has Its Ups & Downs." *Arab Business & Investment Journal* 1 (1997).

Sudarkasa, Michael E. M. *The African Business Handbook: A Comprehensive Guide to Business Resources for African Trade and Investment.* Vol. 3. Washington, D.C.: 21st Century Africa, Inc., 1996.

United Nations. *Reviving Investment In Africa: Constraints and Policies.* Addis Ababa, Ethiopia, 30 March 1995.

U.S.–Africa Trade Flows and Effects of the Uruguay Round Agreements and U.S. Trade and Development Policy. Investigation No. 332-362, Publication 300. Washington, D.C.: U.S. International Trade Commission, 1996.

Whetham, Edith H., and Jean I. Currie. *The Economics of African Countries.* London: Cambridge University Press, 1969.

World Bank. *Adjustment in Africa: Reforms, Results, and the Road Ahead.* Washington, D.C.: World Bank, 1994.

World Bank. *Sub-Saharan Africa: From Crisis to Sustainable Growth.* Washington, D.C.: World Bank, 1989.

INDEX

ABOUT THE AUTHOR

ROBERT A. CLARK is Director, Graduate Studies in Business, and Associate Professor of Finance in the College of Business, University of Tampa. Previously on the faculty of the University of Vermont School of Business Administration, Dr. Clark founded and was the first director of the university's International Business Institute. He has also given lectures at the Business and Econonics University, Vienna, and was a Fulbright Scholar at the Norwegian School of Management.

ISBN 1-56720-149-0

9 781567 201499

90000>

EAN

HARDCOVER BAR CODE